D0289679

ATHOL FUGARD
HIS PLAYS, PEOPLE AND POLITICS

Following his retirement Alan Shelley obtained an MA in African Studies, and was then awarded a PhD for research into the work of Athol Fugard, upon which this book is based. In 2008 his novel *The Colour was Red* was published and his next one, *I Never Met Ernest Hemingway*, will be published in 2009. He lives in Rutland and has six grandchildren.

ATHOL FUGARD

HIS PLAYS, PEOPLE AND POLITICS

A Critical Overview by Alan Shelley

OBERON BOOKS

LONDON

First published in 2009 by Oberon Books
521 Caledonian Road, London N7 9RH
Tel: 020 7607 3637 / Fax: 020 7607 3629
e-mail: info@oberonbooks.com / www.oberonbooks.com

Athol Fugard: His Plays, People and Politics

A catalogue record for this book is available from the
British Library.

Cover photograph by Anton Hammerl

ISBN: 978-1-84002-821-8

Printed in Great Britain by CPI Antony Rowe,
Chippenham

Contents

Introduction: Dublin, 2002

It was an intimate venue, typical of the many small theatrical spaces now to be found in theatres around the British Isles, ranging from the Cottesloe at the National Theatre in London to the B2 at the Belgrade in Coventry, opened in 2007. This one was The Space, a one hundred and fifty-seat auditorium in the Helix, a relatively new performance centre built on the campus of the Dublin City University: an impressive building with elevations of granite and glass and an interior featuring sweeping staircases that twist, like a helix, from one level to another. On entering I thought that however splendid this addition to the City University was, would Dublin's more famous Trinity College, *alma mater* of Oscar Wilde and Samuel Beckett, have been more fitting for the man about to appear, a dramatist that in the past *Time* magazine has considered the best playwright in the Western world? Should this writer, who has exposed human frailties in a different but similarly masterly fashion to the author of *Waiting for Godot,* have been appearing a little closer to College Green? (And, incidentally, where was his Nobel Prize – or, following the opinion of the *New Yorker,* if not in Literature, how about the Peace Prize?)

However, as I took my seat in The Space these thoughts were dismissed: the small-scale venue of the same name in Cape Town had seen the first productions of some of his most important works, and so perhaps he would feel he had in some way come home.

It was 21 November 2002.

Athol Fugard enters and sits at a plain wooden table. A table plays a significant role in his play *Sorrows and Rejoicings* and he has told us in the past of some of the agonies he has undergone at his 'writing table'. In this instance his props are a small sheaf of paper and his spectacles. Under a minimum of stage lighting our impressions are of a relatively small, wiry man who inhabits his whiskers with confidence, allowing us to imagine that without a beard he might not be the man he is. He exudes an aura of warmth in a shade of brown. The flesh we can see is well tanned and his casual apparel is varied between unobtrusive beige and a plain khaki; but he is not in a 'brown study' – his eyes and his energetic movements dispel that idea. The eyes twinkle, evident even from the back row of the seats surrounding this stage, and his hands are never still. He takes his spectacles from their case, places them on his nose and then removes them to use as a conductor's baton, much as Mr M in *My Children! My Africa!* uses his bell.

At first sight the man we have come to listen to appears humble and at the same time confident within himself – but then why not? He is the consummate man of the theatre who, in addition to supplying the words, has directed most all of his own plays, and acted in many of them, so he knows very well how to keep an audience engaged. However, as I look around at this small gathering, I conjecture that to some of them his main claim to fame could be that Richard Attenborough cast him as General Smuts in the 1982 film *Gandhi*.

He reads from his recent diaries – or 'Notebooks' as he prefers to call them. His first were edited by his good friend Mary Benson, published in 1987, and covering the years 1960–1977. They provide a goldmine of superb insights into his earlier works and how they were written. After this major volume, some further entries were published in the scholarly journal, *Twentieth Century Literature*, whose 1993 Winter edition was wholly devoted to Fugard. These later diary extracts covered October, November and December 1990, a period when he was wrestling with the writing of *Playland*. In these he wrote:

> My notebooks have been a complex reality in my life, serving many functions: private confessional, literary finger-exercise, scrapbook, literary workshop where I

jacked-up my plays and examined the problems I was
having in the writing of them. How naive of me to think
I could go on writing without having one open and
ready to receive.   **[p 527]**

In light of this, some update into his current thinking and current
writings is keenly anticipated.

This evening he reads an entry about a real-life happening
and wonders if this could lead to a play. His earlier *Notebooks* are
replete with similar examples: that mother of nine met on the road
to Cradock who was responsible in part for *Boesman and Lena*; the
story of his friend Piet, an alleged informer; incidents from his
own life and the chance meeting with a young woman from Cape
Town – the spark that brought about *The Road to Mecca*. This new
story, taken from a newspaper report, concerned a mother who
had deliberately positioned herself and her two young children in
the path of an express train on the main railway line out of Cape
Town. Little information was given about this family but the
report went on to say that the driver of the train was being treated
for psychological problems. Fugard wondered what distress
this woman could possibly have had to compel this action, and
include her two young children, but even so he concluded that
for some reason there was not in this incident the same seed that
had brought about many of his other works. He did, however,
wonder whether a play could concentrate on the reactions of the
train driver, but then dismissed this idea. This only reinforced
the impression gained from the *Notebooks* that his plays are never
taken from the obvious. The germination from a scrap of information, a fleeting image or a chance encounter to the completed
script is a tortuous process for this man.

By this time, the revelation of the contents of his most recent
diaries became more an act of theatre than a reading. At the
outset there was a quiet and gentle man using the script before
him, but by the end of the evening we were witnessing a theatrical
performance that, even though still low-key, reflected the passion
and sincerity of this septuagenarian giant of the theatre.

This performance was the prelude to an arrangement made in advance that Fugard and I should spend the following morning together, which we did, when the impression gained across the footlights was reinforced by this closer encounter. In his lifetime he has been extremely generous in the provision of interviews, and there was no exception in my case. As expected, he was charmingly articulate and used my questions to reveal his *modus operandi* as a playwright, and his opinion on a wide range of topics. By the end of the morning my long-felt admiration was strengthened and intensified.

The early part of our conversation centred on the fall of the Apartheid State, a state that his drama has portrayed in intimate detail. He made a fascinating comment in this regard, apposite to his work as a dramatist: he thought the theatre in South Africa had played some part in the transition to democratic rule because, he said, drama is concerned with dialogue – 'and in the end what happened was that we finally talked ourselves out of the nightmare rather than trying to kill each other'. He is a master of talk, whether within the family – *Blood Knot, Boesman and Lena, Hello and Goodbye, Valley Song* and *Sorrows and Rejoicings* – or within the other disparate strands of his desperate people. What he looks for in his work, so he said, is 'ambiguity' – which he also considered to be the essence of good poetry – but he could not find that in the tragedy of the suicidal family that he had talked about the evening before. He tried to explain this by two examples from his past.

The first example was *A Lesson from Aloes*, a play based on people he knew. There seemed to be a strong story concerning the friendship between Piet and Steve and the uncertainty as to whether Piet was an informer, but in Fugard's particular way, it was not until he moved Piet's wife, Gladys, to the centre of the account that the play was born. She provided the spark that transformed this narrative of a friendship into the complex work that it became.

The second example concerned a real-life situation that appeared on the surface to be an attractive proposition, but was dismissed – the 'ambiguity' was not there. The facts were these. Fugard has a very special affection for the arid region of South Africa known as the Karoo and has a house there, at New Bethesda, a small *dorp* twenty-three kilometres off the main road between Graaf-Reinet and Middleburg. The contrast with urban South Africa is startling. When my wife and I visited in 2002 we left behind the fortified houses of Johannesburg to stay at a guesthouse in New Bethesda where we were told 'we would find the front door key under the mat'. In this isolated and conservative community, Helen Martins stuck out like a sore thumb. On the death of her father, many years before, this Afrikaner housewife began to decorate the interior of her modest house and cover the adjoining yard with an amazing display of statues and structures that today has become a tourist attraction known as the Owl House. To quote from the Souvenir Guide:

> Hostesses elegantly dressed in elaborately tiered bottle dresses welcome visitors to the 'Camel Yard'. When not attending to the smug and fatuous gentleman in the 'corner of debauchery', these ladies will conduct you on a journey of mystical discovery to a mythical mecca in the East.
>
> The shelves of the pantry inside the house are devoted to rows of jars of crushed glass, meticulously graded according to size and colour. It is this glass that has been applied to boldly patterned paint surfaces on the walls ceilings, windows and other surfaces. The interplay of light and colour are the essence of this elaborate scheme of interior decoration. This is amplified by the myriad lamps, candles and specially shaped mirrors.

This extraordinary woman Helen Martins was surely an ideal subject for the Fugard treatment: on his own doorstep and where the other members of this God-fearing small community, including the Dominee, were antagonistic towards, and even felt threatened by, her highly unconventional behaviour. But not so – and it was only when he met by chance the young woman from Cape Town, who became his Elsa, that the full design fell into place.

Helen Martins, strange as she was, was not enough. It was the relationship between the young teacher of left-wing views and this woman that joined up the pieces. The real Elsa gave Fugard a photograph of herself with her arms around a frail and tiny Helen, and this became the totem that brought about this important play.

He talked about his past: his fight with alcohol – where he has emerged the victor – and his struggles in the early days with the South African authorities who, in 1967, took away his passport. He recalled his boyhood – as partly revealed in *'Master Harold'... and the boys* and this lead him, in typically frank fashion, to talk about his portrait in that play and the relationship he had with his mother's servants. He was, he said:

> A little white boy dealing with his indoctrination in South Africa, turning me into a little racist – because that is what that society tried to do to me. Thank God I had a mother who fought against it – and also Sam and Willie who were teaching me lessons that finally liberated me.   **[Personal interview, November 2002]**

At the end of the morning he provided a final memorable comment that seemed to me to sum up his entire playwriting philosophy:

> I always write out of love – not hatred for the villain but compassion for the victim.
>
> **[Personal interview, November 2002]**

This book validates this statement – as all of his victims in their many forms are revealed – and argues that the South African context of these plays does not affect the universality of his appeal. It is not a work of conventional literary analysis employing accepted forms of literary theory. A commentary on the political background is provided to augment these pictures of the lost and silenced people who look for an identity, or for somewhere to live, or for someone to cherish. In all cases Fugard's men and women display the love and tenderness, despair and desolation, hunger and desire sought by most contemporary humanity, and it is to illustrate his ability to project these emotions onto the world stage that is the defining purpose of *Athol Fugard: His Plays, People and Politics*.

ONE

The Traitor in the Laager

There are certain things about South Africa...which achieve their truest statement from the Afrikaner background. The tragedy is that their love of country has become a passionate but shrivelling emotion. Afrikaans has become the language of violence. The Afrikaner has done this to himself.

Athol Fugard [Benson 1990, p 187]

Athol Fugard is a white man whose antecedents are mixed, just like those of his characters Morris and Lena, but without the tragic consequences of their fusions. As he has said: 'Half of my descent, and maybe all of my soul, is Afrikaner. But I am also the traitor inside the laager.' [Henry 1989, p 56] When asked about his cultural heritage, he explains:

> By and large, because of the strength of my mother's personality the Afrikaner culture was more dominant. It is typical of the Afrikaner, and was perhaps emphasised by my mother's family background as a Potgieter – an old, well known Afrikaner family – that we were very tightly-knit. That in some ways may be the origin of the concern in my work with the nexus of family relationships. [Benson 1977, p 77]

It is this heritage that informs the Afrikaner mindset, so perceptively observed in such plays as *Hello and Goodbye*, *A Lesson from Aloes*, *The Road to Mecca* and *Exits and Entrances*. Fugard's father was English-speaking, of Irish and possibly Polish descent, and the portrait of Hally's father we are given in *'Master Harold'*...

and the boys represents, more or less, Fugard's relationship with his own father. In A *Lesson from Aloes*, Piet quotes from *Romeo and Juliet* saying that he cannot deny his father; in Hally's case this is more complicated, as it was for the author himself, who is reported as saying:

> I was dealing with the last unlaid ghost in my life, who was my father. Our relationship was as complex as Master Harold expresses it in the play. I had resentment at his infirmity and other weakness but as Master Harold says, 'I love him so.'   **[Vandenbroucke 1986, p 256]**

Harold Athol Lannigan Fugard was born on 11 June 1932 at Middelburg, a small town in the Karoo region of South Africa's Cape Province. In 1935 the Fugard family moved to Port Elizabeth, the fourth of the major urban areas in the country after Johannesburg, Cape Town and Durban, known for the motor manufactories set up there (Ford since 1930). This town became the playwright's cultural home, at least during the apartheid years, the place where his touch for 'time and place' was most sure:

> When I stand on a street corner in Port Elizabeth, I can put together a very plausible scenario for any one of the faces passing in front of me on the pavement... I have mastered the code of that time and place; I can 'read' the motley flow of life on that pavement. That street corner is 'home' in the profoundest sense of the word... I belong there, and because of that, because it is mine in a way that no other place in this world can ever be, I have a sense of authority when I write about it.
>
> **[Preface to Port Elizabeth Plays]**

This is particularly so in his play, *Hello and Goodbye*, but it is *'Master Harold'... and the boys* that reveals the backdrop to his own boyhood in Port Elizabeth set in the boarding house and then the tea room run by his mother, who was the breadwinner. She was very important in his life. As recently as 2002 he was still insisting that:

...all of those women I've written about are my mother. All of them in their strength, in their life-affirming qualities that they've got, in their defiance... all of these qualities are actually the telling of my mother's story.

[Walder 2002, p 69]

His alcoholic father had been crippled in an accident – like the father in *Hello and Goodbye*, although Harold David Fugard's injuries had been sustained during an incident at sea as a child rather than as a railway worker – which meant his only contribution to the family exchequer came from occasional fees for playing the piano in public. His role as a musician – and a potential husband – is shown in the 1998 play, *The Captain's Tiger*.

Fugard was a bright boy and gained scholarships to his secondary school and university but in 1953 he left the University of Cape Town before taking his degree, to hitchhike through Africa with a fellow student and poet, Perseus Adams. This expedition culminated in spending time as a merchant seaman and then returning to South Africa in 1955 to begin his theatrical career. Initially he worked as a journalist with SABC radio in Port Elizabeth but moved to Cape Town in 1956 where he married Sheila Meiring, who was already involved with the stage. Together they founded the Circle Players, who performed, amongst other things, Fugard's earliest dramatic efforts, *The Cell* and *Klaas and the Devil*. This latter work was an attempt to transfer J M Synge's *Riders to the Sea* to a South African setting (much as Brecht did with his *Señora Carrar's Rifles* (1937), set in Civil War Spain). Fugard's version was not a success. The couple then moved to Johannesburg where Fugard worked in the Native Commissioner's Court, which dealt with pass offences. As he has said:

It was like a factory. We sent an African to jail every two minutes. It was the ugliest thing I've ever been part of. I think my basic pessimism was born there...

[Gray 1982, p 4]

At this time he became friendly with people living in Sophiatown, resulting in *No-Good Friday* and *Nongogo*, and for a while he was a stage manager with the National Theatre Organisation. He and his wife then left for Europe, but at the time of the Sharpeville massacre in 1960 they returned to Port Elizabeth and his theatrical career began in earnest.

The Plays

His first two plays, *No-Good Friday* and *Nongogo*, made little impact at the time, but with the appearance of *The Blood Knot*, Fugard's career as an international playwright had begun. When the first plays of John Osborne and John Arden were presented at the Royal Court Theatre in the 1950s, these writers, however different, could look to a battery of indigenous dramatic influences, from Shakespeare to Shaw. This was not the case for Athol Fugard, there were no local mentors of any merit for him, but after South Africa's 'angry young man' had presented *The Blood Knot* in 1961, South African theatre in English was never to be the same again. More than forty years later, in *Exits and Entrances*, *Blood Knot* becomes a topic of conversation between the author – in his role as the Playwright – and the great Afrikaner actor, André Huguenet, where the latter refers disparagingly to 'kitchen-sink dramas'. The difference, as the Playwright points out, is that in *Blood Knot* the brothers have no sink of any kind – they could only dream of such a luxury. Fugard's close friend, the actress Yvonne Bryceland, has said about him:

> He has been very much at the disposal of those who need him; we pull lumps off him because we need him. He is the core of theatre in South Africa.
>
> **[O'Sheel 1978, p 75]**

Bryceland first saw *The Blood Knot* in 1962 with her husband, Brian Astbury, who was involved in the founding of The Space Theatre in Cape Town. The play had a major impact on Astbury:

It was extraordinary. We saw it on a night when there was a power cut, so they only had two lights on the stage and it was unbelievably hot. The play was something like nearly three hours long. Athol always said it was one of his most over-written plays but you could have fooled me, I felt it was half-an-hour long! It was one of those pieces that changed my life. It was the first time I'd actually had a sense of a culture that was my own – English-speaking white South African. It's just that you don't seem to have a culture of your own. The Afrikaners have a culture, the blacks have a culture, even the Coloureds have a culture – the Indians definitely have a culture. White South African has this weird thing which is set in America and Britain and you never feel – and suddenly *The Blood Knot* was there and I thought, 'Ah'. Even though it was about a black man and his half-black brother, it was about me for the first time.

[Personal interview, February 2001]

After *The Blood Knot*, and until the present day, Fugard has provided world theatre with a major sequence of plays, mostly set in South Africa, and for the most part reflecting, or influenced by, the politics of apartheid and its legacy. A complete chronology of these plays is provided at the end of this chapter but it is relevant, in considering his development as a theatrical practitioner, to attempt to categorise this evolution. The decade from the formation of the Serpent Players in 1963 until the triumph at the Royal Court in 1973 and 1974 was one of his most productive: six major works that included his two domestic plays, *Hello and Goodbye* and *People are Living There* – with few political overtones – to be followed by one of his finest achievements, *Boesman and Lena*. After this came *Statements after an Arrest under the Immorality Act* and then the two collaborative works with John Kani and Winston Ntshona, *Sizwe Banzi is Dead* and *The Island*. These last four plays are at the centre of his artistic life – works that expose the evils of the political and social life of South Africa more vibrantly than any others – and were followed by the out-of-character *Dimetos*. This play seemed to act as a distancing board, separating Fugard from the collaborative phase and opening up a fifteen-year period from which emerged his next set of major works. The first of these was the psychological drama, *A Lesson from Aloes,* which opened in Johannesburg in 1978, followed by three plays that were first presented away from his homeland: *'Master Harold'... and the boys*, *The Road to Mecca* and *A Place with the Pigs*. This trend was reversed with *My Children! My Africa!* which he said must first be seen in South Africa – hence his words, 'This one is between me and my country' [Time magazine, 10 July 1989].

The locale for *My Children! My Africa!,* one of his most explicitly political plays, was the Eastern Cape where there was more resistance to apartheid than in any other part of the country. In the early formation of South Africa, this area was the first frontier of hostility between black and white as the Boers pressed eastward and the indigenous Xhosa people resisted – as they continued to do into the twentieth century. Of the people detained without trial during anti-apartheid resistance, one third came from this region, which was also the birthplace of the Black Consciousness Movement. Many of the most notorious examples of human rights abuse took place in the shadow of Fugard's Port Elizabeth, including the detention and death of Steve Biko and the assassination in 1985 by the Security forces of the Cradock Four. In *Country of My Skull,* Antjie Krog quotes a friend of hers:

> The funeral of the Cradock Four...changed the political landscape of this country for ever. It was like a raging fire...in a sense it was the real beginning of the end of Apartheid.   [Krog 1999, p 65]

The core of Fugard's political dramas is backgrounded by the reality of this hotbed of political activity.

Since 1990 Fugard, and most other South African writers, have been faced with a very different literary landscape from which to mine their stories; but, as this book demonstrates, Fugard has successfully moved with the times. In 1994 the Truth and Reconciliation Commission (TRC) was set up. While the new Constitution was being debated in the early 1990s, it soon became clear that what went before could not be washed away and the new democracy launched without regard to the injustices suffered by many South Africans in the past. Once this was accepted it was necessary to determine how this should be dealt with. The ANC could not begin to govern the country, and take over the security services, if selected members of those services faced prosecution for their actions during the previous administration, and in any case, the National Party made it abundantly clear during the constitutional negotiations that if this was to be the position, there would be no settlement. There seemed therefore to be no alternative but to set up what became the TRC that would provide some form of forgiveness and limited reparations; in other words, a trade-off – revelation and truth for amnesty. The TRC was generally successful in its quest for the truth, although the efficacy of the reconciliation process was naturally more problematic and few compensation payments have been made. At the end of this process a record of suffering in the shape of a 2,000-page report was published which detailed 31,000 cases of human rights abuse. This report contained the following statement:

> The state, in the form of the South African government, the civil service and its security forces, was, in the period 1960–94 the primary perpetrator of gross violations of human rights in South Africa...
>
> In the application of the policy of apartheid, the state in the period 1960–90 sought to protect the power and privilege of a racial minority. Racism therefore constituted the motivating core of the South African political order...
>
> A consequence of this racism was that white citizens in general adopted a dehumanising position towards black citizens, to the point where the ruling order and the state ceased to regard them as fellow citizens and largely labelled them as the enemy. This created a climate in

which gross atrocities committed against them were seen
as legitimate.

[Quoted in BBC special report, 29 October 1998]

The abuse suffered by Fugard's characters forms a perfect fit with
this excoriating declaration.

His plays after 1990 can be said to reflect the ethos of the TRC,
beginning with *Playland* where the register is one of muted hope
that the past can be lived with, if not erased, much in line with
what the Commission generally concluded. In the playwright's
career there then followed two works of a more personal nature
– *Valley Song* and *The Captain's Tiger* – where he, in one persona
or another, was introduced into the scenario. The success of the
one and the limited success of the other is detailed later; but in
2001, forty years after *Blood Knot*, and seven years after the first
democratic elections, he presented his public with *Sorrows and
Rejoicings,* a further example of political theatre set again within a
small-scale family relationship. This work, for the first time in his
plays, reveals the specific antecedents of a Coloured person, the
girl Rebecca, whose mother Marta is Coloured, while her father,
Dawid, is a white Afrikaner. The mixing of the races, begun in
the seventeenth century, continues. To add to this trio there is
Dawid's wife, Allison, who is of British origins: in other words, the
South African melting pot. Since *Sorrows and Rejoicings*, Fugard
has returned to a personal subject with *Exits and Entrances* but
his latest work, *Victory,* again set in the Karoo, is as pertinent to
the disadvantaged past as it is true to the reality of the 'Rainbow
Nation' of today. At the age of seventy-five, Fugard's dramatic
skills are as sharp as ever.

As its title indicates, this book is concerned with the plays
of Athol Fugard, but they are not all given equal space. All are
important in his dramatic life but in the context of this book
emphasis has been given to a handful of works that have the most
significance.

There have also been excursions into other media. During his
university days he began a novel, which he destroyed, and he also

wrote some poetry. In 1953, while aboard the SS Graigaur, he threw overboard the draft of a second novel he had written about his mother, and since then his only published prose works have been *Tsotsi* and a short memoir, *Cousins* (1994), that provides a limited insight into his family background.

Fugard's only novel, *Tsotsi*, was not published until 1980 but it was first mentioned in the *Notebooks* of December 1960. He maintains that he could not recall the writing process involved in this work; he thought the manuscript had been thrown away, but it was discovered by his wife at Rhodes University in Grahamstown and was then edited by Stephen Gray for publication in 1980 – after some revision by Fugard. 'Tsotsi' is the slang word for a township hoodlum, or gangster, and the story is concerned with one of this breed who, initially, is so uncertain of his origins that the only name he has is that of Tsotsi. He is the leader of a brutal gang of four – there is a graphic description of a murder on a train using a bicycle spoke as a weapon – but they break up when Boston, the most intelligent member, asks questions about his leader's background. As a result, Boston is badly beaten by Tsotsi; this action creates considerable agitation in Tsotsi's mind. He wanders off to the edge of the township where he meets a distraught woman who hands over to him her newborn baby. Tsotsi keeps the child, and this, both mystically and melodramatically, changes him and makes him recall his youth as he tries to find some meaning in his life. He hides the baby in a ruined building, the remnants of a clearance operation by the government in their quest to clear that part of the township. However, the bulldozer returns to finish the job and Tsotsi and the baby are killed as the last of the walls come down.

The transformation in the book from a diabolical wickedness to a state of confused concern for others is unlikely, but the prose contains some examples of the genius of Fugard yet to be uncovered and of situations used later. Forced evictions are observed in *Boesman and Lena*; the man killed on the train had already been formed in the character of Tobias in *No-Good Friday*; and when Tsotsi's memory of his youth begins to emerge he recalls playing on a wrecked motorcar with his brother, as do Morris and Zachariah in *Blood Knot*.

As this book is concerned with Fugard's play scripts, mention of his only novel could have been omitted but it was resurrected in the twenty-first century when used as the basis for a film directed by Gavin Hood that won the 2005 Academy Award for the best Foreign Language Film – the dialogue is shared between Tsotsitaal (the slang language of the townships), Zulu, Xhosa, English and Afrikaans. The film differs from the book in that Tsotsi acquires the baby while stealing a car and he eventually returns the child to the parents in dramatic circumstances.

In 1963 Fugard wrote a television play, *The Occupation*, which was never performed; but in 1968 *Mille Miglia,* for which he wrote the script, was shown on BBC television. This film was based on the victory of Stirling Moss in 1955 in the Italian road race and of the relationship between Moss and a racing journalist named Jenkinson, who was able to assist in the victory by alerting Moss to road conditions ahead using a series of signs, designed by them both. Another diversion was a five-minute piece of mime, called the *Drummer*. This was commissioned by the Actors Theatre of Louisville in Kentucky and performed in 1980; but his most substantial works away from the live theatre were the two films *The Guest* (1977) and *Marigolds in August* (1980), written in collaboration with the director Ross Devenish. As the scripts for these films have been published they are included in this book: *Marigolds in August* in Chapter Three alongside *Blood Knot* and *Boesman and Lena* – the theatrical works that are most in keeping with the film – while *The Guest* is dealt with in Chapter Eight.

Finally, Fugard – the performer and the director. He has never been content to confine himself to pen and paper – indeed with his most experimental work, *Orestes,* there was very little of either. The people who speak his lines, their movements and all of the trappings of a theatrical production, are essential to the final outcome of his dramatic creations. He has been the first director for nearly all of his plays, and as a performer parts range from Father Higgins in *No-Good Friday* in 1958 to, 38 years later, Buks in *Valley Song*. As an actor, he has also appeared in Peter Brook's film, *Meetings with Remarkable Men* (1979) followed by parts in *Gandhi* (1982) and Roland Joffé's *The Killing Fields* (1984).

The Politics

The political and social environment from which these plays are spawned is fully exposed as the individual works are examined, but some general remarks are appropriate, particularly the views of the author himself:

> I myself do not consider my plays to be necessarily political. At one level they say something about social conditions. *People are Living There* and *Hello and Goodbye* are hardly political. On the other hand, *Boesman and Lena* and *The Blood Knot* say a lot about the society we are living in at the moment. I try to relate the very real issues of today to my plays. Perhaps you could describe it as 'theatre of defiance'; yes, my object is to defy. I am protesting against the conspiracy of silence about how the next man lives and what happens to groups other than our own.
>
> But South African audiences are so involved with the situation that it is difficult for them to see beyond the political implications. Yet the very core of a play like *Boesman and Lena* is the love between a man and a woman, embittered though it may have become.
>
> I see *Boesman and Lena* as also making a certain comment about this society and of course my politics are involved here, to the extent to which people can be mutilated by a certain social context. I think that in *Boesman and Lena*, in addition to the responsibility individuals must carry for what they have done with their lives, you also have the view that society must take a certain responsibility in terms of these two rejects, two outcasts, and the extent to which they are bruised and mutilated.   [Gray 1982, pp 51–52]

Fugard has provided, in Ronald Harwood's *A Night at the Theatre*, a corporeal example of political theatre with an account of how in September 1974, two years after the play was first conceived, *Sizwe Bansi is Dead* was given its first public performance in a black township. The venue was St Stephen's Hall in New Brighton, a plain brick building and one of only two usable halls in an area with a population of two hundred and fifty thousand. Until then, performances in South Africa of this play had been restricted to private occasions before an invited audience, prompting Fugard to conjecture how different this experience was likely to be:

> It is one thing to try to educate a comfortable white audience into what the deeply-hated reference book means to a black man and something else to confront, and in a sense challenge, an angry black audience with those same realities.   **[Harwood 1984, pp 29–27]**

It certainly was different. During the description of the Ford Factory incident in Styles' opening monologue, a member of the audience came to the front and raised John Kani's arm, like a boxing referee, and declared that he had knocked out Henry Ford the Junior. When the more serious second half of the play began, before Sizwe decided to surrender his identity and take the dead man's reference book, the audience began a vigorous debate on what Sizwe should have done and the action on stage had to be suspended. This provoked Fugard to write:

> As I stood at the back of the hall listening to it all I realised I was watching a very special example of one of theatre's major responsibilities in an oppressive society: to try to break the conspiracy of silence that always attends an unjust social system. And most significant of all: that conspiracy was no longer being assaulted just by the actors.
>
> A performance on stage had provoked a political event in the auditorium and there was no doubt in our minds as to which was the most significant.   **[Ibid, pp 31–32]**

During the three decades from 1960, Fugard was writing within a censorship regime – particularly in the 1960s and 1970s – that was one of the most all-embracing in the world. However, in a typical piece of South African double-talk, the imposition was referred to not as censorship but as 'publications control', even though the word 'publications' included not just words in books and magazines or speech uttered on stage, but on T-shirts, key-rings, and even shop signs. There were some absurd examples such as the banning of the poster advertising the film of *The King and I* because it showed a white woman, Deborah Kerr, dancing with a man who was of a different colour. From the *Notebooks*:

> So Edward Albee provides us with our first banning in the theatre. Last night's performance in Johannesburg of *Who's Afraid of Virginia Woolf?* was stopped by the Minister of Education.   **[Nb, p 103]**

Fugard's works were, in the main, free from interference from censorship but his international travel was restricted by the removal of his passport from 1967 to 1971. There were some problems with the first performance of *Sizwe Bansi is Dead* when the police prevented this, but on the second night this was overcome by converting The Space Theatre into a private club. However, when attempting to stage the play in 1973 at Witwatersrand University, Security Police chased cast and audience across the campus lawns. Across town, at the Market Theatre, there appeared to be more concern about the protection of public morals, or the joint use of lavatories, than any political issues.

However it was the apartheid of audiences that most concerned Fugard in the 1960s and 1970s. In 1962 he published 'An Open Letter to Playwrights' that by the following year, and with the support of the Anti-Apartheid Movement, had blossomed into an international boycott. Nearly three hundred playwrights from around the world withdrew all performing rights to their works if the audiences in South Africa were segregated. Fugard's state of mind on this question is strikingly exposed in an extract from the *Notebooks* of June 1962:

... Can I any more work in a theatre which excludes 'Non-Whites' – or includes them only on the basis of special, segregated performances – is becoming increasingly pressing.

I think my answer must be No.

That old argument used to be so comforting; so plausible: 'One person in that segregated, white audience, might be moved to think, and then change, by what he saw.'

I'm beginning to wonder whether it really works that way.

What I do know is that art can give meaning, can render meaningful areas of experience, and most certainly also enhances. But, teach? Contradict? State the opposite to what you believe and then lead you to accept it?

In other words, can art change a man or woman?

No.

That is what life does. Art is no substitute for life. It operates on top of life – rendering experience meaningful, enhancing experience.   [Nb, p 59]

At that time mixed casts and audiences were not prohibited, even if rare, but the apartheid authorities presumably paid little heed to the playwright's boycott: in 1965, by an extension of the Group Areas Act, they made performances by mixed casts in front of mixed audiences in public theatres an illegal act. Although condemned by many, in 1965 Fugard changed his mind and allowed some of his work to be seen by segregated audiences. Again his *Notebooks* are revealing – from December 1965:

A letter in the Post...attacks my decision to play before all-white audiences. Refers to me as having become an 'ally of apartheid' and having contributed to the 'erosion of human decency' in South Africa.

Finally I suppose I talk to white South Africa not because they can possibly profit from hearing from me but because I must talk. What is my life without the reality of a 'here and now' in which I belong: how can I cut myself off from it?

... I can't escape talking to South Africa – even under the compromising conditions of segregated performances.

[Nb, p 129]

This dilemma underlines the problems faced not only by Fugard but by many white liberals in South Africa at this time. This question is debated in Chapter Seven but, however politically impotent these people proved to be, Fugard has never allowed the frustration that arises from such a situation to affect the crusade he led for so many years on behalf of the dispossessed.

The Influences

Within his own theatre world – mainly the South African one – his various collaborative phases have influenced his growth as an international man of the theatre, as detailed later, but he does recognise a number of individuals who have been important to him. For instance, Mannie Manim, who is now in charge of the Baxter Theatre in Cape Town, has been associated since he was a fifteen-year-old stagehand at the first production *No-Good Friday*, but the two people who have had most impact have been Barney Simon, an important colleague of Fugard's in the early and middle years of his career, and the actress Yvonne Bryceland.

Simon was about the same age as Fugard and during the 1950s worked backstage, while a student in the UK, for Joan Littlewood's Theatre Workshop in the East End of London. He returned to South Africa in 1960, was employed in advertising and then, in his spare time, worked with the black actors who performed in *No-Good Friday*. After that he helped Fugard with *Blood Knot* and participated in the formation of the Phoenix Players who performed in private to black audiences and in public to all white theatregoers. He spent 1968 to 1970 in the USA. On his return, he produced *Phiri,* a jazz musical of township life and then, in 1974, he was instrumental, together with Mannie Manim, in setting up the Market Theatre in Johannesburg, a venue that became so important in the campaign to provide theatre in South Africa to non-segregated audiences. He was involved in the writing of *Woza Albert*, and other productions that bore his name included *Born in the RSA, Cincinnati, Cold Stone Jug* and, as referred to in the next chapter, *Le Costume*. He died in March 1995 and at the funeral Fugard paid tribute to his old friend:

> In a time when we are all wondering what will become of South Africa, it seems to me that Barney was the only man who really had the answer. His vision of the relationship between theatre and society was such a unique mix of authentic honesty and extraordinary compassion.
>
> **[From the programme notes to the Peter Brook production of *Le Costume*]**

Fugard's 1995 play, *Valley Song*, is dedicated to Barney Simon.

Bryceland was born in 1925. She made her stage debut in 1947 and then began her association with Fugard as the first Milly in *People are Living There*. Since then she has created the original Lena, Frieda in *Statements after an Arrest under the Immorality Act* and Miss Helen in *The Road to Mecca*, for which performance she won a Laurence Olivier Theatre Award. In addition to being the first lady of South African theatre, she was also closely involved with her husband Brian Astbury in the setting up of The Space Theatre in Cape Town. It could be said that Barney Simon was mostly concerned with the mechanics of the theatre but Yvonne Bryceland was more at the heart of Fugard's artistic development – helping with the words in the rehearsal room, and by her interpretation of them on stage. As a particular example, she was closely involved in the workshopping of *Orestes* and on stage, to take one instance, on her performance as Lena, Fugard described this as: 'awesome in its range and authenticity, in the blunted bewilderment which she used as the dominant tone' **[Nb, p 235]**.

Fugard has in the past recognized the influence of other writers and thinkers external to his own country. Although very different in style, he admired William Faulkner and has acknowledged that what he learned from the American Nobel Prize winner was that an artist can be unashamedly regional. Port Elizabeth was just as essential to Fugard's early work as was Yoknapatawpha County, however imaginary, to Faulkner. One critic makes a case for comparison with Anton Chekhov and in an interview in 1983 Fugard said:

> ...there was a very specific requirement in the case of *A Lesson from Aloes* that had me going back to study and learn from someone else, whom I admire most profoundly – Chekhov. This need to go back to Chekhov arose from the fact that, more than in the case of other plays I've written, the creational concept operated under a bland surface of words, particularly in that very strange first act, where, with the exception of one or two little explosions, the real movement is taking place subterraneously.   [Daymond 1984, p 25]

He also admired Albert Camus, whom he saw as a man of the South, much like himself:

> You know, ever since I first read Camus – I have never visited his world, but I just read about Algiers – it is the sunshine, and the hard light, that severe landscape, that has struck me. I think there's a resonance there, especially if you go into our stark hinterlands, like the Karoo. Now for me that really becomes the territory where you can see Sisyphus rolling one of his rocks up to the top of a koppie – only to see it roll down again...   [Brink 1990, p 77]

There is ample evidence in the *Notebooks* that this geographical affinity is more than matched by his respect for Camus's written work:

> How dared I assess Camus's *The Rebel* after reading only about forty pages! The further I get into it the more light does it bring into those dark and obscure corners of my

> thinking. So great is my impression, now, that I almost
> want to speak of an 'inward illumination'.   [Nb, p 61]

> His importance to me is monumental. Reading Camus
> is like finding, and for the first time, a man speaking my
> own language.   [Nb, p 94]

There are some signs of the influence of Greek theatre in Fugard's dramaturgy, besides those instances where there is a direct reference to the Greeks in *Orestes,* and *The Island* and a less than direct one in *Dimetos.* Classical playwrights often centred their work at the heart of the family – families that more often than not were visited by tragedy – as does Fugard, although most of his disasters tend to lead to a sense of helpless resignation rather than unmitigated despair.

One writer who influenced Fugard perhaps more than anyone else was Samuel Beckett. In 1981, Fugard's collaborators, John Kani and Winston Ntshona, played the lead parts in a memorable version of *Waiting for Godot* at The Old Vic in London, but two decades earlier, in 1962, Fugard had directed this play at the Rehearsal Rooms in Johannesburg with an all-black cast. At the time he considered this production as important to him as *The Blood Knot* and it is recorded in the *Notebooks* that he told the cast that:

> ... Vladimir and Estragon must have read the accounts of
> the Nuremberg trials – or else they were at Sharpeville...
> Choose your horror – they know all about it. [Nb, p 62]

A few years later he was back with *Waiting for Godot* and the Serpent Players when he highlighted, in a 1967 interview, how germane this play was to black South Africans: 'When we did *Waiting for Godot,* that image of disoriented man, dislocated man, of absurd man, pointlessness and meaninglessness, the Africans took the play and made it their own statement.' [Seidenspinner 1986, p 133] The prisoners on Robben Island obtained a copy of *Waiting for Godot.* One of them, PAC activist Kwedi Mkalipi, said:

'Is that tramp trying to show us that we can go on hoping against hope.' [Sampson 1999, p 285]

In the *Notebooks* for 1962:

> Read Beckett's *Malone Dies* over Christmas. Hard to describe what this book, like his *Godot, Krapp* and *Endgame*, did to me. Moved? Horrified? Depressed? Elated? Yes, and excited. I wanted to start writing again the moment I put it down. Beckett's greatness doesn't intimidate me. I don't know how it works – but he makes me want to work. Everything of his that I have read has done this – I suppose it's because I really understand, emotionally, and this cannot but give me power and energy and faith.
>
> Talking to Sheila about Beckett's humour, I said, 'Smile, and then wipe the blood off your mouth.'
>
> Beckett has for me succeeded in 'making man naked again'. How to be clearer in what I mean? When it rains – the rain falls on the skin of Beckett's characters.
>
> [Nb, p 67]

A further description of *Waiting for Godot* – 'a meditative rhapsody on the nullity of human attainment' [Fletcher and Spurling 1978, p 68] – could so easily be applied to *Boesman and Lena*, and to most of Fugard's other plays, and it is therefore unsurprising that the story of these two outcasts is often directly compared with Beckett's work. One critic, to accentuate the similarity, suggested a new title for Fugard's play – *Walking for Godot*! – and it could be said that for Boesman and Lena the white man is their Godot: they wait on his command. The word 'Godot' is possibly taken from 'Godillot', French slang for a boot – hardly appropriate for the barefooted Boesman and Lena, but apt if their life is seen as being under the heel of an oppressor. Beckett does not provide the 'time and place' as given in such detail in *Boesman and Lena,* although Oscar Lewenstein, who brought *Sizwe Bansi is Dead* to the Royal Court Theatre, told Fugard that as far as he was concerned, *Waiting for Godot* is set in Ireland [Personal interview,

November 2002]. However, when Estragon asks Vladimir 'where are we now' and receives the reply 'Where else do you think? Do you not recognise the place?' he replies, in Lena mode:

> Recognise! What is there to recognise? All my lousy life I've crawled about in the mud! And you talk about scenery! (*Looking wildly about him.*) Look at this muck-heap! I've never stirred from it!   **[Beckett 1979, p 61]**

Lena makes a similar comment: 'Put down your foot and you're in it up to your knee' **[p 194].**

Both these playwrights have sparse sets and a small number of players, but the famous ending of *Waiting for Godot*:

> VLADIMIR: Well? Shall we go?
> ESTRAGON: Yes, let's go. (*They do not move.*)
>
>   **[Ibid, p 94]**

is not repeated in *Boesman and Lena* where Fugard's Didi and Gogo leave the stage; an important difference. Beckett's characters could be said to be in limbo but in the case of Fugard's couple, we know they are destined to continue their sorry existence in a real and cruel world, as in the past, but with some hope, unlike Beckett's generally pessimistic vision. However, the Swedish Academy had a somewhat different view. When Beckett was awarded the Nobel Prize for Literature in 1969 the citation read: 'Beckett has exposed the misery of our times through new dramatic and literary forms. His muted minor tone holds liberation for the oppressed and comfort for the distressed.' Fugard also writes in a 'muted minor tone' with strands of hope running through, even if there is no more obvious 'comfort for the distressed' than in Beckett's plays. Fredric Jameson refers to the post-Auschwitz desolation often identified in Beckett's work – another parallel with Fugard whose scenarios are replete with extremes of desolation **[Jameson 2000, p 62].**

References and glossary

The plays dealt with in *Athol Fugard: His Plays, People and Politics* are not presented in a chronological sequence but the record of all of the major dramatic works provided at the end of this chapter are listed by the date of first performance. Where in this book references are made to play texts, they refer to the editions listed at the start of the bibliography (page 282). In 1983, Fugard's *Notebooks* covering the years 1960–1977 were published, edited by the writer and veteran anti-apartheid campaigner, Mary Benson. She has been important in his life, providing encouragement and friendship over many years. These *Notebooks* provide a valuable insight into the thought processes of the playwright and no apologies are offered for the fact that they are quoted at some length throughout this book. All further references to the *Notebooks* are indicated by 'Nb' and the page number.

This book is primarily based on a close reading of the published text of these plays which means that performance elements cannot be afforded the same importance. However, stagings of sixteen of the twenty-four works listed below have been seen, some more than once. As a result this analysis has been able to take some account of the extra dimension provided by the actor's interpretative ability and the director's skills, the set, the sound effects, the costumes, etc.

In *A Lesson from Aloes*, Piet quotes from the Bible that the first thing that Adam did in Eden was to name his world. However, in South Africa, and principally as a result of apartheid, this was not an easy task as race nomenclature became a complicated and sensitive subject around which both confusion and anger arose. In the broadest of terms the word 'Native' was used for the Bantu-speaking people, of whom the Xhosa and the Zulu were the majority, while for those whose origins were from Europe, however remote, were described as 'Europeans'. This book uses a capital 'C' for people of mixed race and a capital 'A' for black Africans (where appropriate), except when the word 'Bantu' is required. For the white populace, 'Afrikaner' is obvious but for the remainder, titles are more cumbersome – 'Europeans', 'British', 'English', 'English speaking', 'English settlers', etc – and each instance is rendered on its merits, or as appears appropriate.

A glossary is provided of the words and phrases in Afrikaans that are used in this book. Fugard writes in English for mostly English-speaking audiences, but in South Africa, these audiences would have been able to understand most of the Afrikaans phrases which, in some plays, add considerable strength and realism to the dialogue; particularly as in most cases they replicate the language of the Master – phrases that represent power, discrimination and oppression. Barney Simon described Fugard's scripts as: 'arbitrary in his use of Afrikaans... So what he gives you is the sweat of the dialogue, rather than the dialogue – the sweat of the encounter between the people, the feel.' [Gray 1982, p 48]

Play	Venue and date of first performance	Cast of characters
No-Good Friday	Johannesburg 30 August 1958	REBECCA, a young women living with Willie
		GUY, a young jazz musician and friend of Willie's
		WATSON, a township politician
		WILLIE, a man in his thirties
		FATHER HIGGINS, a white priest
		TOBIAS, a 'blanket boy' or a rural migrant on his first visit to the city
		PINKIE and PETER, backyard characters
		MOSES, an old blind man
		SHARK, a township gangster
		HARRY, one of his thugs
		A SECOND THUG

Nongogo	Johannesburg 8 June 1959	JOHNNY, a young salesman QUEENY, a shebeen propri-etress in her forties BLACKIE, her hanger-on SAM, a friend of Queeny's PATRICK, one of Queeny's customers
The Blood Knot	Johannesburg 3 September 1961	MOSES ZACHARIAH
Hello and Goodbye	Johannesburg 26 October 1965	JOHNNIE HESTER
The Coat	Port Elizabeth 28 November 1966	LAVRENTI MARIE ANIKO JINGI HAEMON
People are Living There	Glasgow 13 March 1968	MILLY, a Johannesburg landlady DON, one of her lodgers SHORTY, another of her lodgers SISSY, Shorty's wife
Boesman and Lena	Grahamstown 10 July 1969	BOESMAN, a Coloured man LENA, a Coloured woman OUTA, an old African
Orestes	Cape Town 24 March 1971	OLDER WOMAN YOUNG WOMAN YOUNG MAN
Statements after an Arrest under the Immorality Act	Cape Town 28 March 1972	A WHITE WOMAN (Frieda Joubert) A COLOURED MAN (Errol Philander) A POLICEMAN (Detective-Sergeant J du Preez)

Sizwe Bansi is Dead	Cape Town 8 October 1972	STYLES SIZWE BANSI BUNTU
The Island	Cape Town 2 July 1973	JOHN WINSTON
Dimetos	Edinburgh 27 August 1975	DIMETOS, an engineer LYDIA, his orphaned niece SOPHIA, his housekeeper DANILO, a young man from the city
A Lesson from Aloes	Johannesburg 30 November 1978	PIET BEZUIDENHOUT, an Afrikaner in his mid-forties GLADYS BEZUIDENHOUT, his wife, at the same age STEVE DANIELS, his friend, a Coloured man, the same age
'Master Harold'... and the boys.	New Haven, USA 12 March 1982	HALLY, a seventeen-year-old white boy SAM, a black man in his mid forties WILLIE, also black and about the same age
The Road to Mecca	New Haven, USA 5 May 1984	MISS HELEN ELSA MARIUS BYLEVELD
A Place with the Pigs	New Haven, USA 24 March 1987	PAVEL PRASKOVYA
My Children! My Africa!	Johannesburg 27 June 1989	MR M THAMI ISABEL

Playland	Johannesburg 16 July 1992	MARTINUS ZOELOE GIDEON LE ROUX 'BARKING BARNEY' BARKHUIZEN (off-stage voice)
My Life	Grahamstown 8 July 1994	SIVAGAMY GOVENDER RIANA JACOBS HEATHER LEITE RESHOKETSWE MAREDI ELLEANOR BUSI MTHIMUNYE
Valley Song	Johannesburg August 1995	THE AUTHOR, in his early sixties ABRAAM JONKERS, 'BUKS', in his seventies VERONICA, his grand- daughter, seventeen years old
The Captain's Tiger	Pretoria 5 August 1997	THE AUTHOR / TIGER DONKEYMAN BETTY
Sorrows and Rejoicings	Princeton, USA May 2001	ALLISON OLIVIER, a white woman, forties MARTA BARENDS, a coloured, forties REBECCA, Marta's daugh- ter, eighteen DAWID OLIVIER, the writer, a white man, fifties and then younger
Exits and Entrances	Los Angeles, USA 2004	THE PLAYWRIGHT ANDRÉ
Victory	Cape Town 2007	VICKY FREDDIE LIONEL

TWO

Sophiatown

Sophiatown, Softtown, Kofifi, Kasbah, Sophia... Place
of Freedom Square, and the Back of the Moon. Place
of Can Themba's House of Truth. Place of the G-men
and Father Huddleston's Mission. Place on Balansky's
and the Odin cinema. And let's never forget Kort Boy
and Jazz Boy and the Manhattan Brothers, and Dolly
Rathebe singing her heart out – here in Sophia...

Sophiatown. *Junction Avenue Theatre Company*

I t could be said that, as a writer, Fugard was born in Sophiatown,
a place described by Loren Kruger as 'Part ghetto, part cultural
bazaar, a meeting place of black radicals, bohemians of all
colours, and organised and disorganized criminals' [Kruger 1999,
p 87]. Certainly, contact with the black intellectuals living there
was an important ingredient in Fugard's political education, but
it would appear that the black theatre that had gone before him
– or was contemporary to him – had little influence on his development as South Africa's premier playwright. Until the second
half of the twentieth century, the received wisdom was to assume
that there was no such thing as a black culture in South Africa.
Similarly, it was taken for granted that black theatre be dismissed
because, even if evidence of its existence could be shown, it
was not worthy of consideration as it failed to follow any of the
Western or European conventions. However, elements of early
black theatre modes have been carried forward into contemporary South African works with the successful melding of dance
and song and narrative and mime – to be seen in a number of

plays contemporaneous with Fugard, significant examples being *The Hungry Earth* (1979) and *Woza Albert* (1981).

Sophiatown was established close to Johannesburg before the 1913 Land Act, which meant that a small number of the black occupants owned freeholds. Many of the black writers contributing to *Drum* magazine lived there, as did Trevor Huddleston and Desmond Tutu, together with a sprinkling of gangsters and shebeen owners: a new species of black African, second- and third-generation detribalized city people. The majority of the inhabitants were working class but there was a small and influential black middle class who deliberately distanced themselves from their rural and tribal antecedents. This middle class was nowhere better typified than in the writers who lived there during the 1950s, what Lewis Nkosi called the 'fabulous decade', an African version of New York's 'Harlem Renaissance' of the 1920s. These writers produced some of the most influential Black literature of the 1950s and 1960s including the autobiographical works *Blame Me on History* (1963) by Bloke Modisane, *Chocolates for my Wife* (1961) by Todd Matshikiza and *Down Second Avenue* (1959) by Es'kia Mphahlele. One of the most talented was *Drum's* assistant editor, Can Themba, a graduate of the University College of Fort Hare, founded in 1916 by Scottish missionaries – the first university in all Africa for black students. He died in Swaziland where he had gone after his work was banned in South Africa and was perhaps the most representative of the Sophiatown group, as reflected in his colourful writing and his heavy-drinking lifestyle. However, he is interesting in retrospect because of *The Suit,* one of his most famous short stories. This was written in 1963 and then thirty years later was adapted by Barney Simon and Mothobi Mutloatse as a play for the Market Theatre in Johannesburg; nearly ten years further on, Peter Brook's company *Bouffes du Nord* presented the play in French.

No-Good Friday

Sophiatown was the location for Fugard's first full-length play, *No-Good Friday*, which had its debut performance at the Bantu Men's

Social Centre on 30 August 1958 with the author playing Father Higgins, who was modelled on Trevor Huddleston. This play provided Fugard with valuable experience in working with other individuals in the theatre that eventually resulted in the significant success of the two collaborative plays, *Sizwe Bansi is Dead* and *The Island*. *No-Good Friday* was conceived after his university friend, Benjamin Pogrund, had introduced him to a number of the black *Drum* writers, including Lewis Nkosi and Nat Nakasa, who were keen to form some sort of theatre company as an outlet for new playwriting. It was at that time that Fugard also met Zakes Mokae, a musician with an interest in the theatre and who, in due course, created Zachariah in *The Blood Knot* and was the first Sam in *'Master Harold'...and the boys*. It is not clear what contribution his collaborators at this time made to the evolution of *No-Good Friday*, but we do have a pertinent comment from Zakes Mokae:

> Since Athol was going to direct the thing, it made sense that he also write it, though he had to do so as we went along. If he had said 'Listen fellows, I'll go off and write the play and see you again in four weeks,' our momentum would have stopped, the group would have dissolved, and he might never have seen any of us again.
>
> There was a lot of exchange between Athol and the actors, but basically he was our pen man. If something didn't work, we'd throw it out and come up with something else. You had the stuff written, you had an idea, and if it didn't work you changed it around.
>
> [Vandenbroucke 1986, p 28–29]

With the exception of Father Higgins, all the characters in the play are black. When it was presented for one performance only before an all-white audience at the segregated Brooke Theatre, the cast was required to be all black, so Lewis Nkosi was drafted in to play Father Higgins. At about the same time across the continent, in Nigeria – and before the age when world theatre became colour-blind and it was not uncommon to see a black Henry V – two amateur theatre groups, one with white members only and the other with black, were engaged in a joint production of Peter Ustinov's *Romanoff and Juliet*. To fit the parts to the skin colours available, all of the Russians in the play were white actors while the American ambassador's family and the citizens of Ustinov's Ruritania were black. In real life, Christopher Kolade, who played the American ambassador, had recently been the Nigerian High Commissioner in London. Tension between the races was not a major concern in Nigeria – unfortunately, as time was to tell, it was tribal and religious differences that became paramount – but this theatrical comparison provides a graphic instance of the lunacy of apartheid where an audience in South Africa was required to suspend belief to accept a black Father Huddleston.

No-Good Friday does not have a complicated plot. Willie is studying for a BA by correspondence course and has been living with Rebecca for the last four years. The first scene is in the backyard of his house peopled by a variety of characters but principally, in addition to Willie and Rebecca, by Pinkie and Guy, a saxophonist and an old friend of them both. It is Friday night – pay-day. The first conflict on display concerns Pinkie, who tells the yard's inhabitants that he has been ordered by his white boss to apologise to another white employee, or lose his job, for something Pinkie is alleged to have done – but had not. What is more important, Pinkie's pride or the job? It is no contest; as Buntu in *Sizwe Bansi is Dead* was to say fourteen years later: 'If that is what you call pride, then shit on it! Take mine and give me food for my children.' **[p 191]**

However, this problem pales into insignificance compared with the next action. Shark, who is described as a township gangster, calls with his thugs each Friday night to collect five shillings from everyone as protection money. There is a newcomer to the gathering, Tobias, who has just arrived from the East Transvaal, looking for work. He has left his home – '...there is no work there and the soil is bad' **[p 12]** – for the big city where the Johannesburg earth is rich; 'Egoli', the city of gold – but none of it belongs to the black man. Tobias fails to comply with, or even understand, Shark's demand and so is killed on the spot. None of the onlookers react, at least not then, but afterwards Willie reports the murder to the police although he knows they are complicit with Shark and will take no action. Willie does this because Father Higgins asks him to write a letter to Tobias' wife but in the circumstance he finds he cannot. Rebecca fails to understand what is happening to Willie and so she leaves and when Shark returns on the next Friday, Willie refuses to pay which can only result in another pointless death.

No-Good Friday differs from Fugard's later work in that there are two sets and a stage full of characters. Nevertheless, signs of the powerful writing yet to come are on display in this picture of township life, even if the characters are not as memorable as some of his later portraits. The play is about an intelligent black man who is only able to find peace of mind by opposing the system, but in this instance the system has been created within, and by, the black community itself.

Many of the inhabitants of Sophiatown were strongly influenced by the United States of America – their films, jazz and black authors –and it would be easy to compare the protection racket on display in *No-Good Friday* with that imposed by gangsters like the American Mafia. However, in Fugard's case he provides a character with an intellectual approach that provides no happy ending; there is no Gary Cooper to repel the bad man at high noon. Willie refuses to accept what is happening but he takes no practical action to change things, other than to offer himself as a sacrifice. Mr M in *My Children! My Africa!* does the same thing but his motives, and the outcome of his actions, are more complex than in Willie's case. As Willie says: 'we helped to make it, the way it is', but he is no longer prepared to avoid this fact as he tells Rebecca: 'I've been running away my whole life', and now: 'For once there is something I'm going to work out for myself' [pp 51–52].

There is no attempt to give any depth of character to the denizens that converge on this backyard – or to Shark and his thugs; for instance, the criminals in *Tsotsi* are drawn in considerably more detail. Guy is a survivor, an early portrait of Buntu in *Sizwe*

Banzi is Dead, but the character that most bears the stamp of the future Fugard is Willie. The large cast helps to provide a picture of township life, particularly in Scenes 1 and 2, but at the centre is the story of one man – a man alone. It could therefore be argued that this play is one of Fugard's most sparsely occupied; there is certainly nothing to compare with the relationships, yet to come, between the equally tortured minds of two brothers, a brother and a sister, or a pair of ill-fated lovers. That between Willie and Rebecca or Willie and Guy has little impact as we are given the journey of an individual through three phases. In Scenes 1 and 2 he generally accepts the conditions of his life. Even the murder of Tobias makes little dent in this compliant attitude and it is only when he fails to write the letter to the victim's wife that the agonies begin. He is then just as tortured of mind as a Hester or a Morris, but in this early work Fugard does not leave the agonised in limbo, to an uncertain destiny, because in this play death provides the solution. In *Hello and Goodbye*, when Hester is most distraught, Johnnie dares her to commit suicide. In *No-Good Friday* this happens.

Nongogo

Nongogo is set in 'a Johannesburg township', though not specifically Sophiatown. Nevertheless, it is a partner-play to *No-Good Friday*. It was first performed on 8 June 1959, again at the Bantu Men's Social Centre, when it attracted some interest in the wake of the enthusiasm at the time for depictions on stage of an African way of life acceptable to white audiences at home and abroad. The prime example was the musical *King Kong* (1959), written by Harry Bloom and with a Sophiatown background. The only person involved within the all-white production team who had any theatrical experience was Leon Gluckman, who had worked at the Nottingham Playhouse, but nevertheless *King Kong* was a considerable success, playing to theatres all over South Africa, where colour restrictions allowed, and at the Princess Theatre in London. Works of this nature, particularly the much later *Ipi Tombi* (1974) – referred to disparagingly as 'Zulu showbiz' – were heavily criticised by black intellectuals in the same way that Lewis Nkosi commented that *Nongogo* could have taken place anywhere. This remark might be justified except that the shebeen, the crucial backdrop to this play, can be seen as unique to South Africa.

Shebeens are unlicensed establishments that deal in the sale of illicit liquor to black people. Alcohol figures in a number of Fugard plays – and in his life (a subject returned to in Chapter Eight). Milly, in *People are Living There*, tries to establish a party with half a bottle of Muscatel and Zachariah in *Blood Knot* fantasizes about the 'jollification' of his time with Minnie and 'Golden Moments at fifty cents a bottle' [p 58], but this is precisely that – a momentary escape from the everyday drudgery. In the case of Boesman and Lena, alcohol is constantly used to anaesthetize them from the real world they inhabit, and it is ironic that they collect empty bottles – even if not all of them had contained alcohol – to earn enough to purchase full ones: *Weg wêrald, kom brandewyn* [p 213]. No doubt this liquor was marketed by the shebeen owners or Indian shopkeepers, but there is some history of the control of alcohol production by the authorities going back to the situation in the Witwatersrand mining industry in the nineteenth century. For nearly two decades from the 1880s, agriculture and the mining industry co-operated – at least initially – over the supply of cheap liquor to black miners. This situation was the subject of the Junction Avenue Theatre Company's 1978 play, *Randlords and Rotgut*, which was based on the work of social historian Charles van Onselen. In more contemporary times, some homeland development was financed by profits made from municipal liquor sales to black Africans and Coloureds.

When *Nongogo* was revived at the Laager Studio of the Market Theatre in 1981, the director, and the actress who played Queeny, did some research on shebeen queens which provided an interesting point of view relevant to Fugard's representation written twenty years earlier. Quoting from an article by Barry Ronge in the Johannesburg newspaper, *The Star*, of 24 November 1981:

In researching the play actress Thoko Ntshinga and director Lucille Gillwald uncovered some facts about these women which run exactly counter to the conventional image of the shebeen queen as a mercenary prostitute and bootlegger, raking in the shekels by ripping off the township dwellers. Thoko, who spent time in a shebeen run by her aunt when she was younger, reminds us that the shebeens are not pits of vice and iniquity, and are certainly not regarded with horror in the townships. They are rather more like the local pubs in the British style, and are an integral part of social life.

But the most fascinating discoveries they made were about the women themselves, who are by no means the victims we imagine them to be. Thoko suggest that they are probably the first and most completely liberated group of women the township has produced.

'In many ways,' says Lucille, 'the shebeen queen expresses the dilemma which faces the contemporary black woman. She is looking for personal and financial independence in a confused, confined environment, yet she also respects and yearns for the traditional family and husband.'   [Gray 1982, pp 37–38]

Fugard's version hinges on how genuine is Queeny's yearning 'for the traditional family and husband'. Her hopes in this direction are centred on Johnny, a young man who entered her life only yesterday, but who is about to depart when he discovers what Queeny was doing before setting up her shebeen five years ago:

JOHNNY: Don't stall, Queeny! Tell me or let me go.
(*Evasions are past. QUEENY realizes that she can no longer avoid the truth.*)
QUEENY: Where do I begin?
JOHNNY: There is a name for everything.
QUEENY: Nongogo.
JOHNNY: Jesus!

QUEENY: Yes... Nongogo...a woman for two and six.
Don't you think that was a bargain? Me for two and
six? And you're seeing me when I'm older and fat.
You should have seen me then... Maybe you would
have joined the queue.

JOHNNY: No!

QUEENY: Yes... I'm telling you yes!

JOHNNY: Stop it.

QUEENY: You wanted to know so I'm telling you,
Johnny, and now you got to listen. I did it because
I was hungry, because I had sworn to myself I was
going to make enough to tell the rest of the world
to go to hell. And nothing makes money like Sam
organizing the business. We started with queues
around the mine dumps at night. I can also tell you
a few things about compounds, Johnny. But we
ended big...one man at a time. That's how I got here
and Sam got his shop across the street and that's
the ten pounds that bought you rags and the first
decent thing I've ever had in my life. Because if you
think I liked it or wanted it that way you're so far
away from knowing what a woman is, you can forget
them. I'm a woman, Johnny. I never stopped being
one, but no one's given me a chance. I've had men
but never one who treated me like I mattered far
more than just a night in bed. Because that man I'll
love. If he'll just take me, for what I want to be, and
not what I was, I'll make him happy. God's been
generous in what he's given me. In body, in feelings,
in the need for love...give me a chance...

[pp 117–118]

The day before Johnny had come into the shebeen selling tablecloths. He is very different from the shebeen's usual visitors
– he is described as 'neatly, but quietly dressed' – and before
Queeny enters he signifies his appreciation of the expensive,

but neglected, furniture. When she does appear he points at the stains on the table and suggests his tablecloths could protect them in the future. These stains, mostly caused by the innumerable glasses and bottles consumed by her male customers, can be seen to represent the stains made by men during her career as a prostitute and Johnny's tablecloths are going to cover these up – wipe them out. (An impressive theatrical image concocted by Fugard so early in his career – particularly as the tablecloths and Johnny fail in their tasks. Forty years later, the table in *Sorrows and Rejoicings* is equally symbolic.) Johnny makes Queeny laugh. She buys a tablecloth and he leaves for home. When he returns soon thereafter, he has missed the bus, Queeny is delighted and he tells her about his ambition to be an interior decorator. Initially this will entail selling pieces of colourful cloth that Johnny can buy as scrap from large clothing factories. Queeny gives him ten pounds to finance this purchase, much to the disgust of Sam, who had been her pimp and helped set up the shebeen. Johnny returns with the material next day but when he is away selling it, Sam arranges for Patrick, one of the shebeen's regular customers, to hint to Johnny that Queeny has a past. When this is revealed Johnny leaves and Queeny gives up the dream of a legitimate business – and perhaps a husband.

Johnny's departure is the more tragic because he also has a past, but one he told Queeny about when they first met:

> … I was a kid. Seventeen years old. It was the big story about the mines. The good food, the clean rooms, the money. My parents bought that one all right. Money! So I came here, ten years ago. I stood just one year in that place.
>
> … There's no women in those compounds and they don't let you out. There's big bursting men in those compounds and there's no women. So they take the boys, the young ones, like me. That's what they take.

[P 95]

He wants a clean woman, but how clean is he? Nkosi said this
story could happen anywhere; Johnny's one-sided reaction can
be seen as a universally typical male attitude, but here is a case
where the South African background is more crucial than in most
of Fugard's later plays. It is a tale of thwarted love that has, at
the fall of the curtain, and like *No-Good Friday*, more abject pessimism on display than in the plays yet to come. Willie is killed and
Queeny is in agony so that as Johnny leaves, she applies cosmet-
ics and jewellery to re-create her former persona as the prostitute. As the other Johnnie in *Hello and Goodbye* uses his father's
crutches to effect a resurrection, for Queeny it is Johnny's hate
that brings this about – and it is painful to her, and to the audience, to witness her re-birth manifest itself as the disintegration of
an essentially good woman. Just before he leaves he says, sancti-
moniously: 'Some of us try to crawl out of it.' Queeny replies:

> What do you think I've been doing for five years? It
> has ended, Johnny, it was dead and buried when you
> walked in here. But you won't let it stay that way, will
> you? You'd be worse than Sam, who just sighs when he
> passes the grave. You've dug it up. You've performed a
> miracle, Johnny. The miracle of Jesus and the dead body.
> You've brought it back to life. The warmth of your hate,
> the breath of your disgust, has got it living again.
>
> [p 118]

Fugard's wheel of theatrical fortune is beginning to move. This
play may not contain too many indicators of the strengths to be
found in his next, but some of the images he creates in the future
are beginning to emerge in *Nongogo* from out of the mists of the
over-populated and more melodramatic stage of *No-Good Friday*.

THREE

God's Stepchildren

'We are all God's children', he said.
'But is God Himself not white?' asked Cachas.
And, as the Rev Andrew Flood hesitated for a reply, she made a suggestion:
'Perhaps, we brown people are His stepchildren,' she said.

Sarah Gertrude Millin

Applying Sarah Gertrude Millin's description 'God's Step-children' to the title of this chapter is wholly appropriate, concerned as it is with the characters in Fugard's plays who are Coloured. Millin, who was a confidante of the Afrikaner establishment and a friend of General Smuts, published in 1924 her fifth novel, *God's Stepchildren*, an invective against miscegenation. These 'brown people', the Coloureds of today, are a direct result of the very origins of South Africa. When Cape Town was first settled the founders of that society needed labour and so, while elsewhere slaves were being exported from Africa, Jan van Riebeeck, the commander of the station, was importing them into the continent, mainly from the Far East. The officers of the United East India Company, then the world's largest commercial enterprise, did not generally take their wives to the Cape. In 1663 there were said to be only seventeen white women amongst the population and so these officers, and eventually the free burgher farmers, bred from female slaves and the indigenous Khoikhoi these 'God's Stepchildren' – a mixed ancestry destined to occupy, both materially and psychologically, a no-man's land between the white farms and suburbs of the privileged and the African tribal kraal. In the first twenty years of occupation by the 'white tribe of Africa', 75 per cent of the children born at the Cape were non-whites, adding to the stock of slaves at little cost to the establishment. Morris and Zachariah Pietersen in *Blood Knot* and Boesman and Lena (not afforded the dignity of surnames) are of this stock.

Fascinated, week after week, as if by a snake

Fugard's masterly skill in revealing complex human relationships during an hour or two on the stage is nowhere better shown than in his first triumph, *Blood Knot*. The action of the play is confined to the interior of a *pondok* in Korsten, on the outskirts of Port Elizabeth, built with a patchwork of scraps of wood, cardboard, and corrugated iron. The play covers a period of a week or so in the lives of two brothers, who evidently share the same mother, but probably have different fathers. Morris is sufficiently light-skinned to pass for white while Zachariah is palpably black. Morris left his brother ten years ago to see if he could exist in the 'white world' away from Korsten, but returned unexpectedly a year before the action of the play begins. Zachariah has a menial job in a local park while Morris stays at home and performs the role of housekeeper. Before Morris's return, Zachariah had spent any surplus from his weekly wage on drink and women, but now Morris controls the purse strings as he saves for the 'impossible dream' of getting away from Korsten and buying a small two-man farm. In Scene One, Zachariah remembers his happier days and tells his brother, 'I want woman'. Morris quickly diverts Zachariah's desires into the idea of a female pen pal, and to this end Morris writes a letter on behalf of his illiterate sibling. Eventually Zachariah warms to the idea, but Morris's scheme for a safe substitute for the real thing backfires when they discover that Ethel, the pen pal they choose, is white and has a police-man brother. This makes the game more exciting to Zachariah and so, when Ethel threatens to visit Port Elizabeth, he uses their savings to buy, from the shop of Mr Moses, suitable cloth-ing so that Morris can take his place and pretend to be a white

Zachariah. The practical danger of exposure by Ethel evaporates when she writes to say that she has become engaged, but the more lasting danger of a serious rift between the brothers is acted out as Morris, donning the new clothes, becomes the white man and treats his brother as the subservient black. Zachariah eventually rebels at this play-acting but the ring of the alarm clock brings them back to reality – a reality with very little future.

The first four-hour version of the play, under the title *The Blood Knot,* had its initial performance in Johannesburg on the evening of Sunday 3 September 1961 before a black and white invited audience – only sixty or so people, according to Mary Benson, with the windows draped with blankets to keep out the noise of drumming from a nearby mine compound. However, the text used in this chapter is of the considerably shortened version, now entitled *Blood Knot* and published for the first time in 1985. Members of this first audience may have been familiar with two earlier South African plays that dealt with the taboo of sex across the colour line, namely *Kimberley Train* (1958) by Lewis Sowden and Basil Warner's *Try for White* (1959), although in both cases the relationship was between Coloured women and white men. There is no record that either of these works had any influence on Fugard, but the Coloured heroine in *Kimberley Train* has some lines that contain an important message relevant to *Blood Knot,* namely that there are more differences between the white and the non-white than simply the colour of their skin:

> Don't you understand: It's not enough to pretend to be white. You have to know of the colour within you and not care a damn! That's what makes people white. I wasn't able to do it...   **[Orkin 1991, p 88]**

However, theatregoers at this time are unlikely to have recalled an even earlier and less controversial example of this genre, a 1938 play by H I Dhlomo, called *Ruby and Frank*, a story of love between a Coloured woman and an African man, and only the Afrikaans speakers would have known of Bartho Smit's play *Die Verminktes* which exposed the hypocrisy of the Afrikaners' condemnation of

inter-racial sex while indulging themselves in the secret exploitation of black and Coloured women [Kruger 1999, p 104]. Although
Fugard may not have been persuaded by, or even aware of, earlier
South African plays dealing with sex between men and women of
different ethnicities, there was one work on the subject of passing
for white with which he was directly involved. While in Europe
he performed in a play called *A Kakamas Greek* written by David
Herbert, an actor Fugard had met in Cape Town. The play concerns
three men: Gabriel, an albino black trying for white, Akadis who
claims to be Greek but is actually a Coloured man called Okkie,
and Skelm who, like *Boesman and Lena*'s Outa, is black but says
nothing during the play. Athol Fugard played Okkie. Critics saw
the influence of *Waiting for Godot*; Herbert had played Estragon in
Pretoria before leaving South Africa [Vandenbroucke 1986, p 41].

After the opening at the Rehearsal Room of the African Music
and Drama Association's Dorkay House, with Fugard playing
Morris and Zakes Mokae Zachariah, *The Blood Knot* was performed
one hundred and forty times in South Africa in 1961 and 1962
where, according to Nadine Gordimer, the principally white,
English-speaking audiences 'sat fascinated week after week, as if
by a snake' [Kruger 1999, p 110]. It was then brought to the New
Arts Theatre Club in Hampstead, London, with Zakes Mokae
and Ian Bannen. After performances at a number of venues in the
USA, it spent nine months off-Broadway in 1965 and was voted
'Best Play of the Year' by the *New York Times*. Since then it has
been performed many times in the USA, the UK and the rest of
the world and, with some restrictions during the apartheid years,
around South Africa.

The long arm of the Apartheid State

Lewis Nkosi, often critical of some aspects of Fugard's work,
wrote in *Home and Exile* on the subject of *The Blood Knot*: 'In some
passages the vigour of the writing – the lyricism, imagery and
rhythm – approaches the level of pure poetry.' [Nkosi 1983, p 142]
There was, however, no poetry in the policies of the National Party
that surprisingly came to power in 1948. South Africa was already

deeply divided by race when the rest of the world, appalled at the
excesses of National Socialism in Nazi Germany, had begun to
discard the white supremacist view. As the West withdrew from
Empire and the US Supreme Court found against segregation in
public schools in America, Afrikaners were now in power and any
earlier fears that miscegenation might lead to racial equality were
to be dealt with by legislation. Hendrik Verwoerd, who was the
principal architect of the apartheid edifice built on earlier segregation precedents, introduced much of this. Like many Afrikaners
he unequivocally asserted that his authority was derived from God
and as such he had no qualms about the policies he pursued. In
reply to a reporter from a Nationalist newspaper he said: 'I do not
have the nagging doubt of ever wondering whether, perhaps, I am
wrong' [Bunting 1969, p 148]. In *Blood Knot*, Morris and Zachariah's
relationship with God provides no such certainty. Their prayer to
the Father recognises the long arm of Verwoerd's State:

> Furthermore, just some bread for the poor, daily, and
> please let your Kingdom come as quick as it can, for
> Yours is the power and the glory, ours is the fear and the
> judgement of eyes behind our back for the sins of our
> birth...   [p 122]

Blood Knot poignantly exposes the extent to which the State, the
'eyes behind our back', controls the lives of Morris and Zachariah
and punishes them for the sins of their birth, determining where
they live or do not live, where they work or do not work, and,
even more crucially, insidiously influencing the relationship they
have with each other.

William Beinart, in his book, *Twentieth Century South Africa*,
considered that the apartheid system rested on seven pillars:

> ...starker definition of races; exclusive white participa-
> tion and control in central political institutions (and
> repression of those who challenged this); separate insti-
> tutions or territories for blacks; spatial segregation in
> town and countryside; control of African movement to

cities; tighter division in the labour market; and segregation of amenities and facilities of all kinds from universi-
ties to park benches.   [Beinart 2001, p 148]

Most of these seven pillars of Afrikaner wisdom impact upon the
lives of Morris and Zachariah, and *Blood Knot* provides a fertile
ground for illustrating the sinister effect of the labyrinthine State
apparatus on the lives of just two of its insignificant and marginal
subjects. The play has flashes of humour, but the most important action on stage shows how, within this Korsten *pondok*, the
awesome power of the authorities 'out there' exerts so much influence on the brothers. On stage there are no direct instances of a
violent intrusion by the State, as in *Statements after an Arrest under
the Immorality Act*, but it is not difficult to imagine the two brothers being overlooked by Jeremy Bentham's idea of a 'Panopticon'
prison where the inmates learn to be self-regulating; where just
the suspicion of surveillance can persuade the watched to police
themselves. There is no need for Ethel's brother, or any other
agent of white authority, to appear in person; Morris acts out the
role for them exactly in accordance with the prevailing ideology.
Michel Foucault describes the impact of the Panopticon in the
following terms:

> He who is subjected to a field of visibility, and who
> knows it, assumes responsibility for constraints of
> power; he makes them play spontaneously upon himself;
> he inscribes in himself the power relation in which he
> simultaneously plays both roles; he becomes the princi-
> pal of his own subjection.   [Foucault 1991, pp 202–203]

In *Blood Knot*, Morris in particular as 'the principal of his own
subjection' plays the role to perfection. Following Orwell, the
apartheid Thought Police have transplanted their own telescreens
into the minds of the overseen who can be led to believe that, for
them, surveillance is always there, as described by Aimé Césaire:
'I am talking of millions of men who have been skilfully injected
with fear, inferiority complexes, trepidation, servility, despair,

abasement' [Fanon 1986, p 9]. The bulldozer driver notices Boesman
long enough to tell him to *Voetsek*' and *Vat jou goed en trek*', but as
Zachariah perceptively says of the white man: 'That sort doesn't
even see me' [p 116]. To the oppressor, Zachariah (any more than
Boesman and Lena) does not exist as an individual; as Buntu tells
Sizwe in *Sizwe Bansi is Dead*, they only see a ghost [p 185]. Herein
lies a fundamental truth about the position of the non-white in
apartheid South Africa: the all-seeing eyes of the white State are
never closed, the oppressed are under constant surveillance, but
the individual is ignored and rendered invisible. The oppressor
sees little human worth in the likes of Morris and Zachariah, but
the extreme evil is that these subjugated people find it difficult to
discover any real human worth in themselves.

Tread softly because you tread on my dreams

A major theme in this play is contained in the following speech by
Morris about how the all-enveloping and all-seeing 'they' are ever
present and will even participate in the dreams of Zachariah and
enter his mind, awake or asleep – and judge him guilty:

> What have you thought, Zach! That's the crime. I seem
> to remember somebody saying: 'I like the thought of
> this little white girl.' And what about your dreams, Zach?
> They've kept me awake these past few nights. I've heard
> them mumbling and moaning away in the darkness.
> They'll hear them quick enough. When they get their
> hands on a dark-born boy playing with a white idea,
> you think they don't find out what he's been dreaming at
> night? They've got ways and means, Zach. Mean ways.
> Like confinement, in a cell, on bread and water, for days
> without end. They got time. All they need for evidence is
> a man's dreams. Not so much his hate. They say they can
> live with that. It's his dreams that they drag off to judge-
> ment [...]   [p 92]

Fugard refers to dreams in a number of his plays – a device used
to underline that, in many instances, these are the only posses-

sions his victims own. Lena dreams of condensed milk – 'Sugar's not enough man. I want some real sweetness' – while Zachariah dreams of what he might do to Ethel as an alternative to shaking hands. In *Valley Song*, the more optimistic Veronica, a citizen of the new South Africa, has her own view:

> Oh yes. What's the use of a little dream. A dream must
> be big and special. It much be the most special thing
> you can imagine for yourself in the whole world.   [p 54]

In *Statements after an Arrest under the Immorality Act* Errol Philander persuades Izak Tobias, using 'old bricks and things', to build a five-room house: 'If you're going to dream, give yourself five rooms, man'. However Morris, with his dreams, tries like Prospero to manage their lives within their Korsten domain, but he cannot because control is in the hands of the Apartheid State, and Morris has no magic wand. They are poor like Yeats's unhappy lover:

> But I, being poor, have only my dreams;
> I have spread my dreams under your feet;
> Tread softly because you tread on my dreams.
> **[W B Yeats, 'He Wishes for the Cloths of Heaven']**

Coloured author Bessie Head fled to Botswana because she could not write 'in a land whose laws enacted fear and hatred', 'a place that crushes dreams' [Head 1995, p ix], but for the brothers, we know that the dream of a 'two-man farm' is as remote as the fantasy of a possible relationship between Zachariah and Ethel. These are dreams that cannot be lodged in the strong room of Styles whom we will meet in *Sizwe Bansi is Dead*. However, what is not in doubt are the consequences of the two dreams – one, a relationship between Zachariah and Ethel, suicidal; the other, becoming a landowner, totally illusory:

> Here, I want to show you something. You want to know
> what it is? A map...of Africa. Now, this is the point,
> Zach. Look – there...and there...and down here... Do
> you see it? Blank. Large, blank spaces. Not a town, not

a road, not even those thin little red lines. And, notice, they're green. That means grass. I reckon we should be able to get a few acres in one of these blank spaces for next to nothing.   [P 59]

There are no blank spaces, green or otherwise, thanks to The Natives' Lands Act. Apartheid had in effect begun with the conquest by the whites of the land occupied by black Africans. By the end of the nineteenth century, the frontier wars were over and the gun had begun to be replaced by the social and political domination over the black and Coloured people that eventually manifested itself as apartheid. Segregation was practised in the diamond fields from more or less the time discovery was made when white workers, many of whom were skilled miners from Britain, sought to protect their rights against black labour. However, segregation throughout South Africa substantially began with The Natives' Lands Act of 1913 – further amplified by the Native Trust and Land Act of 1936 – which decreed that non-whites could not own or lease land outside the Reserves established by this legislation. These Reserves covered around 7 per cent of the total land-mass of the country, which was gradually increased to about 13 per cent. The equation was a simple one: approximately 20 per cent of the population enjoyed more than 80 per cent of the land.

Morris must surely have known this, but the text does not make it clear whether he is deceiving his brother so as to save money or simply to keep him away from real sex and liquor. His unrealistic territorial ambitions contain no threat to the all-powerful State whose hegemony in the field of land ownership is total and inviolable. Or perhaps not? Nadine Gordimer, prior to winning the Nobel Prize, had gained the Booker Prize for *The Conservationist* (1974), a novel mainly located in a rural setting. Gordimer's modernist work is projected through the consciousness of Mehring, the white man who lives in the city but who owns a farm primarily as 'A place to bring a woman'. The principal concern of the novel centres on who the real owner of the land is. Is it Mehring's, or does the dead black man, who is twice buried on the farm, have the proper title? Mehring ponders to himself:

> That bit of paper you bought yourself from the deeds office isn't going to be valid for as long as another generation. It'll be worth about as much as those our grandfathers gave the blacks when they took the land from them. The blacks will tear up your bit of paper.
>
> **[Gordimer 1978, p 177]**

Twenty years later, in *Valley Song*:

> ...and after the usual formalities between lawyers, I finally had it in my hand... The Title Deed! The land was mine!
>
> Or was it? Had my few thousand Rand really bought me ownership of that land? Remember the Psalm? 'The Earth is the Lord's, and the fullness thereof.'
>
> I would have felt a lot better if God had countersigned that Title Deed. Because you see, Buks put his first seed into that soil when he was only a few years old...   **[p 31]**

Nevertheless, in the life time of Morris and Zachariah, they are never going to be landowners, and even their title to the Korsten *pondok* is probably as unsecure as the many dwellings of Boesman and Lena.

Morris, anguish and 'passing for white'

The character whose identity is the most problematical is Morris. According to Mel Gussow, from a review in the *New York Times* of 2 February 1977, 'The plays of Athol Fugard make such painful political statements – they prove the validity of art as a social instrument'. In *Blood Knot,* one of these political statements is crucially concerned with the impact of the Population Registration Act of 1950 on racial categorisation, which is fundamental in understanding Morris, his relationship with his brother and his experience of attempting to 'pass' as a white man. The wording of Section 5 (1) of the act underlines the uncertainty relating to colour in South Africa. A 'white person' is defined as meaning: 'a person who in appearance obviously is, or who is generally accepted as a white person, but does not include a person who, although in appearance obviously a white person, is generally accepted as a coloured person.' Morris appears to have been one who has failed this test both to himself and to the outside world. His dilemma is far from unique; at the end of Scene Five, he pleads with Zachariah not to see him as a Judas, but he cannot wipe out this stain – 'be forgiven' – by simply wearing his brother's coat. To quote Albert Memmi, the first move by the colonized to reject the situation is 'by changing his skin':

> The first attempt of the colonized is to change his condition by changing his skin. There is a tempting model very close at hand – the colonizer... The first ambition of the colonized is to become equal to that splendid model and to resemble him to the point of disappearing in him.   [Memmi 1990, p 186]

Morris has clearly not succeeded with the disappearing trick; he does not know who or what he is.

From the very first conception of the play, as indicated at the beginning of Fugard's *Notebooks*, Morris resists the temptation to use his lightness because it is easier to live without fear and uncertainty but in the final version of the play, a more complex Morris has emerged. Fugard writes about John Berry, who produced the play in Hampstead in 1963:

> The many moments when he said something about Morris and Zachariah that made me realise how much he understood, how total was his understanding – '... those two impoverished, mutilated bastards.' 'Don't you understand' he said to Ian Bannen, who played Morrie... 'something's missing. They're not complete. Who the hell for that matter is? That's what the play is about, man. They *want something*.'

Something else he said to Ian Bannen about Morrie: 'There's one question present, if unspoken, behind everything this man does in that room. 'What am I?' That question is his life – at all levels. Is he white or is he black? Is he friend or is he enemy? Is he real or is he a dream? And who the fucking hell knows the answers to that lot! Do you, Ian? We are dealing with a search for identity.'

And then John suddenly: 'Christ, man! Do you know what this is – this is what Sartre calls anguish...'

It seemed to me that behind everything John said about Morrie was the recognition of his, Morrie's anguish.   **[Nb, pp 70–71]**

As the incomplete Morrie tries to answer the question, 'What am I?' he, to some extent, regrets his pale skin and yet as he berates his own beginnings: 'I wish that old washerwoman had bruised me too at birth' **[p 94]**, he is acknowledging to himself that the white man is his superior. The antithesis of Morris passing for white is seen in the attitude of Zachariah to his blackness. As Morris harshly calls upon his brother to atone for the sin of dreaming that he can have a white woman, Zachariah says, with a cry of despair:

> The whole, rotten, stinking lot is all because I'm black! Black days, black ways, black things. They're me. I'm happy. Ha Ha Ha! Can you hear my black happiness? What is there is black as me?   **[p 94]**

In the *Notebooks* Fugard writes: 'Morris, if anything, hates himself. Zachariah hates the world that has decided his blackness must be punished.' **[Nb, p 9]** Morris's hatred is the more complicated; he can fume against the petty legislation imposed by the State but he appears to suffer the added burden of ambivalence, using Homi Bhabha's description, a desire to be 'in two places at once'. A year after Morris returns to live with his brother after ten years' absence, Zachariah asks him why he came back, and in

reply Morris says: 'I was passing this way'. We can only conjecture as to how deliberate the author's use of the word 'passing'
was, but what is clear is that for twelve months Zachariah seems
to have enquired little into what Morris was doing during that
time, or expressed any curiosity about the society he inhabited.
However, as the text reveals, Morris spent some part of this
decade attempting to 'try for white' and indeed Zachariah eventually acknowledges the fact when in his imaginary conversation
with their mother he tells her that Morris: 'came back quite white'
– but evidently not white enough. Morris is even more of a step-
child, to use Sarah Gertrude Millin's description, than his brother
or Boesman and Lena: he is 'not quite' part of the real (white)
family.

In the play-acting at the end of Scene Five, when Morris,
wearing the clothes from Mr Moses, calls his brother 'swartgat',
Zachariah is startled and says: 'I thought I was looking at a different sort of man'. This prompts Morris to confess that he had tried
to be different but was stopped by thoughts of his brother:

> But don't you see, Zach? It was me! That different sort of
> man you saw was me. It's happened, man. And I swear, I
> no longer wanted it. That's why I came back. Because…
> because… I'll tell you the whole truth now…because I
> did try it! It didn't seem a sin. If a man was born with a
> chance at changing why not take it? I thought…thinking
> of worms lying warm in their silk, to come out one day
> with wings and things! Why not a man? If his dreams
> are soft and keep him warm at night, why not stand up
> the next morning? Different… Beautiful! So what was
> stopping me? You. There was always you. What sort
> of thing was that to do to your own flesh and blood
> brother? Anywhere, any place or road, there was always
> you, Zach. So I came back. I'm no Judas. Gentle Jesus,
> I'm no Judas.   [pp 106–107]

During his ten-year absence, the thought of Morris disowning his
brother clearly took some time to percolate into his conscience:

the facts are more likely to be that the anguish he endured – like many others – in trying to imitate all of the nuances of being white was eventually too hard, as it was for the heroine of *Kimberley Train*: 'you have to know the colour within you'.

> Well, the suit then. Look, Zach, what I'm trying to say is this. The clothes will help, but only help. They don't maketh the white man. It's that white something inside you, that special meaning and manner of whiteness. I know what I'm talking about because... I'll be honest with you now, Zach... I've thought about it for a long time. And the first fruit of my thought, Zach, is that this whiteness of theirs is not just in the skin, otherwise... well, I mean... I'd be one of them, wouldn't I? Because, let me tell you, Zach, I seen them that's darker than me.
>
> [p 103]

As Morris says, you cannot be: 'white-washing away a man's facts', much like theatre critic Harold Hobson observed (his review in the *Sunday Times* of 24 February 1963): '...the more Morris Pietersen demonstrates his whiteness, the more and more apparent grows his blackness' and, as this occurs, his guilt eases and he becomes more stable like Zachariah, not defeated, but resigned to join the ranks 'of people getting by without futures'.

Zachariah's initial indifference about Morris' activities during his ten years absence is mirrored in the play text itself by the absence of detail as to what actually happened. He admits to trying for white but protests to Zachariah that trying to be a different sort of man was not a sin and uses the analogy of silk worms that lie dormant and then one day come out as beautiful creatures: or does he truly want us to believe that 'the worm had turned' and he gave up the delights of living life as a white man because of Zachariah? Were those ten years a happy or a sad experience? Whatever, there is sufficient evidence to show that he now prefers the Korsten *pondok*, even if this is only made tolerable by the ambition of owning a two-man farm, and actually wishes, *with absolute sincerity* (as the stage instructions have it) that he had been born black. If the tie to his brother was not genuinely the reason for his return, the title chosen for this play is stridently ironic, but the text appears to indicate that, at the last resort, it was brotherly love that brought Morris back.

What is less clear is Morris' sexuality. There is anguish in his make-up but is there any latent homosexuality involved? Away from Korsten, did Morris ever 'come out' like the silkworm and was he seen, either in the white world or the non-white world, as a 'moffie'? In *A Dictionary of South African English*, a 'moffie' is defined as: 'Homosexual, sometimes a male transvestite'. A possible origin is from British seaman's slang *mophy* – 'a delicate well groomed youth' **[Branford 1980, p 180]**. Fugard is silent on the question of Morris's sexuality, but this may be an example of his preferred ambiguity; although when Zachariah asks if Morris has ever had a woman, the stage instructions say that Morris pretends he hasn't heard. When the subject of women comes up in the next scene, Zachariah asks: 'Wasn't there ever no white woman thereabouts?' **[p 81]** Morris fails to respond, but his monastic role in that Korsten shack can be questioned. Is he just the housekeeper – why doesn't he go out to work? He was mixed up outside in the white world and now he cannot fit into the black one. It can be accepted that there is a different openness today on the question of homosexuality than in the 1960s when Fugard was writing *Blood Knot* but compared to Zachariah's no-nonsense attitude towards women and sexuality, Morris is something of an enigma. His brother comments on Morris's shyness – he always undresses in the dark: 'Always well closed up. Like a woman.' **[p 95]** – and even when he is trying on the white man's suit, he requires Zachariah to close his eyes. It would be perfectly reasonable to accept that Fugard's lack of detail about Morris's ten-year absence and the apparent unconcern about his sexuality is deliberate, a silence that the author refuses to elaborate upon; or is it that the playwright sidelines this question as being of no import in transmitting to audiences the central message of this play? It could be further argued that this unknown is in fact answered in the text where, like John and Winston in *The Island*, there is perhaps inevitably a sense of a homo-erotic relationship on view where two men alone are deliberately confined within a small room, be it a *pondok*, or a prison cell.

The world of *Blood Knot* is apparently an overwhelmingly male one, with any female participation off-stage, and restricted to the periphery of the action. Ethel, 'snow-white Ethel', vividly represents, by written word and photograph, 'the eyes behind' the brothers' backs; an unlikely and yet powerful agent of the regime. An eighteen-year-old girl, whose motto is 'rolling stones gather no moss' and with interests extending to 'nature, rock & roll, swimming, and a happy future', hardly appears to constitute a credible voice of authority but, however banal, she is white and as such represents all the power of the malevolent State. This is chillingly exposed in *Statements after an Arrest under the Immorality Act* where Fugard shows the psychologically dangerous impact, on an educated Zachariah and a mature Ethel, when the relationship is consummated – and the full weight of the State's control is applied. However, in *Blood Knot* there are some moments when the spectre of the non-appearing Ethel becomes nearly as real and dangerous as Detective-Sergeant J du Preez, the invading force in *Statements*. She is no less the unseen eye of Bentham's Panopticon than Hendrik Verwoerd himself. Nonetheless, although the external State invades and permeates the realm of Morris and Zachariah with the menace represented by Ethel, there are elements of a minor rebellion by the brothers when they fantasise about sex with a white woman:

> ZACHARIAH: It's because she's white! I like this little
> white girl! I like the thought of this little white
> girl. I'm telling you, I like the thought of this little
> white Ethel better than our plans, or future, or foot
> salts or any other damn thing in here. It's the best
> thought I ever had and I'm keeping it, and don't try
> no tricks like trying to get it away from me. Who
> knows? You might get to liking it too, Morrie.
> (*MORRIS says nothing. ZACHARIAH comes closer.*)

> *Ja.* There's a thought there. What about you,
> Morrie? You never had it before – that thought?
> A man like you, specially you, always thinking so
> many things! A man like you who's been places!
> You're always telling me about the places you been.
> Wasn't there ever no white woman thereabouts? I
> mean...you must have smelt them someplace. That
> sweet, white smell, they leave it behind, you know.
> (*Nudging MORRIS.*) Come on, confess. Of course,
> you did. Hey? I bet you had that thought all the
> time. I bet you been having it in here. Hey? You
> should have shared it, Morrie. I'm a man with a
> taste for thoughts these days [...]   **[p 81]**

But all is fantasy, just like owning a 'two-man farm' away from the restrictions of Korsten, or as unlikely as being able to grow marigolds in August in the windy environs of Skoenmakerskop.

Marigolds in August?

After Fugard had co-operated with Ross Devenish in the production of one film, *The Guest* – discussed in Chapter Eight – they came together again with a second, *Marigolds in August*. It was shot in 1979 and first exhibited in 1980 – the first major screening being at the Berlin Film Festival in that year. There are three principal characters in the film, all male. Daan, a black man in his late forties, is unmarried and described in the film text as: 'A striking and unforgettable personality – alternating between a radiant childlike innocence and garrulous distrust. The former expresses itself in his dealings with nature...the latter in his dealing with people.' **[p 5]** He works as a gardener for a variety of white householders within the community of Skoenmakerskop where he waters marigolds that he forecasts will die tomorrow when the wind comes. He has been in prison a number of times for pass-book infringements and has no valid work permit for Skoenmakerskop. He shows his 'garrulous distrust' when dealing with another black man, Melton, who is looking for work on Daan's patch.

Melton is younger and married and he is first introduced when digging a grave for one of his two children who has died. His family lives in utter poverty and despair; and their remaining child is ill:

> (*His wife is trying to pacify the crying and obviously sick child. She has an empty medicine bottle and a spoon in one hand. She cries quietly. Melton closes his eyes. Suddenly her grief erupts in a spasm of violence.*)
> WIFE: (*Hysterically.*) Finished... (*Shakes empty bottle.*) ...finished...finished...finished...finished...finished... (*She hurls the medicine bottle against the wall smashing it. Melton stares at her. She holds out the crying infant.*) Do you want this one too? (*Pause.*) Then do something, find work, you're a man, why don't you do something. [pp 14–15]

The third character, Paulus Olifant, is somewhat unique in Fugard's pantheon as he represents the playwright's interest in the natural world. He is a man of nature; the bush is his habitat and he lives off the land, obtaining what cash he needs by catching snakes and selling them to the Snake Park in Port Elizabeth. He is Coloured but described as being totally at peace with himself, in striking contrast to the anguish of Morris and the confused and frustrated Boesman.

What is in keeping with Boesman is the walking. The film opens with a series of street and road scenes as Daan walks from the Walmer location on the outskirts of Port Elizabeth to Skoenmakerskop. His traverse is mirrored by Melton who walks from his shack, soon to be demolished, situated 'in the dense coastal bush of Lovemore Park'.

When Daan sees Melton asking for work at the properties he regards as his territory, he becomes aggressive, but thanks to the intervention of Paulus, he comes to realise that they are brothers who suffer the same indignities imposed by the oppressor. Like

Fugard's other outcasts, they own nothing except their manhood, a point stressed in this instance where they meet three *Abakwetha*, recently circumcised Xhosa initiates still living apart in the bush. However, their relationship with the whites are no more assured than with Morris or Zachariah or Boesman, even though in this script the responses from the white folk seem uncharacteristically polite. What is revealed in this film is the concept that even the water that falls from heaven is reserved for the white tribe. They lock up the water tanks, so Melton says: 'It's water, boetie. We got to steal water. Even the rain belongs to them.' [p 37] This point is reinforced when Daan is encouraging Melton to burgle the store. You need to take for yourself because even if the rain does not belong to them: 'It won't ever belong to you.' [p 49]

The film ends when Melton, in desperation, breaks into the Ocean View Tea Lounge that is always closed in August. He only steals canned goods – food for his family – but the film script provides an instruction to the actor who must show Melton's reaction, not to his crime, but to the realisation of the gulf between his environment and that of the owners of the tea lounge:

> *He looks at everything carefully...the refrigerator, the record player, the television set, the comfortable furniture...and we realise that this is most probably the first time that MELTON has encountered the whiteman's life this intimately. In what is obviously the lounge he approaches a table covered with a collection of framed family photographs...the happy and smiling faces of husband and wife, children of various ages, uncles, aunts and pets. He studies them for a second and then in a moment of anger sweeps them violently to the floor.*
>
> [p 54]

We can understand Melton's action. When Paulus tells him there is a good chance he will be caught, the father replies: 'I buried my baby yesterday. Good chance I'll bury another tomorrow.' [p 49]

The sub-plot concerns the interruption to Paulus's way of life that is about to occur – his terrain has been designated as a nature reserve. They pass a group of black labourers erecting a notice

board. A white foreman is sitting in a lorry reading a newspaper.
The notice reads:

> DECLARED NATURE RESERVE
> All bait collecting, fishing, hunting prohibited.
> Picking of wildflowers prohibited.
> Lighting of fires is prohibited.
> By order.   [p 11]

When this restriction is discussed later, Daan suggests that Paulus
can overcome the problem by posing as a white man – he is
evidently sufficiently light-skinned. Llike Morris, Paulus says he
has tried it, but it did not work. Daan then compares this to trying
to grow marigolds in August – not very likely – as nature will
out. As with Fugard's work of a similar character, he leaves the
film audience asking whether this handful of characters engaged
in the slightest of stories have any hope for a better future. The
meeting with Melton may have resulted in Daan acquiring a more
trusting nature towards other people, and we can hope that the
thief is undetected and the child lives, but in reality there is as
little likelihood of an improvement in their prospects as there is
in trying to grow flowers out of season.

Real room, with a door and all that

The minimalist scenery in *Blood Knot* is taken to a further extreme
in *Boesman and Lena* where there is no set other than the imagined
stark mudflats adjacent to the Swartkops River. Unlike the mud
literally coating the stage in Robert Lepage's striking production of *A Midsummer Night's Dream* at the National Theatre in
1992, the Swartkops River mud only materialises as that caught
between Lena's toes which she squashes in her fingers saying:
'Mud! Swartkops!' The real mud on the National stage was used
to facilitate the physical action of the play, but in Lena's case the
invisible mud she finds clinging to her feet only symbolises the
deprived existence and muddied relationship of the two itinerants. As to plot and action, there is virtually none. Boesman and
Lena have walked that day from Korsten – home to Morris and

Zachariah – where the couple's shack has been demolished by the authorities who have told them to: '*Vat jou goed en trek*'. Lena wearily complains: 'Another day gone. Other people lived it. We tramped it into the ground. I haven't got so many left, Boesman.' [p 196] They spend part of a night on the mudflats where an old Xhosa man, Outa, joins them. His entrance exacerbates the tension between Boesman and Lena but his very presence miraculously provides an infusion of hope into Lena that enables her to turn the tables against Boesman. At the end of the play, she emerges with the strength to continue her life with him, still in what Fugard describes as the 'camaraderie of the damned', but in a more equal relationship, released from the chain of Boesman's violence. Outa dies during the night and before dawn they pick up their 'things' and trek on.

Boesman and Lena had its first performance at the Rhodes University Little Theatre in Grahamstown on 10 July 1969 with Fugard both as director and playing Boesman and Yvonne Bryceland taking the part of Lena. According to a review of 12 July in the *Cape Argus* there were eight curtain calls on the first night. The reviewer wrote of 'a grim and powerful play with a sustained flow of wit and joy shining off its surface of misery and desolation'. It was then staged in Cape Town and presented on two occasions in New York in the same year, with Zakes Mokae firstly as Outa and then as Boesman. John Berry, who became an influential friend of Fugard, directed the off-Broadway production. Berry had left the USA as a result of the McCarthy witch-hunt and then lived, off and on, in Paris for the rest of his life. However, he returned to America to produce *Blood Knot* off-Broadway in 1964 and then again in 1970 to champion Fugard's work and introduce *Boesman and Lena* to American audiences with what was described in Berry's obituary in *The Times* of 11 December 1999 as a 'landmark' production. No doubt his insights into these works of Fugard were nurtured when, as early as 1942, he acted in, and assisted Orson Welles in the direction of, a stage version of Richard Wright's novel of racial prejudice, *Native Son*. After Berry had directed *Blood Knot* in London in 1963, Fugard wrote in the *Notebooks* that Morris's anguish had been recognised by Berry because he was also an 'anguished man'. Fugard conjectured: 'To what extent did John's experience of McCarthyism in Hollywood enable him to understand what a corrupt society does to individuals?' [Nb, p 71]

Immediately after a version of *Blood Knot* was shown on BBC television in 1967, Fugard had his passport withdrawn, but when it was returned to him in 1971 he travelled to London to produce *Boesman and Lena* at the Royal Court and the Young Vic. Since then, the play has been presented all over the world and, in 1974, a film version was shown at the Edinburgh and Berlin Film Festivals. A new film was issued in 1999, made in the USA and directed by John Berry, who died that year at the age of 82.

The eyes behind the backs of the two itinerants are as potent and pertinent to them as for Morris and Zachariah, but in the case of Boesman and Lena these materialise as the headlights of a yellow bulldozer:

> Slowly it comes...slowly...big yellow *donner* with its jawbone on the ground. One bite and there's a hole in the earth! Whiteman on top. I watched him. He had to work, *ou boeta*. Wasn't easy to tell that thing where to go. He had to work with those knobs!
>
> In reverse...take aim!...*maak sy bek oop!*...then horse-power in top gear and smashed to hell. One push and it was flat. All of them. Slum clearance! And what did we do? Stand and look.   [p 227]

At least Morris and Zachariah had some shelter; a basic human right. Even the 'birds of the air have nests' but, while Lena envies the birds she looks for at the opening of the play, she dreams, not of a two-man farm, but of a 'Real room, with a door and all that' [p 208]. The main reason for their homelessness is poverty, but the other culprit is the Group Areas Act of 1950 whereby Boesman and Lena are denied any permanent home, due to the spatial segregation imposed by the Apartheid State.

There had been a degree of residential segregation in urban areas for Africans as far back as 1923. This also affected Coloureds, and Indians in some places, but the geography of the Coloureds was ambiguous – they had no tribal ancestry such as that used in the case of black people to justify the creation of the Reserves. However, that was not allowed to stand in the way of the Government's determination to achieve complete segregation of the races, at least as pragmatically complete as the demand for cheap labour allowed. To take just one instance: in Cape Town, during 1966 and 1967, Coloureds were moved from District Six, Simonstown and Kalk Bay when these areas were declared to be for white residents only. Amongst people forcibly removed were some families whose ancestors had lived there for centuries – since the time of the Dutch East India Company.

This widespread dispersal was the subject of an unofficial five volume report in 1983 entitled the *Surplus People Project* – an evocative title – where a group of researchers estimated that to promote homeland development, and for other reasons, around 3.5 million people had been moved between 1960 and 1982, with perhaps a further two million threatened with removal in the near future. In May 1984 the Government refuted these figures and said that only 1,971,908 people had been moved and they could not estimate future numbers. These figures need to be viewed from the perspective that the total black and Coloured population of the country in 1980 was 23.5 million, which means that at least 10 per cent of these had felt the direct impact of the Group Areas Act. Black and Coloured property owners in areas now declared 'white' were forced to sell at low prices, but those without title were dealt with under the Prevention of Illegal Squatting Act 1951, as amended in 1971, which allowed the demolition of property without warning – a fate suffered more than once by Boesman and Lena.

In addition to the impact of the Group Areas Act, or as an indirect result of this legislation, the pattern of the lives of this couple appear to have been determined by their penury. Fugard's *Notebooks* provide in detail a possible history of their inexorable descent into abject poverty:

Coega to Veeplaas	–	the first walk. One night in an empty shed at the brickfields. At Veeplas Boesman got a job at the Zwartkops Salt Works. To begin with rented a small pondok – later built one of their own. Lena's baby born – six months later dead. First miscarriage. Three to five years.
Redhouse	–	working for Baas Bobbie – farmer. One year.
Kleinskool	–	Job with Vermaak the butcher. Labourer for building contractor. One year.
Bethelsdorp	–	Farm labourer. Brickfields. Two years.
Missionvale	–	Salt works. Aloes. Lena's second miscarriage. One year.
Kleinskool	–	Odd jobs. Theft – six months in jail. Lena did house-work for Vermaak. Two years.
Veeplas	–	Odd jobs. Saltpan. Chinaman. Prickly pears. Two years.
Redhouse	–	Farm labourer. Six months.
Swartkops	–	Building labourer. Odd jobs. Bait. Two years.
Korsten	–	Odd jobs. Empties. Lena's third miscarriage. Boesman in jail again – knife fight. One to two years.
Veeplas and Redhouse	–	Prickly pears. Six months.
Swartkops	–	Bait – odd jobs. Six months.
Korsten	–	Empties. One year.

[Nb, p 169]

At the beginning of the play, when Boesman is in the ascendancy, he taunts Lena as she tries to recall the sequence of their fruitless wanderings, their pointless existence, criss-crossing the periphery of Port Elizabeth – going round in circles. One of the most evocative words in the play is the first one. As Lena appears on stage: '...*reduced to a dumb-animal like submission by the weight of her burden and the long walk behind them*', she passes Boesman before she realises that he has stopped and intones: 'Here?' [p 193] Eighteen years

of relentless decline, back into the mud of Swartkops, symbolic
of the muddy fate of the dispossessed who have no 'here' on a
permanent basis. They are not permitted possessions, except for
the junk they carry on their backs, and they are most certainly not
allowed a freehold or leasehold tenure over any one square foot
of the land they traverse; any more than Caliban, 'This thing of
darkness', can reclaim the island usurped by Prospero. They are,
as Boesman describes it, 'whiteman's rubbish':

> ... Make another hole in the ground, crawl into it, and
> live my life crooked. One push. That's all we need. Into
> gaol, out of your job...one push and it's pieces.
>
> Must I tell you why? Listen! I'm thinking deep
> tonight. We're whiteman's rubbish. That's why he's
> so *beneukt* with us. He can't get rid of his rubbish. He
> throws it away, we pick it up. Wear it. Sleep in it. Eat it.
> We're made of it now. His rubbish is people.   **[p 231]**

This situation, all too familiar in apartheid South Africa, provides
a devastating piece of theatre, saturated with political reality.
Fugard's *Notebooks* detailing the inspiration for the play gives
examples of a number of real-life itinerants that he has met, in
particular one Coloured woman who clearly serves as a model for
Lena – and for Patience in *The Road to Mecca*:

> The old woman on the road from Cradock... We picked
> her up about ten miles outside the town – she was carry-
> ing all her worldly possessions in a bundle on her head
> and an old shopping bag. About fifty years old. Cleft
> palate. A very hot day.
>
> Her story was that she had been chased off a farm
> after her husband's death about three days previously.
> She was walking to another farm where she had a friend.
> Later on she told us that she had nine children but didn't
> know where they were. She thought a few of them were
> in PE [Port Elizabeth]...

Finally only this to say: that in that cruel walk under the blazing sun, walking from all of her life that she didn't have on her head, facing the prospect of a bitter Karroo night in a drain-pipe, in this walk there was no defeat – there was pain, and great suffering, but no defeat.   [Nb, pp 123–124]

His *Notebooks* also reveal doubts Fugard had as to whether his play sufficiently condemned the regime that spawned people like Boesman and Lena:

The 'social' content of *Boesman and Lena*. Nagging doubts that I am opting out on this score, that I am not saying enough. At one level their predicament is an indictment of this society, which makes people 'rubbish'. Is this explicit enough?   [Nb, p 181]

Some critics share Fugard's view but an informed reading of the play reveals that in *Boesman and Lena*, one of his finest achievements, the political and sociological impact of the Group Areas Act are most effectively and skilfully evoked. This vividly portrayed political scenario is also the background for what is undoubtedly the heart of the play, the relationship between two desperate people whose desperation results from the politics of the country of their birth. As Fugard himself has said: 'It has always been desperate people who have fascinated me', but in addition, a major influence was his own marriage:

I am on record as saying that Boesman and Lena is the story of my marriage. I have never beaten my wife in my life, and I have no intention of doing that. It's a profound marriage – it has lasted forty odd years – but in the sense of a selfish male and of a woman who has to try and fight for her identity against that suffocating selfishness of the male – that relationship. That is the story of my relationship with Sheila, and Sheila liberated herself in a way that I tried to suggest that Lena

might, because I think, at the end of Boesman and Lena,
Boesman is defeated and Lena has actually risen above
her predicament.

[Personal interview. November 2002]

Lena does rise above her predicament and as she makes her
exit, some two hours after arriving in a physically and mentally
exhausted state at the mud-flats, she does so in a form of triumph
that can be expressed as a victory over apartheid.

Lena's epiphany

The confused recital by Lena of their repetitive cycle of walking,
given at the beginning of the play, represents a series of forced
marches as surely imposed upon them as are the orders of Hodoshe
requiring John and Winston in *The Island* to undertake their cycle
of non-utilitarian labour. Boesman and Lena's Sisyphean wanderings are just as useless and unrewarding. As Fugard wrote in his
Notebooks: 'How many put all of their life that they haven't got in
their hearts onto their heads and make that walk' [Nb, p 124]. Most
critics' readings of *Boesman and Lena* see little hope for Fugard's
wandering couple – they are destined to complete their remaining days to a pattern of a repetitive cycle of walking: 'Just crawl
around looking for a way out of your life' [p 244]. However, what
Lena does have is the inner spirit of the survivor, like the woman
on the road to Cradock – 'great pain and suffering, but no defeat'.
Lena rebels and liberates herself.

The influence of Camus in Fugard's work is well recorded;
for instance in the case of Hester, which could equally apply to
Lena, Fugard said: 'Camus helped me understand my Hester…
"courageous pessimism" – a world without hope but you've got
to have courage…you carry on, you live.' [Blumberg 1998, p 129]
Camus explored the notion of 'the absurd', which he saw as the
conflict between a desire for rationality and justice and an indif-
ferent universe. Little wonder Fugard was influenced – most of
his characters look for justice in the face of the State's indifference. Boesman hates Lena because he hates himself but, as one

critic wrote, he is defined by shame while Lena is defined by pain.
However, the humanity she shows towards Outa, and her final
ascendancy over Boesman enables her to shrug off her bruises and
tiredness and take the bucket from Boesman because it 'Hasn't
got a hole in it yet. Might be whiteman's rubbish, but I can still
use it.' [p 246]

The aimless drift around Port Elizabeth imposed upon Lena
can be compared with those of a real-life Afrikaans-speaking oppressed woman, Poppie Nongena, as described in Elsa
Joubert's 1987 book *Die swerfjare van Poppie Nongena (The wanderings of Poppie Nongena)*. Joubert had begun her career writing
travel books but in a complete change of genre, her *Poppie
Nongena* documents the life of a black Afrikaans-speaking woman
in apartheid South Africa. The book was formed out of a series
of interviews, taped by Elsa Joubert, of the poignant memories
of Poppie Nongena (not her real name). Instead of the eighteen years of nomadic existence of Lena, Poppie spends ten
years trying to keep herself and her family in the Cape, where
they have lived for generations, until she is eventually forced to
relocate to one of the Homelands. Although a powerful work in
itself, its importance at the time stemmed from the extraordinary
reception the book received when it was published in Afrikaans
in 1978. It won three literary awards, was reprinted three times
in six months and translated into English, French, Spanish and
German. It was even serialized in *Rapport*, an Afrikaans Sunday
newspaper. It can only be assumed that this reception came
about because although the work highlights the evils of apartheid, the establishment appears to have decided that it was an
apolitical piece and because it was the biography, or autobiography, of a black woman who only spoke Afrikaans – and referred
to herself as an Afrikaner – they were prepared to accept the work
as 'one of theirs'. To quote Ampie Coetzee: 'Poppie, Afrikaans-
speaking Xhosa woman, has become appropriated for Afrikaans,
has become an Afrikaans "Mutter Courage" and was praised and
accepted by the hegemony, revered and canonised.' [Coetzee 1990,
p 348] Whatever its position in the political maelstrom, it is a fasci-

nating example of 'oral history'. This work was translated into a successful play, *Poppie,* and was performed in South Africa and elsewhere. To continue the paradox, the play was produced by Performing Arts Council of the Transvaal, one of the few plays with black participation that had ever been performed at that time in a Government theatre.

Although Outa has no dialogue in *Boesman and Lena*, his presence on stage has just as much impact on the events and strength of the play as does the unseen Ethel or the dead father in *Hello and Goodbye*. He illustrates how anomalous is the position of the Coloured population in South Africa where even though they are way down the racist hierarchy, compared with the whites, they consider the black man their inferior. However, more importantly, his very presence acts as the sounding board that brings about Lena's awakening. At least she is face to face with Outa; with Boesman she mostly only sees his back. She acknowledges Outa's difference, but without the embedded prejudice of Boesman as Fugard gives her the word 'apartheid' – the only time it appears in his work: 'Sit close. *Ja! Hotnot* and a *Kaffer* got no time for apartheid on a night like this.' [p 233]

Outa also fulfils another most meaningful function in the action; he is Lena's congregation as she shares her bread with him: 'Look at this mug, *Outa*...old mug, hey. Bitter tea, a piece of bread. Bitter and brown. The bread should have bruises. It's my life.' [p 225] 'It is my life' echoes the Sacrament 'through your goodness we have this bread to offer... It will become for us the bread of life.' In the *Notebooks* Fugard wrote:

> The accident in writing: A powerful example when sorting out my ideas and images for the ending of Act I – Lena at the fire with Outa, sharing her mug of tea and piece of bread – kept hearing her say, 'This Mug... This Bread... My life...' Suddenly, and almost irrelevantly, remembered Lisa the other day reading a little book on the Mass – and there it was = Lena's Mass...the moment and its ingredients (the fire, the mug of tea, the bread)

because sacramental – the whole a celebration of Lena's
life. **[Nb, p 173]**

Lena also uses Outa as her audience when she gives a distressing
and yet resigned account of her experience of motherhood:

> *Yessus, Outa!* You're asking things tonight. (*Sharply.*)
> Why do you want to know?
> (*Pause.*)
> It's a long story.
> (*She moves over to him, sits down beside him.*)
> One, *Outa,* that lived. For six months. The others
> were born dead.
> (*Pause.*)
> That all? *Ja.* Only a few words I know, but a long
> story if you lived it.
> (*Murmuring from the old man.*)
> That's all. That's all.
> *Nee, God, Outa!* What more must I say? What you
> asking me about? Pain? Yes! Don't *kaffers* know
> what that means? One night it was longer than a
> small piece of candle and then as big as darkness.
> Somewhere else a donkey looked at it. I crawled
> under the cart and they looked. Boesman was too
> far away to call. Just the sound of his axe as he
> chopped wood. I didn't even have rags! **[p 219]**

Such are the joys of motherhood – for six months only – and the
tragedy of miscarriages. This speech graphically illustrates Lena's
experience of childbirth, matched by that of the other oppressed
black and Coloured mothers. The position outside the Homelands
may have been less severe, but according to a survey conducted in
1966, almost half the children born in most Reserves were dying
before the age of five.

A hopeless cry for freedom

In contrast to Lena, by the end of the play Boesman, like King
Lear and Hamlet, is uncertain, confused and misguided. Boesman
intones, 'Why?! Why?!!!' [p 232], because he cannot understand
the relationship between Lena and Outa, while Lear, the architect
of his own misfortune and with the dead Cordelia in his arms,
cries: 'Howl, Howl, Howl!' On the surface, Boesman is far from
being the architect of his own misfortune – the hand of the State
is all too evident – but he displays all of Hamlet's uncertainties.
As Fugard says in the *Notebooks,* Boesman represents self-hatred
and shame that by the end of the play descends into panic and
the grotesque. Two stage directions on the last pages of the text
describe this: *Barely controlling his panic... He stands before LENA, a
grotesquely overburdened figure.* At the end of the play Lena initially
refuses to leave with Boesman, which generates this panic and
in a mixture of anger and uncertainty, he determines to leave
nothing for her as he attempts to place on his shoulders their
sorry possessions. He is consequently 'overburdened' physically,
but, in addition, Fugard is illustrating symbolically that, with or
without Lena, Boesman is a typical member of the dispossessed,
shouldering all the freight that the Apartheid State effortlessly
weighs upon him, and all the other black and Coloured people
in South Africa.

Just before Outa dies, Boesman, in frustration that Lena prefers
the company of Outa to the comfort of *brandewyn,* also recalls
the tragedy of their stillborn children as he begins to reveal his
true pessimism, in contrast to the fake bravado and subservience
shown that morning as the white man destroyed their shack:

...We're not people any more. Freedom's not for us.
We stood there under the sky...two crooked *Hotnots.*
So they laughed.
Sies wêreld!
All there is to say. That's our word. After that our life
is dumb. Like your *moer.* All that came out of it was
silence. There should have been noise. You pushed out

silence. And Boesman buried it. Took the spade the next morning and pushed our hope back into the dirt. Deep holes! When I filled them up I said it again: *Sies*.

One day your turn. One day mine. Two more holes somewhere...   **[p 238]**

Echoes of Beckett where Vladimir says: 'Astride of a grave and a difficult birth. Down in the hole, lingeringly, the grave-digger puts on the forceps' **[Beckett 1979, pp 90–91]** or as Fugard wrote in a letter to Norman Ntshinga, who was incarcerated on Robben Island: 'Jump into your coffin and pull down the lid yourself' **[Nb, p 149]**. When Boesman says, 'Freedom's not for us', he is repeating one of the sorry truths that permeate these representations on stage of the lives of the oppressed, although freedom, in whatever form, is perversely and ironically a recurrent theme in *Boesman and Lena*.

No one, least of all Boesman, believes that he has acquired any real form of freedom, either from his own nature or from the oppression or indifference of the State. For him this is a complete deception, totally illusory; a very different freedom from that quietly won by Miss Helen in *The Road to Mecca* or very publicly achieved by Nelson Mandela, who entitled his autobiography *Long Walk To Freedom*. As the play shows, Boesman can no more attain any remnants of independence than Morris can purchase a two-man farm but, by the end of the play, the change in Lena's status brings some benefit to him; she acquires the strength, the freedom, to elect to stay with him. The heart of the play shows how, while Boesman sees his so-called freedom disappear as quickly as the two bottles of wine he consumes, Lena gains her freedom both within herself and in her relationship with Boesman. At the beginning of the play she curses the freedom of the birds but at the end it is she who has found that she has freed herself of the weight of her past life:

What's your big word? Freedom! Tonight it's Freedom for Lena. Whiteman gave you yours this morning, but

you lost it. Must I tell you how? When you put all that
on your back. There wasn't room for it as well.
(*All their belongings are now collected together in a pile.*)
   You should have thrown it on the bonfire. And me
with it. You should have walked away *kaal*!
   That's what I'm going to be now. *Kaal*. The noise I
make now is going to be new. Maybe I'll cry!!... Or
laugh? I want to laugh as well. I feel light. Get ready,
Boesman. When you walk I'm going to laugh! At you!

                                                    [p 245]

The freedom that Lena acquires has not changed her material
position, but she has decided to be different, to interact differently
with her situation and thereby (perhaps) change it. However,
what the play clearly shows is how, despite the poverty imposed
by outside sources, this abject couple have a relationship as strong
as the blood knot that binds Morris and Zachariah, a relationship
that transcends the reality of their existence and, further, makes
the audience care. During that one night on the mudflats, Lena is
transformed, and it is this transformation that binds the knot of
their relationship even tighter.

The silent witness

The introduction of the old Xhosa man acts as a catalyst that in a
most extraordinary way makes the epiphany of Lena believable,
even though the only understandable word that he contributes to
the dialogue of the play is her name. Lena pleads with Boesman
– 'Talk to me' and 'I want somebody to listen' [pp 199-200] – but
to no avail, and so when, in a sagacious piece of theatre, Fugard
provides her with the silent Outa, her desperation for human
contact is conspicuously highlighted. As Fugard sees much of his
work as 'bearing witness' on behalf of the oppressed, so Outa
bears witness to the sufferings of Lena's life. The silence that is
Outa – and to some extent Boesman, who is described in one of
the stage instructions as '...*in a withdrawn and violent silence*' [p
232] – also represents, in the wider context, the silencing of the

entire non-white population of South Africa, silenced socially and politically by the equally silent but all-seeing 'eyes behind their backs'. Winston in *The Island*, when representing this non-white population in his role as Antigone, tells Creon that the people of his State see the burying of her brother as an honourable action, and they would say so, '...if fear of you and another law did not force them into silence...' **[p 226]**. However, by the end of some of Fugard's plays it is possible to see that this 'silencing' has been broken. His characters in *Boesman and Lena* may not have been granted the privilege of a fully-unfettered voice but during that night on the mudflats, the new understanding of themselves, particularly in the case of Lena, is in itself some form of articulation; they have symbolically spoken out against the forces that have directed them to the Swartkops River, even if for the time being their lot in life is not essentially changed.

In *Boesman and Lena*, several minutes elapse before there is any dialogue, an opening silence used evocatively in a number of Fugard's plays. For this play, Fugard has said: 'My whole sense of the play is that it must have a core of silence'. In *Blood Knot,* there is an even longer period of quiet which is only broken by the alarm clock but even when Zachariah arrives, the stage instructions say: '*Their meeting is without words*'. It could be conjectured at one extreme that this is a deliberate device by Fugard to suggest that, even before we meet these examples of the dispossessed, the State has silenced them. In the case of *The Island* there is no need for conjecture; John and Winston are not allowed to speak while the audience is provided with a mimed dumb show of useless labour for fifteen minutes, or more in some productions: a vivid dramatic message without words.

In 1992, Dennis Walder published an article in the *New Theatre Quarterly* – 'Resituating Fugard: South African Drama as Witness' – that provided a thoughtful and wide-ranging discussion of Fugard's role as a witness on behalf of the silenced. A paradoxical example is the place of Outa in this campaign of 'bearing witness'. Although he cannot speak for himself, in *Boesman and Lena* he acts as a form of witness to the lives of those who, like him, are silenced. At the end, Outa is totally silenced by death, and when Boesman tries to avoid any involvement in the Xhosa man's demise, Fugard gives to Lena the symbolic words: 'Now you want a witness too' [p 241].

Fugard's plays are notable for the paucity of characters on stage – and off stage for that matter. Augusto Boal, in his book *Theatre of the Oppressed*, asks: 'Where were the people...when Lear divided his kingdom? These are questions which do not interest Shakespeare.' [Boal 1985, p 65] The 'people' are similarly not seen on Fugard's stage but, unlike Shakespeare, he is passionately interested in those of them that inhabit the land of the dispossessed, and he delivers this interest through incisive portraits of typical and yet individual inhabitants of that land. This limitation of characters in a society where the 'extended family' is the norm is also significant, as it tends to emphasise their isolation. Fugard does not provide his characters in these plays with any relations except for the brothers' mother and the other unseen and unquoted off-stage presence in the shape of their father – or fathers. It is not clear in the play whether there is a common father – although Morris uses the singular when he says: 'What is there for us in... Father? We never knew him' [p 66], which is repeated in the pastiche of the Lord's Prayer and in Fugard's *Notebooks* he specifically writes: 'It was the same mother! The same father!' [Nb, p 10] On the other hand is there a clue to their paternity from the differing names they were given, Morris more anglicised than the biblical-sounding Zachariah – although more likely named after Zakes Mokae? However, when the play was filmed by the BBC in 1967, with Fugard playing Morris, the text was changed to allow Morris to say: 'Different fathers but the same mother, and that's what counts...brothers' [Wertheim 2000, p 240]. The ultimate degradation, the last victory of the State, is achieved as Morris blames his black mother for the condition of his life, and not his possibly white father, who epitomises the white paternalistic State.

The final lines of the play resign the brothers to their fate and their blood. From the *Notebooks*: 'The blood tie linking them has chained them up. They are dead or dying because of it.' [Nb, p 10]

Morris accepts that they have no future but Zachariah asks if there is any other way, echoing the plaintive cry of Milly in *People are Living There*: ' Is this all we get?' **[p 60]** and Hally's scepticism when he says: 'But is that the best we can do, Sam...watch six finalists dreaming about the way it should be?'**[p 37]** Is this all that the brothers can expect? Fugard ponders whether they are any freer than the prisoners on Robben Island:

> The loss of Freedom that imprisonment involves. What is 'Freedom'?
> > Two men in a cell on the Island
> > Two men in New Brighton.
> > What is the difference?   **[Nb, p 211]**

As for Boesman and Lena – from the *Notebooks*: 'Boesman and Lena facing each other across the scraps and remnants of their life – "I'll carry my share." "This is all we are, all we've got."' **[Nb, p 155]** – or is there some hope? If there is any Christian belief in the hearts of the oppressed featured in *Blood Knot* and *Boesman and Lena*, there are some lines in Tennyson's *In Memoriam* that might be appropriate to seekers after hope who, like Boesman and Lena in particular, try to avoid being 'cast as rubbish to the void':

> O yet we trust that somehow good
> Will be the final goal of ill,
> To pangs of nature sins of will,
> Defects of doubt, and taints of blood;
>
> That nothing walks with aimless feet;
> That not one life shall be destroy'd
> Or cast as rubbish to the void,
> When God hath made the pile complete.

The sad reality is that despite the incipient hope in Lena's breast, she and Boesman are unlikely to be treated any differently in the future – they will continue to be treated as rubbish – just as

Morris and Zachariah will still be controlled by 'the eyes behind their backs' as they tolerate the conditions of their *pondok* home.

FOUR

Is this all we get?

MILLY: (*Summoning up all her control to ask the question for the last time.*) You are telling me this is all I get?
DON: Yes!
MILLY: (*Almost a cry.*) Then somebody is a bloody liar. Because there were promises. The agreement was that it would be worth it.

People are Living There [p 61]

Survival, admixed with hope, is a frequent theme in Fugard's work, even though in many cases to find the elusive quality of hope requires a sensitive intelligence. There are some who do not survive: Willie and Tobias in *No-Good Friday*, and of course Sizwe Bansi is dead. Lydia in *Dimetos* takes her own life as, indirectly, does Mr M in *My Children! My Africa!*, but in the principal corpus of his work both survival and hope rise from what appear to be the ashes of despair and doubt. There may seem to be very little positive to observe in *Blood Knot, Boesman and Lena, People are Living There* and *Hello and Goodbye*; the people in these plays are sad creatures, mostly to be pitied, but Fugard does not readily accept this interpretation: they are separate individuals all with their own separate nightmares. They have their own ghosts – and their own salvations. These dramas form a group that might be termed 'family and failure', but we are challenged to look deep into the psyche of these failures and understand them. One of the best arenas for this exercise is provided in *Hello and Goodbye* and *People are Living There* and these two plays are dealt with in this chapter.

Fugard was developing his craft at considerable speed. *Blood Knot* is still considered to be one of his finest works and this was staged only two years after *Nongogo*. Two years later, in 1963, he began the improvisations with the Serpent Players while writing *Hello and Goodbye* which had its debut in Johannesburg in October 1965, directed by Barney Simon and with the author playing Johnnie. When it played in New York in 1969, it starred Colleen Dewhurst – who received a Drama Desk award for her performance as Hester – and Martin Sheen. *People are Living There* was not staged until 1968 but a first draft, with an initial title of *Silkworms*, was completed in 1963.

It is unlikely that Arthur Miller would have been aware of *Hello and Goodbye* at this time, but there are some striking similarities with his 1968 play *The Price*. In this, two brothers who have enjoyed differing fortunes in their careers – one is a policeman and the other a surgeon – meet after many years to deal with their dead father's effects. He, like Mr Smit, has been affected by the depression of the 1930s but, unlike the Fugard play, Miller provides more characters than just the siblings.

On the other hand, perhaps *Hello and Goodbye* could be seen as not altogether a new work, being simply another version of *Blood Knot*, moved from Korsten to a white area of Port Elizabeth; but this is not the case. The actions of the 'second-hand Smits of Valley Road' are not controlled by the eyes behind the backs, as with Morris and Zachariah; the Smits' despair and survival and future are manipulated by forces that are not directly concerned with the politics of the time. In this play it is class and not race that is at work and the circumstances of what happened, or is happening, at Valley Road can be directly linked to the 'Bad Years', the economic depression in the 1930s that impacted on the entire Western world, including Miller's fictional father – and South Africa, where conditions were exacerbated in the early thirties by the worst drought of the century.

The Bad Years

To recognize the force of this economic slump on the Afrikaner, it is necessary to trace the differences between the ancestors of the Smits and the English settler, represented in Fugard's plays by Gladys in *A Lesson from Aloes*, Elsa in *The Road to Mecca* and Allison in *Sorrows and Rejoicings* – whose origins stem from the beginning of the nineteenth century. The first substantial number of English immigrants arrived in 1820 when they were promised an uninhabited African Eden in the Eastern Cape. However, what they got was a sour-grass coastal plain with no market nearer than Cape Town, five hundred miles away; and as for uninhabited, the territory had been fought over by the Boers and the Xhosa for years – there were five frontier wars before 1820. This is important. The English that arrived were not farmers. They were conservative and middle-class, products of the age of mercantile capitalism who had left Britain in the midst of the world's greatest industrial revolution. These proved to be the characteristics they took forward into the twentieth century, where the English-speakers continued to dominate the commercial world as many Afrikaners became more and more destitute.

In the 1930s a commission, partly funded by the Carnegie Corporation of New York, was set up to investigate this problem and report on the economic conditions that had created, principally amongst the Afrikaners, what were known as 'poor whites'. When published, the report estimated that of a white population in 1931 of 1.8 million, of whom one million were Afrikaners, three hundred thousand were living as paupers. Mr Smit, who was a railway-man, was one of these. Employment at the South African Railway was seen as an Afrikaner sinecure but during the 1930s this did not seem to have done him much good. The Africans watched him doing their work, laying sleepers, and this impacted on his behaviour as he became a husband and a father – and then a cripple. He was injured at work – or, more precisely, when absent without leave from his labours picking prickly pears. This may be precisely relevant. The accident was more his fault than that of the South African Railway and as a result, the monetary compensation Hester searches for may never have existed.

The Parents

At the beginning of the play Johnnie says that the year is 1963 but there is some confusion about this. Nevertheless, the most important date is not the now, but the past, the hard times of the 1930s when the father's character was formed and the fates of the children determined.

Hester and Johnnie are the children. She has returned to the family home when Johnnie allows her to believe that their crippled father is still alive and bedridden in the next room. Hester's life in Johannesburg as a prostitute has reached such a pitiful state that she has returned in the hope, to begin with, of obtaining her share of the compensation she believes was paid to their father as a result of the accident when he lost his leg. At least this is one reason, but more is at stake within Hester than avarice; what she really seeks is her heritage. For Fugard this was crucial:

> The major question – why and what does Hester find in the boxes when searching for her father's 'compensation'? When I know the answer, I have got my play.
>
> **[Nb, p 118]**

To keep Hester away from the unoccupied bedroom, Johnnie brings into the living room all the boxes and old suitcases stored in the adjoining room so that she can search them for hidden treasure. She finds nothing but forlorn memories and when, near the end of the play, she goes into the bedroom, that is also empty. She then returns to her old life leaving Johnnie resurrecting his father and using his crutches. This action takes place over a period of around two hours – during late afternoon and early evening – between Hester's 'Hello' and 'Goodbye'.

During the bad years the family existed on the wages earned by the father when he was in work, or his disability pension after the accident, but Hester's view is that these times were made worse by the nature of the parents, one or both:

HESTER: Anything. Everything. There wasn't enough
of anything except hard times.
JOHNNIE: Because we were hard up. Breadwinner out
of action.
HESTER: Other people are also poor but they don't live
like we did. Look at the Abels – with only an *Ouma!*
(*Shoes in her hands.*)
Even the birthdays were buggered up by a present
you didn't want, and didn't get anyway because it
had to be saved. For the rainy day! I've hated rain
all my life. The terrible tomorrow – when we're
broke, when we're hungry, when we're cold, when
we're sick. Why the hell did we go on living?

[pp 165–166]

'It had to be saved.' One of the boxes explored by Hester is full
of shoes, including those of the left foot of a man who has had his
left leg amputated.

Both Hester and Johnnie are aware of the trials their father
endured in the work place:

1931, or '30 or '32. Don't you remember? The Bad Years.
1931 onwards. When he worked on the line to Graaff-
Reinet. You remember, man. Daddy. He was always
telling us. Something terrible had happened somewhere
and it was Bad Times...no jobs, no money. That's what
he dreams about now.   [pp 170–171]

But is it that simple? Can all the blame be accorded to the 'Bad
Years'? Were the characteristics of Johannes Cornelius Smit and
his wife-to-be, Anna Van Rooyen, defined by this event – or were
their fates, and those of their children, predetermined?

To explore this it is first necessary to try and understand the
father, particularly as his creator includes this play in the trilogy
called 'The Family' on the basis that the familial relationship is of
'child and parent' [Nb, p 174]. This is significant. On the surface
the play could be viewed as another story about two siblings, just

as in *Blood Knot*, but as a result of Fugard's remarks, the unseen father needs to be included as a major contributor to this drama.

In *Blood Knot*, Ethel is the spectre offstage and out of sight, but now the siblings' father, who is equally invisible, has to be accorded a more significant role – as he has done throughout their lives. What do we know about him? Would this question be easier to answer if Fugard had allowed him to appear in person? According to the *Notebooks*, this matter was the subject of some thought:

> First problem: do we see the old man? Or only Johnnie and his sister?
>
> Even if not seen, his 'presence' must be felt – a hate, bigotry, resentment, meanness – as twisted and blind as the physical reality.   **[Nb, p 99]**

Fugard's final decision to keep him hidden was the correct one. The play is stronger with the father acting as an unseen presence, but even away from view he has a crucial role to play. If Fugard thinks Hester is strong, how much more so the father. There is no sense that he is physically cruel or even overtly domineering but he seems to have been able to exert a most baleful influence from within his strict Calvinistic persona – in Johnnie's case even after death. Hester's memory is of:

> ...all our life it was groaning and moaning and what the Bible says and what God's going to do and I hated it! Right or wrong? Right! And it was hell. I wanted to scream. I got so sick of it I went away. What more do you want? Must I vomit?   **[pp 135–136]**

This is described by Loren Kruger as 'the dead weight of their father and his impoverished material, psychological, and existential legacy.' **[Kruger 1999, p 111]** He appears to have been able to exercise the same psychological control over the children as the eyes behind the backs of Morris and Zachariah.

While alive he is directly involved in Johnnie's choice to abandon an ambition to be an engine driver – or was this decision totally self-induced? Johnnie sets out for the Kroonstad Railway School with his packed suitcase that includes a gift from his father – one of his railway shirts – but only gets as far as the bridge:

> So, back there. Simple as that. Here. I told him I missed the train. We agreed it was God's will being done. He helped me unpack. Said I could still keep the shirt.
>
> **[p 180]**

God's will – or that of his earthly father who rewards the son by permitting him to keep the shirt? What a trade-off! An old shirt for the chance of a life away from Valley Road. When Fugard himself left home to hitchhike through Africa, he did not turn back, but there was one parallel: as a parting gift Fugard senior gave his son a present of a shirt that the son had given his father as a Christmas present a few months earlier. **[Fugard 1994, p 82]** Johnnie's return may not enable us to advance too far in understanding the father, but such knowledge is essential if we are to comprehend why Hester and Johnnie develop as they do. The most cogent insight into his character is given in the following:

> JOHNNIE: Daddy never beat Mommie. He was never drunk.
> HESTER: Because he couldn't. He was a crock. But he did it in other ways. She fell into her grave the way they all do – tired, *moeg*. Frightened! I saw her.
>
> **[p 176]**

It is difficult to recognize from the reminiscences of Hester and Johnnie what those 'other ways' were. For instance, with Hester, did he hate her because she rebelled as a young girl, 'stayed out late and brought those soldiers home' **[p 151]**, or did she rebel because of his nature? According to Johnnie, he found a reason for Hester's waywardness:

> When you left he said, 'We won't speak about her any more.' You weren't a real Afrikaner by nature, he said.

> Must be some English blood somewhere, on Mommie's
> side. He hated you then.   **[p 151]**

Ironically it is of course the Afrikaner blood – and their status
– that has created this dysfunctional family, although eventually
Hester does not limit the responsibility to him:

> And I don't blame him! Look at it. Who the hell would
> have wanted anything to do with us? We weren't just
> poor. It was something worse. Second-hand! Life in
> here was second-hand…used up and old before we even
> got it. Nothing ever reached us new. Even the days felt
> like the whole world had lived them out before they
> reached us.   **[p 172]**

Looking for other reasons that converted this family from being
merely poor to something worse, second-hand, little blame can
be attributed to the mother. Hester shows affection for her, but
if she added to the ills of 57A Valley Road because she was frightened, who or what had frightened her? Hester recalls:

> See for yourself. There's a picture in the album – it's
> here somewhere. Smallish. None of her things fitted me
> when I was big. Always working – working, working,
> working…
> (*Pause.*)
> Frightened. She worked harder than anybody I ever seen
> in my life, because she was frightened. He frightened
> her. She said I frightened her. Our fights frightened her.
> She died frightened of being dead.   **[pp 174–175]**

Daddy has to be the primary cause and Hester finally comes
out with it: 'I hate him! There, I've said it, and I'm still alive. I
hate my father.' **[p 180]** What is clear is that this man was partly
moulded on Fugard's own father, who was also crippled: '*Hello
and Goodbye* – a dedication: "To my father, who lived and died
in the next room."' **[Nb, p 121]** Fugard had a love/hate affiliation
with his father but in that between Hester and hers there was very

little love; her father was more influential in the path her life was to take than the playwright's. On the other hand, the relationship Johnnie had with his father was very different; and the reasons why this was so form an essential element in this intriguing play.

The Children

Johnnie is a paradox. In the harshest light, he could be seen as another piece of the junk stored away in the boxes and old suitcases Hester searches through, but he genuinely grieves for his father. He does not want to think about the death, but for the audience it is quite difficult to pin him down. At one moment he seems to be astute. When Hester walks into the house at the beginning of the play he asks her to prove who she is. She describes a birthmark he has to which Johnnie replies: 'But all of that's me. I know I'm Johnnie. It's *you*. You say you are Hester. Prove it.' [p 135] On the other hand his speech is littered with infantile puns, jokes and sayings: gently does it, peace not pieces, hospitaliTEA, truth is stranger than fiction, ants in pants, etc. What is clear is that he is asexual. He is interested in what Hester does: 'On average, how many times a week?' and 'How much did they pay you?' – referring to her clients, whom he naively calls boyfriends [pp 160, 159]. At the opening of the play he talks voyeuristically about an amorous bus conductor, but he apparently accepts his situation:

> So he kissed her. Just like that. And I thought, there are things to think about, which I did and still do, things to happen which hadn't and don't seem to. Other things happened to me. I am not complaining. I'm happy with my lot. [p 131]

In his opening monologue he stresses, 'Here' as does Lena, but her 'here' is the muddy bank of the Swartkops River and only one stop during her itinerant life. For Johnnie, his 'here' has been the scenery of his life to date. 57A Valley Road is consistently referred to as a home. On the surface, for Johnnie it is 'my doorstep', 'my house' [p 134], but for Hester the Proustian memories that emerge when she searches the boxes of rubbish are such that she describes the house as a place where 'Nothing in here knows what happy means' [p 148]. Johnnie refers to the contents of the boxes as their inheritance but Hester's response is to say: 'All I'm inheriting tonight is bad memories' [p 66]. These are evoked by tangible objects – such as a pair of girl's shoes or an album of old photographs. As a comparison in Beckett's *Krapp's Last Tape*, the recollections are more powerful as they are registered by voice; even though they appear to give as little comfort to Beckett's man as the rubbish of the Smits gives to Fugard's unhappy Hester.

Even for Johnnie it is not truly 'Home, sweet home'. We begin to realize early in the play that he is living a lie, particularly as to his view of this house: 'Back home. No place like here. That's a lie.' [p 128] He says he never looks back, but of course he does. He recalls the funeral and the difficulty moving the coffin from the house where he could not help: 'all of me useless' [p 129]. He also remembers his frequent and familiar jaunts around Port Elizabeth – or journeys by the Number six bus to Summerstrand (Europeans only). He repeats the bus stops which read as a litany of despair, as poignant in its own way as Lena's list of her peregrinations. He refers to himself as useless, but is that correct? He has nursed his father for many years, but the picture we are given of this man shows that even if the care he has provided is motivated by love, the absence of any alternative way of life could be seen as an equally compelling motive. The only regular human contact he has had for many years has been his father, and Hester's impingement on this drab existence – where the penury is really a poverty of spirit – results in the play ending with Johnnie bringing his father back to life. The risen man stands, using his father's crutches, and the senior Smit is resurrected. The last word of the play is 'Resurrection'. Hester could see this happening as she tries to deny her brother the crutches:

> HESTER: YOU don't need them!
> JOHNNIE: (*Anguish.*) I NEED SOMETHING! LOOK
>   AT ME!

> (*HESTER lets go of them and JOHNNIE goes on to them
> with feverish intensity.*)
> *Aina! Aina!*
> HESTER: Then take them. Be cripple!
> JOHNNIE: God's will be done...
> HESTER: You already look like him...
> JOHNNIE: ...in hell as in heaven...
> HESTER: ...and sound like him...
> JOHNNIE: I am his son, he is my father. Flesh of
> his flesh.   [p 181]

As already discussed, the picture of the father is somewhat blurred
but the portraits of the brother and sister are more clearly focused.
If the senior Smit has any malevolence it can be described as
passive in nature – as static as Johnnie's existence. An empty life,
the highlight of which is an occasional trip to the beach with a
bottle of beer and a packet of biscuits – lemon creams – but Hester
is different. She has some spirit even if she leaves her second-hand
existence at Valley Road to become second-hand goods available
to any man with money in his pocket. As a result she is full of
hate, as Johnnie recognizes:

> ...your hate! It hasn't changed. The sound of it. Always
> so sudden, so loud, so late at night. Nobody else could
> hate the way you did.   [p 136]

In this regard there is a direct comparison with Morris. He hates
his ambivalent self but Hester hates both her Valley Road memories, particularly of her father and what her life has become.
Morris' hate is reflexive but hers is a full-throated.

> And you're my brother and I'm his daughter so we must
> all love each other and live happily ever after. Well I got
> news for you, brother. I don't. There's no fathers, no
> brothers, no sister, or Sunday, or sin. There's nothing.
> The fairy stories is finished. They died in a hundred
> Jo'burg rooms. There's a man. And I'm a woman. It's as

simple as that. You want a sin, well there's one. I *Hoer.*
I've *hoered* all the brothers and fathers and sons and
sweethearts in this world into one thing... Man. That's
how I live and that's why I don't care.   **[p 158]**

This hate is shadowed by guilt, again like Morris. He felt guilty
for leaving his brother but Hester's cannot be explained so simply.
Hers is a godless world apparently reflecting Fugard's own position. From the *Notebooks* for 1963:

> It is Good Friday. I read the paper, observe the solemn
> silence in the street outside – but it all means nothing
> to me. I am an alien to this Christianity. Too much has
> been written on to the label 'Christian' for me to tie it
> around my neck...
>   In any case I still spell god with a small 'g' – and I
> suppose that settles it.   **[Nb, p 77]**

There is no connection between the Christian Good Friday
and the day of the week referred to in his first major play but
then again, Fugard's indifference may have changed with time.
Religious references are not infrequent in these plays, and if they
are examined, changes in view might be charted. As a result of the
murder he has committed, Martinus in *Playland* has a strong belief
in a biblical heaven and hell; but Morris' nightly reading from the
bible has little impact, and his recital of the Lord's Prayer is in
fact used to highlight the unseen power of the State, rather than
any belief in a Christian salvation. Any religious brotherhood
Outa gives to Lena is short-lived as she tells him that Boesman
says: '...there's no God for us'.

   Nevertheless, there is perhaps some more tangible evidence of a
change of view by the writer. *The Road to Mecca* can be considered
a quasi-religious play, and he has also written, but not apparently
published, a work about Hildegard of Bingen (1098–1179), the
German abbess, composer and mystic. Extracts from this latter
work, *The Abbess*, can be heard on the internet covering a reading
of a section of this play that Fugard gave to the University of

California and where some sympathy with a Christian faith seems evident.

Whatever his stance, in reality the Christian faith was important for the black and Coloured peoples in apartheid South Africa as, perversely enough, it was largely used by the Calvinist Afrikaner to legitimize the very system that appears to have exiled Morris and Zachariah and Boesman and Lena to a Godless world. It also provides no comfort for Hester who exclaims, with some vehemence and, perhaps in her case, some justification: 'THERE IS NO GOD! THERE NEVER WAS!' [p 181]

The two acts of the play take place in a room of the Smit's family home, described as a lounge-cum-kitchen, to be renamed kitchen-cum-bedroom when Johnnie became too big to sleep with his sister. This room contains only four chairs and a kitchen table with a solitary electric light hanging above. The chairs are significant. Only one is occupied throughout the play, and this fact can be seen to underline how barren and self-centred is life in this house, revolving firstly around the father and now around the lonely Johnnie. However, even these spare and frugal surroundings might be seen as a paradise compared to where Hester has spent her rootless and unhappy existence while she has been away:

> There's no address! No names, no numbers. A room somewhere, in a street somewhere. To Let is always the longest list, and they're all the same. Rent in advance and one week's notice – one week to notice it's walls again and a door with nobody knocking, a table, a bed, a window for your face when there's nothing to do. So many times! Then I started waking in the middle of the night wondering which one it was, which room…lie there in the dark not knowing. And later still, who it was. Just like that. Who was it lying there wondering where she was? Who was where? Me. And I'm Hester. But what's that mean? What does Hester Smit mean? So you listen. But men dream about other women. The names they

call are not yours. That's all. You don't know the room,
you're not in his dream. Where do you belong?   [p 154]

Was her father the only agent responsible for the awfulness of her
sorry life? The sister in *Nongogo* became a prostitute so as to be
able to feed herself but the circumstances in Hester's case were
not that dire. Was the sad atmosphere of the family home so terrible that she was prepared to exchange it for a room of her own,
like the one so described? Whatever, at the end of the play she
goes back to that world – Valley Road has not provided her with
any alternative. She has become as much a fatalist as her brother
but for a moment, as she leaves, there is a hint of something positive, something worthwhile, with her parting advice to Johnnie:

> Anything! Anything's better than this, *Boetie*. Get a job,
> a girl, have some good times...
>   ... Read the newspapers, plant the seeds, have a
> garden...
>   That's it!... Live happily. Try, Johnnie, try to be happy.
>   [p 187]

The audience leaves the theatre thinking that Johnnie is unlikely
to act on this advice, but the fact that Hester offers it provides just
a glimmer of a more hopeful future.

Night at the Braamfontein Circus

In the memoir *Cousins*, Fugard regrets that he has never been able
to write what he referred to 'as a full-blooded comedy' although
he does suggest that *Hello and Goodbye* and *People are Living There*
have their moments. He continues:

> At one point had a quote from Charlie Chaplin on the
> title page of *People are Living There*:
>   If the flesh does not laugh in mockery and delight at
>   the world and at itself, then it will die.
>
>   [Fugard 1994, p 67]

There are certainly comic moments in *People are Living There* but close examination shows that the play is still deep in familiar Fugard territory, down amongst life's failures. It is, however, splendid theatre. The dialogue sparkles as the players provide, according to Polonius, the 'tragical-comical' that veers from a glimpse of the Marx Brothers – or Chaplin – to a measure of the menace found in Edward Albee. Milly, at the centre of Fugard's play, wears a dressing gown throughout the action. The 1957 film, *Woman in a Dressing Gown,* was described by the writer, Ted Willis, as a film about: 'good honest fumbling people caught up in tiny tragedies'. *People are Living There* is rather stronger than that; more akin perhaps to the bitterness of the characters searching for their youth in the Australian play *Summer of the Seventeenth Doll.*

Like other Fugard dramas, there is another offstage character who, like the senior Smit, is pulling the strings that cause the action to develop as it does, although this is not too difficult to achieve when the puppets onstage comprise two frustrated women, a pimply pseudo-intellectual and a simpleton. The kitchen-sink setting is not much of an improvement on that at 57A Valley Road, and as to the moment of the play, the audience can envisage as background music Frank Sinatra quietly crooning 'Saturday night is the loneliest night of the year'.

As already mentioned, although this play was not seen on a stage until 1968, its composition preceded *Hello and Goodbye.* Indeed, Fugard has said that he could never have produced his Hester if he had not already conceived Milly [Nb, p 131]. *People are Living There* was first performed in Glasgow in March 1968 and the South African premiere was in Cape Town on 14 June 1969 with Fugard directing and playing Don and Yvonne Bryceland, in their first collaboration together, as Milly.

Millicent Constance Jenkins – Milly – is a fifty-year-old menopausal woman who lives in Braamfontein, as did Sheila and Athol Fugard for a time in 1958. She is based on someone they knew. Milly is more prosperous than anyone else in Fugard's early plays. Although Braamfontein is an unfashionable district in central Johannesburg, she owns the two-storey house big enough to accommodate her and four lodgers and she does appear to have a maid or washerwoman called Emily. The most important of the lodgers, at least from her point of view, is Mr Ahlers with whom she has had a sexual and social relationship for ten years. When she tells him of the biological change that is taking place, he suddenly decides he would like to have children:

> Because of the business and Ahlers being a good name
> to keep alive through the ages. We better stop now, he
> said. But we can still be friends   [p 62]

The first move in the change towards 'just being friends' is that on this Saturday night they will not be going to the Phoenix for their usual beer and sausages because he will be spending his evening with a German acquaintance; we never discover for certain whether male or female but a lady is suspected (just conceivably Hester – or someone like her). Milly is distraught and determined that, with help from the other lodgers, she will have a good time without him and when he returns to the house he will discover his ex-lover the mistress-of-ceremonies at a happy and raucous party. However, she has some unlikely – and partly unwilling – accomplices. The most important of these is the unkempt Don, a would-be intellectual at the age of twenty who is studying for a degree – like Willie in *No-Good Friday*. The final partygoer is Shorty, a postman who is also an aspiring boxer and nurturer of silkworms. He is not very bright and often finds his weekly wage has been cut because of a habit of losing letters. He cleans the shoes of Mr Ahlers – the ones that are used for walking out on Milly or for walking over the diffident Shorty.

The South African background is made clear at the outset when Shorty wishes for a Native sparring partner, preferably a Zulu. Later, Don is alleged to have called his fellow lodger '...a perfect specimen of a retarded poor white'. This opinion is then amplified:

> Here we have Natives to do the dirty work. You're saved
> by your white skin. Because, examine the facts. You

can just about read and write. You can't carry out the
simple duties of a postman. I don't think you could do
anything complicated. You blunder on from day to day
with a weak defence – yet you survive. You even have a
wife.   **[p 58]**

Yes, he does have a wife, Sissy, who comes from one of the poorer
white suburbs of Johannesburg. She is twenty years old and, like
Mr Ahlers, is also going to miss the party; she is going out with
Billy, said to be her cousin. She and Shorty have been married six
months, possibly unconsummated:

MILLY: (*To SHORTY.*) Do you understand? He doesn't
    think you know how to do it. I think you do, but
    that Sissy doesn't want it from you, because we *both*
    think that Billy knows how.   **[p 59]**

During the party the character of the three principal participants
is exposed with a mixture of cruelty and farce. Don has absorbed
sufficient philosophy, mainly of the existential variety, to decide
that he has given up on life:

DON: Purpose was dead in me. When I lay down at
    four o'clock there were a hundred reasons why I
    should have got up. When you saw me not one was
    left. I had systematically abandoned the lot. Sartre
    calls it Anguish.
MILLY: Still looking for it are you?
DON: I've told you before the expression is 'finding
    oneself'.
MILLY: What's the difference?   **[p 4–5]**

He dreams he is an awkward outsider, all arms and legs, that he
uses to try and explain his inertia: '...How can I put it? The fit. A
feeling that things don't fit. Either life is sizes too big or you're
too small. Something's wrong somewhere.' **[p 34]** He talks about
an 'Age of crisis' but does not specify how this is caused. No
doubt it is the arrogance of youth – he is only twenty years old,

but to create a proper foil for Milly, he needs to appear old for his years. Milly's counter to Sartre is: 'Put out the light and you're as good as in your grave.' [p 7]

She is – from the opening stage instruction – '...*dressed in an old candlewick dressing gown, her hair disordered, her face swollen with sleep.*' and during the first exchange with Don talks about getting 'dressed in a mo' so she can pop out for a bit of fresh air. Five hours later she is still in her dressing gown; the party is over and we are drawn back to the potency of cheap music:

> The Party's Over, it's time to call it a day.
> They've burst your pretty balloon and taken the moon
>   away.

Sissy appears briefly and, before she leaves, puts on her stockings in full view of her husband and Don which gives the latter another opportunity to display some of his philosophical wisdom. He sees her action as a deliberate act to arouse both of the men in her role, and their part in it, as:

> The aggressive female and the submissive male. The loss
> of male virility and the woman's rebellion. The neurosis
> of our time.   [pp 15–16]

The next departure is that of Mr Ahlers. As he leaves, offstage, Milly harangues him, in '*a pose of studied indifference*' and tells him:

> ... I've got a surprise for you, Mr Big Shot. I'm also
> going to have a good time tonight. You bet. I'm going
> to have the best good time of my life.   [p 24]

However the trio of partygoers have a problem in deciding where to go, and what to do, in pursuit of a 'good time'. Milly becomes frustrated. They reject the movies and she looks out of the window at the Saturday night revellers and asks:

> Where are they going? They're going to have a good
> time. Every Saturday night they drive past on their way

> to have a good time. And don't try to tell me they're
> going to the movies! So what I want to know is, where
> is it?   [p 25]

They never do discover where to find it and Don does not help when he presciently tells Milly that her good time is an illusion – a hoax. Nonetheless, she is determined to take revenge for what she sees as ten years of her life put to waste. However difficult, a party will be in full swing when Ahlers returns. Don's response is to say that a party cannot be produced out of thin air, even with half a bottle of Muscatel, a cake and some Christmas decorations; but, with some reservations, he agrees to participate when Milly finds an excuse and says it is to be a celebration for her birthday. Act One closes at this point.

The party is all of the fiasco Don portends. Shorty is sent out buy cake and only manages to return just in time to prevent the event being transformed into a 'midnight supper'. There is some attempt at a sing-song but the affair is so depressing Milly has to insist: 'Nobody goes to bed until I've laughed!' [p 53] She is asking for the impossible but in the process some cruel opinions are voiced on the subject of her party-going accomplices. This then leads to the heart of the play as Milly, crying to anyone who will listen, implores: 'Is this all we get?' Don tells her it is and, 'what's more you've had it', but Milly refuses to accept: 'I'm owed,' she says, 'pay up or be damned.' [pp 60–61] She does not get paid even though she makes some feeble attempt to revive the celebrations when Ahlers returns, but with little success. Her laughter is very hollow; tonight's events have begun to make clear to her the absurdity of the human condition.

The action on stage rarely flags but if the audience has time, it might try to consider how, more than with any other Fugard play, the olfactory constituent within that kitchen is well signposted. At this Braamfontein location, it is the variety of perfumes that catches the attention. Shorty may have washed himself after sparring at the boxing club – although he has been charged an extra shilling for his laundry because of smelly socks – but when the gloves are off, in the bout between Don and Milly, the following exchange takes place:

> MILLY: Now we're getting somewhere. The rock-
> bottom boxing match! Get out your gloves and
> hit! But first... Let's tell him if he wants to see a real
> psychological curiosity, to have a good look in the
> mirror next time he squeezes his pimples. That's
> why no decent, clean-living girl will ever stomach
> the sight of you. Furthermore, you also blow your
> nose on the sheets, I've seen you use the washbasin
> in the bathroom as a W.C., and I've a strong suspi-
> cion that, as regards positively filthy habits, that is
> still not the worst. Sometimes when I think of your
> hands I want to vomit...
> DON: You finished?
> MILLY: If you've hit the bottom with a bump – yes.
> DON: Because there's a few things that could be said
> about you.
> MILLY: Go ahead. It's a free-for-all.
> DON: (To SHORTY.) Come on. Let's tell her.
> MILLY: Christ, you're yellow.
> DON: You've started to get old woman odours. You
> should use scent. It's unpleasant being near you
> at times. That's why I've got no appetite left. And
> maybe that's why Ahlers doesn't want to marry
> you...   [pp 59–60]

Sissy is described as 'Dressed with cheap extravagance' and no doubt she is also doused with a cheap and cloying perfume. Even the offstage member of this smelly crew, who has a new suit and has taken an unusual bath for a Saturday, does not escape:

> Putting on his hair oil. Ever seen that? If you want to
> lose your breakfast one morning go up and have a look.
> It's enough to make any decent person sick. He sort of
> washes those big paws of his in the stuff, smoothes down

the few hairs left on his nut and then smiles at the result.
It's revolting. Greenish. Looks like peppermint liqueur.

[p 8]

Time's wingèd chariot

Fugard has said that it is secrets 'that generate all the significant
action in my plays' [Fugard 1994, p 74], as is shown for example in
The Road to Mecca and with Gladys in *A Lesson from Aloes*; but for
Milly, it would seem that there are no striking revelations from the
past that cause her any torment. She tries to explain her behaviour by pretending to Don that there really are incidents from
the past 'that would make your hair stand on edge' [p 26]. Don is
not convinced; he believes she is 'compensating for a colourless
existence...' [p 31] but he agrees to play her game. He begins by
asking if her father was the Prince of Wales and then moves on to
provide verbal pictures of rape – of either Milly or her mother –
climaxing with an assault on her by a drunken father. She avoids
answering the question – to Don or herself – by perversely saying
that it would not be a secret if she knew what it was. All she does
know is that the picture in her mind of a little girl in a white dress
now hurts because she has achieved nothing except for a state of
inertia, personified in her current attire.

What principally concerns her is the agony of rejection at a
significant point in middle age – and the realisation that time is
passing. Fugard's grasp of the unity of time and place is well in
evidence for this play with, like the alarm clock in *Blood Knot*,
a timepiece as an essential prop. This, as unseen as Mr Ahlers,
is a malfunctioning grandfather clock which needs to be beaten
on the hour to persuade it to give out the correct number of
chimes. This object is first encountered at seven o'clock in the
evening and then throughout the play; as the beatings continue,
it symbolises the importance Fugard attaches in his work to the
concept of time. This is very strong in *People are Living There*. It is
Milly's biological clock that has prompted tonight's crisis and we
can readily accept the reluctant chimes as the indicator that time
is running out for everyone on view. Is the marriage of Shorty

and Sissy destined to survive? If Don doesn't rise up from his bed
and complete his studies, does he have any future? And what of
Milly? She believes life owes her something but if she goes to
bed too often having worn her nightwear all day, is the debt ever
likely to be paid? Halfway through Act Two Fugard provides her
with one of his finely-crafted monologues. This includes:

> So you see, it's gone. Or just about. A little left but
> mostly in the way of time. The rest just gone. Not broken,
> or stolen, or violated – which might make it sound like
> there's been no crime, I know. But I did have it and now
> it's gone and nobody ever gets it back so don't tell me
> that doesn't make us victims.   **[p 62]**

The off-stage Ahlers is not the villain – it is time represented by
the off-stage grandfather clock. 'Time's wingèd chariot' is moving
fast for her but once again, as the audience leaves the theatre,
they know she is a Fugard heroine – a defiant survivor. In the
Notebooks he wrote:

> Ultimately – Pessimism. But heroic. Heroic Pessimism.
> 'Courage in the face of it all' – Milly in *People are Living*
> *There*: Surrender? Never!   **[Nb, p 96]**

It is Don that points this up:

> DON: If I were to sit down somewhere, unseen, and was
>   quiet for a very long time, and the instinct to return
>   to the herd petered out. All you need is four walls,
>   and a lid.
> MILLY: (*Looking around.*) In here?
> DON: It's a likely spot. It's got the feel.
> MILLY: But there's a street outside their, Don! All the
>   people! Rush-hour traffic. Right outside that front
>   door!
> DON: Yes. But you've got to open it, Milly. (*Pause.*) Did
>   you today?   **[pp 72–73]**

At the end of the play we believe she does.

Who's Afraid of Virginia Woolf?

In contrast to an apparently happy ending when we conjecture she follows Don's advice and opens the door – or as happy as it can be in the circumstances – the play has a strong heart of potential peril where the comparison with *Who's Afraid of Virginia Woolf?* is conspicuous. Don, like George in Albee's play, knows where they are heading if not careful:

> DON: I know, and that's why I'm nervous. It won't work. Take my advice and call it a day. Nothing's happened yet...
> MILLY: Exactly!
> DON: (*Trying to ignore her.*) We are intact, in shape. We can still retire with grace. But beyond this lies the point of no return.
> MILLY: Good! I've always hated going back.
> DON: For the last time I'm warning you – this is getting dangerous.   [p 54]

In the end no one gets seriously damaged and the contest between the two main opponents ends in a draw even though, with the arrogance of youth, Don says he was not trying too hard:

> MILLY: ... What's the score for tonight?
> DON: (*Looking at his notes.*) On paper it looks like a draw. But I stopped halfway. It's a pity. You came out with some good things towards the end.   [p 73]

Albee's play is considerably more high-octane than Fugard's, and where rather more drink is consumed than half a bottle of Muscatel, but George issues similar warnings to Martha that she is treading on dangerous ground. She breaks the rules by talking about the child she and George never had, but at the end of Act Three, entitled *The Exorcism*, there is a resolution. George tells his guests and his wife that the party is over as he and Honey between them deliver the benediction: Requiem aeternam dona eis, Domine. Et lux perpetua luceat eis. (For to Thy faithful people, Lord, life is changed, not taken away.) [Albee 1967, p 138]

For Milly, her act of revenge against Ahlers has failed dismally but more importantly, her protestation to the world that people are living there is much more of a success and she is given her own benediction; laughter – enormous laughter – as described in the final stage instruction:

> (*MILLY's amusement breaks into laughter. Repeating random images from the picture just drawn – kangaroo, boxing gloves, blue bums, etc, etc. – her laughter grows enormous. At its height and with DON watching her...*)
> *CURTAIN*   [p 74]

FIVE

The Fractured Family

In a sense another version of Boesman's predicament: the constant emasculation of Manhood by the South African 'way of life' – guilt, prejudice and fear, all conspiring together finally to undermine the ability to love directly and forthrightly.

Athol Fugard [Nb, p 194]

Their creator considered that the trio of plays *Blood Knot, Hello and Goodbye* and *Boesman and Lena* should be called 'The Family'. His next play – if it can be so described – was *Orestes*, where the family connection between the three actors involved is taken from Greek mythology. However, their affiliation, one to the other, is not self evident to the audience and needs to be teased out. It is not a happy family. In the second play dealt with in this chapter, *Statements after an Arrest under the Immorality Act*, the relationship on display is one of the closest – that of lovers – but mainly because of the world in which they live, it is doomed to failure.

Greeks bearing gifts

With *Orestes* there is no text for the reviewer to use and it has been seen by very few people – the first time being in Cape Town on 24 March 1971. What is available in printed form is a description of Fugard's intentions in a letter he wrote to an American, Bruce Davidson, and published in 1978 in a collection entitled *Theatre One*, edited by Stephen Gray. There is no text because that was the playwright's design: a piece of experimental theatre using three hand-picked actors – a young man, a young woman and an older woman – a minimum of props and with references to Greek mythology and recent South African history to create a public performance. After ten weeks in a rehearsal room, Fugard and the three performers emerged with an article of theatre that lasted about eighty minutes and used less than four hundred words – although the spectator was given the following information in advance:

> From Greek mythology comes the story of Clytemnestra. Her husband was Agamemnon. She had two children, Electra and Orestes. Agamemnon sacrificed their third child, Iphigenia, so that the wind would turn and the Greek fleet could leave Aulis for the Trojan War.
>
> Agamemnon returned to Clytemnestra ten years later when she murdered him. Orestes and Electra avenged his death by killing their mother.
>
> From our history comes the image of a young man with a large brown suitcase on a bench in the Johannesburg station concourse. He was not travelling anywhere.

Fugard's letter amplifies this as follows:

> For your benefit I would like to add this: For most South Africans the young man with the suitcase suggests John Harris, a twenty-six-year-old white South African. In an appallingly desperate protest about the world in which he found himself, he took a suitcase full of dynamite and petrol, wired to a time fuse, into the Johannesburg Railway Station and left it beside a bench. It exploded, killing a young child and severely burning an older woman. He was caught, tried and executed.
>
> **[Gray 1978, p 84]**

Even if the small audience – about seventy seated on a single row of chairs around the acting area – knew who the young man was meant to represent, it is impossible to determine whether they fully understood what was happening. The boy plays games with a matchbox. This goes on for what must have seemed an interminable length of time, reminiscent of John and Winston in *The Island*, until the girl says: 'Let's dream about the sea!' Eventually this leads to an impression that the older woman is at the seaside with her two children. The younger girl mimes smoothing a patch of sand and then asks: 'How do you spell "Orestes"?' The mother (played by Yvonne Bryceland), whom Fugard hopes is now seen as Clytemnestra, is shown giving birth to Iphigenia and then at every performance she pulls a chair to pieces to represent her killing of Agamemnon. Bryceland then collapses in the debris and the children try to restore their world to what it was, but fail. She rises and moves towards other chairs representing a railway station bench where she is joined by the children. The boy now has a brown suitcase filled with newspapers. He uses these to make bombs and places one in each of the older woman's hands. The action then shows the bombs exploding and the mother falls to the floor and drags herself away from the scene using her heels and her backside; the soles of her feet have been burnt away by petrol. The piece closes with short speeches by the three actors, that of the young man taken from the official testimony of John Harris.

Fugard was particularly influenced at this time by Grotowski and his Polish theatre laboratory. The South African has repeated more than once that for him the gospel of the theatre is that propounded by Grotowski who contended that all 'Poor Theatre', all true theatre, requires is an actor and an audience; and so, if nothing else, *Orestes* acted as a bridge in Fugard's quest for true theatre as he moved from the limited scope of experimental theatre, devised in collaboration with others and seen in *The Coat*, to the triumphs of his middle period, *Sizwe Bansi is Dead* and *The Island*. As he was to bring *Antigone* into relevance in *The Island*, in this play the mythology is related directly to the tragedy of John Harris' action with, to quote from the *Notebooks*, 'Clytemnestra as reflected in the cracked, tormented mirror of our twentieth century awareness of self'. From this same entry: 'We saw our spectators seated...on brown station benches (*Whites Only*)...' Fugard then goes on to write:

> Among many things, we wanted in this way to say to our
> audience of white South Africans: 'You could have been
> the person beside whom a young man left a large brown
> suitcase.'   [Nb, pp 188–189]

In itself, *Orestes* is relatively unimportant in a survey of Fugard's
theatrical output, but its influence on his work since then, at least
in his view, is paramount. In a chapter in *Modern African Drama*,
published in 2002, he wrote:

> *Orestes* was my first, and remains my most extreme excur-
> sion into a new type of theatre experience, in which we
> attempted to communicate with our audience on the
> basis of, for us at least, an entirely new vocabulary. It has
> defied translation onto paper in any conventional sense.
> I have tried. At the moment it is 'scored' in three large
> drawing-books. It is one of the most important experi-
> ences I have had in Theatre and I will be living with it,
> and using it, for as long as I continue to work. I can
> think of no aspect of my work, either as a writer or direc-
> tor, that it has not influenced.
>
> [Jeyifo 2002, p 526]

Adultery and a white skin

Fugard chooses the titles for his plays with considerable care, some
more obvious than others, and in the case of *'Master Harold'... and
the boys* this even extends to punctuation and format. Is 'Harold'
a master and are the boys – lower case 'b' – an afterthought?
In most cases his appellations are short except for the case of
Statements after an Arrest under the Immorality Act and, in keeping
with the legal phraseology in this title: 'It is hereby agreed that
this play shall hereinafter be referred to as: "*Statements*"'.

The content of this work would appear to be fully reflected in
its label. Or is it? This is one of Fugard's more difficult plays,
partly because the fully descriptive title is to some extent a
smokescreen that hides what is at the heart: a doomed love affair

similar to those that have graced world literature in the past from Madame Bovary and Anna Karenina to the two railway passengers in *Brief Encounter*. Fugard never loses sight of this, and the story of the affection that Frieda and Errol have for each other is as bitter-sweet as in similar tales; but in this instance the South African context cannot be ignored. Their relationship is doomed because it is the State that determines who can be loved, and who cannot. The divisiveness is not caused by questions of morality or honour or loyalty. Causes are not from differences in age, or class or biology – or even colour; Errol could easily have been as white of skin as Frieda. No. Their love is forbidden primarily because of the Afrikaner's pathological fear of miscegenation.

Many of Fugard's best-known works are re-staged at regular intervals all around the world but *Statements* is rarely performed, perhaps because more than most it appears to be particularly relevant to the South African political landscape and the conservatism of the Karoo, the first of many of his plays to be set in this region. No doubt we could have had a story about the consequences of sex across the colour line set in Johannesburg, or in Tennessee, but what Fugard gives us is not just another pair of his people who transgress one of the most fundamental of the apartheid laws but a couple who are, in their own way, as disadvantaged as Morris and Zachariah and as equally affected by the Group Areas Act as were Boesman and Lena. This would not be self-evident for audiences outside South Africa, but even so, the sympathetic viewer would soon understand the frictions in this relationship and the causes of these. These lovers are not Romeo and Juliet; romance is not a word that sits comfortably in a darkened room in this small South African desert town.

Statements was introduced to the theatre-going public at The Space Theatre in Cape Town, a performance area evolved from the joint enthusiasms of Brian Astbury, his wife Yvonne Bryceland and Fugard himself. Astbury, a photographer by calling, was principally involved in the practical task of finding somewhere to stage experimental works and this came to be in a converted warehouse, named after the seminal text by Peter Brook, *The*

Empty Space, and from the Open Space in Tottenham Court Road in London. Initially Astbury contemplated a revival of *People are Living There* but Fugard did not want to direct this and promised a new play, which became *Statements*. The premiere in 1972 had Fugard as Errol Philander and Yvonne Bryceland as Frieda Joubert. It was first seen in London during the Royal Court season that included *Sizwe Bansi is Dead* and *The Island*, opening on 22nd of January 1974 with the Yvonne Bryceland continuing in her role but with Ben Kingsley as Philander.

The stage instruction at the beginning of the play reads:

> *A man and a woman on a blanket on the floor. Both of them are naked. He is caressing her hair. Dim light.*

As the audience assembles, the explicit title of the play would have given them a strong hint as to the subject matter of what they were about to see, but many in South Africa would have been shocked when the curtain rose to reveal this nudity. There had been an Immorality Act on the statute books since 1927 but an amendment in 1950 outlawed all sex between South African men and South African women of different races. One of the first prosecutions under the revised legislation involved a minister of the Dutch Reformed Church who was discovered with a domestic worker in a garage that had been erected by his parishioners. This man of the church was given a suspended sentence but his angry congregation destroyed the garage. The Immorality Act was seen by many as the most diabolical in the catalogue of apartheid legislation but the diehard Afrikaner was still unreasonably fearful of the mixing of the bloods and abhorred the thought of inter-racial skin contact. Such contact was now to be seen on stage.

The high-minded view of the architects of this legislation can be contrasted with a reality that is pungently expressed in one of Fugard's plays written twenty years after *Statements*. In *Playland*, the apparently typical Afrikaner young man is represented by Gideon Le Roux, who mocks the black nightwatchman who has murdered a white man for raping his girlfriend:

Story my arse! It's a fucking joke man. A bad joke. You
killed that poor bugger just for that? Just for screwing
your women? (*Laughter.*)

You people are too funny. Listen my friend, if screwing your women is such a big crime, then you and your
brothers are going to have to put your knives into one
hell of a lot of white men...starting with me! Ja. What's
the matter with you? Were you born yesterday? We've
all done it. And just like you said, knocked on that door
in the backyard, then drag her onto the bed and grind
her arse off on the old coir mattress. That's how little
white boys learn to do it. On your women!   **[p 36]**

Gideon may well have been boasting, but the situation in the 1972
play is totally different.

Errol Philander is Coloured and the principal of the location
school. He is a married man with one child and is taking a correspondence course to try to better himself. He goes to the back
door of the town library – where he cannot be a subscriber – and
meets the Afrikaner librarian, Frieda Joubert, a spinster six years
older than he. He asks her for a book needed for his course. He
then returns to the library a number of times to use her office
to read and they become attracted to each other. He is sexually
experienced and she a virgin spinster but in the small town of
Noupoort the fact that she is white and he Coloured turns the
situation upside down. We learn that it is she who first switches
off the light. Errol returns frequently. A neighbour, Mrs Tienie
Buys, sees him entering the back door to the library, keeps watch
and then, after six months, reports these activities to the authorities. As a result, policemen force the window and shine torches on
the two lovers lying on the floor who jump to their feet, startled
and frightened.

The police action was true to life. In *The Apartheid Handbook*,
Roger Omond wrote:

What police techniques were used to catch offenders
and prove guilt?

Special Force Order 025A/69 detailed the use of binoc-
ulars, tape recorders, cameras and two-way radios to trap
offenders. It also spelled out how bed-sheets should be
felt for warmth and examined for stains. Police were also
reported to have examined the private parts of couples
and taken people to district surgeons for examination.

[Omond 1985 p 29]

There are two distinct halves to the play. In the first the lights
are low and we are treated to a typical Fugard situation of two
people in close quarters, like Moses and Zachariah, who are to
reveal themselves as they discuss a myriad of subjects. What sort
of a day have they had; the book he is reading; her earliest memories; their uncertainties, their joys and their fears; the shortage of
water. They are an ill-matched couple, joined only by the love they
have for each other and the fact that although of different races,
they are probably the only two educated people with interests in
common in this small dusty town. Except for the fact that they
are laying nakedly side-by-side on a blanket, their conversation
could be seen as commonplace – and typically Fugardian. They
both say: 'I love you'. The man has forty three cents in his pocket
and they conjecture what such a sum might purchase. There is
also a frank conversation on a subject very commonplace in situations like this when one of the couple is married. Frieda asks him
if he would ever leave his family and in reply, and after some hesi-
tation, he says: 'No. I would never leave them. I'm not...strong
enough to hurt them, for something I wanted.' [p 90] In many
ways this is the crux of the play. It is not the sexual relationship
between Frieda and Errol that predominates, it is the personal
intercourse between these two people who are in love – but live
in South Africa. They naturally talk about sex, shyly for the most
part, but like Boesman and Lena or Piet and Gladys or Moses
and Zachariah, the system will not allow them to be commonplace. He hates the location where he is forced to live, she is beset

by guilt and both are, to quote critic Jeanne Colleran, 'sundered by their own insurmountable dread' [South African Theatre Journal, September 1995, p 48]. We have seen such dread before in Fugard's world, particularly in the case of Morris. His comes about because of an imagined intervention by authority, but in the later play the intervention is real and forbidding and brings into the theatre the realisation that in South Africa what we have just witnessed is as fragile as a feather.

After the intimate first scene, authority enters in the form of Detective Sergeant J du Preez, followed by an intense light from camera flashes and torches that reveal the couple: their fears have come to pass. The man tries to dress himself but the woman ignores her nakedness as she tenderly tries to explain the relationship she has had with Errol. He is then shown as being more scared than Frieda, perhaps understandably so; she and the policeman are white and he is not. This results in the male half of hitherto equal partners failing to make any sense as he keeps repeating the same words about water shortage until he is totally broken. The stage instruction at this point reads:

> (...*The man's 'performance' has now degenerated into a grotesque parody of the servile, cringing 'Coloured'.*)
>
> [p 96]

At this point some normality is introduced into the action as they talk about how they met, but this is a false normality; what they say to each other will form part of the eventual court dossier. After this sequence the action moves to a question and answer session – with Frieda in the role of both the interrogated and the interrogator – where she gently recounts how they first kissed. The play ends as the woman, knowing the affair is at an end, recognises that her only legacy will be pain. Errol has the final speech, alone on the stage, where his recognition of the consequences of this intervention by authority is to quietly rage against this force that can do anything to him, take away all his rights, all his senses; but in this instance they have deprived him of one of nature's fundamental gifts, the right to love.

For most of the play there are two naked lovers on stage, post-coital, and yet *Statements* is almost non-erotic. It is however, very political as it underlines the real evil in South Africa – the deliberate separation of the people. The man is interested in the theory of evolution and you could almost believe these two have created their own Garden of Eden – their own Adam and Eve – but the first half of the play takes place in virtual darkness which epitomises the furtive basis of this relationship and the way in which the oppressed in South Africa are kept in the dark.

Fugard deliberately includes the fact of adultery, not to point up any transgression of the Ten Commandments, but to add to the burdened nature of the situation:

> ... My adultery? And yours? *Ja*. Yours! If that's true of me because of you and my wife, then just as much for you because of me and your white skin. Maybe you are married to that the way I am to Bontrug.   [p 90]

In the Fugard canon we have met Errol before, either in his guise as a Coloured man, or as an impotent one. At least that is Fugard's view:

> Sudden and clear realization at this table of how, almost exclusively, 'woman' – a woman – has been the vehicle for what I have tried to say about survival and defiance – Milly, Hester, Lena…and even Frieda in a way; that, correspondingly, the man has played at best a passive, most times impotent, male. Image occurred to me of the large female spider and shrivelled, almost useless, male – there only for his sexual function. Thus Johnnie, Don, Boesman, Errol – all unable to 'act' significantly – the image of the castrated male culminating of course in Errol Philander's nightmare in *Statements*.   [Nb, p 198]

Fugard is accurate in describing Errol as the castrated male but in his case this cannot be seen as a counter to a Frieda eptomising survival and defiance: he is brutally castrated by the State – not by his partner. She does not want to be seen and reacts when her lover strikes a match. She is desperate to avoid the social and political implications of being observed in this situation, but Errol wants Frieda to see all of the elements of his humanity. When the police light up the lovers' nest she cannot avoid being seen and Errol is given no opportunity to preserve his dignity. Their relationship as two people who love each other is destroyed and Frieda speaks, not only of losing her lover, but of losing what he added to her being:

> I am here. You are not here… The pain will come. I'm holding it far away. But just now I will have to let it go and it will come. It will not take any time to find me. Because it's mine. That pain is going to be me. I don't want to see myself. But I know that will also happen. I must be my hands again, my eyes, my ears…all of me but now, without you. All of me that found you must now lose you… In every corner of being myself there is a little of you left and now I must start to lose it.   [p 102]

SIX

Collaboration and the Invisible

I am a faceless man
who lives in the backyard
of your house

'The Master of the House' from Sounds of a
Cowhide Drum *(Oswald Mtshali)*

F ugard's works invariably have a recognisable source, whether
an introspection from his past or his own critical observation
of other people or events of history, but his plays' origins
are not harvested from the wide and varied field that Shakespeare
used; Fugard's backgrounds are more limited in their geography
and humanity. The people are generally the society's outcasts, often
in a familial relationship. *My Children! My Africa!* comes directly
from the political history of the time, while *'Master Harold'...and
the boys* and *A Lesson from Aloes* are from the playwright's youth
experiences or adult acquaintances. It is not revealed whether the
inspiration for *Blood Knot* came from a newspaper report about
a twenty-two year-old African house-boy found guilty of a crime
by writing a love-letter to an eighteen year-old white girl, but
Boesman and Lena is, according to the *Notebooks*, firmly grounded
in the woman Fugard gave a lift to in 1965.

However, the plays in this chapter, where poet Oswald Mtshali's
faceless men are specifically featured, are no less the product of
personal history but in this instance there was a different first
step. In the case of *The Coat, Sizwe Bansi is Dead* and *The Island*, the
defining moment was a knock on the door that gave birth to the
Serpent Players. In Fugard's words:

I was back in Port Elizabeth writing a new one, *Hello and Goodbye*, when there was a knock on the door and into our lives trooped five men and women from the township. They had read about my success with *Blood Knot* and had come to ask me to help them to start a drama group. With some reluctance, because I resented anything that would interfere with my concentration on the new play, I agreed and Serpent Players was born.

[p vi]

The Serpent Players were allowed to use the old snake pit at the Port Elizabeth museum, hence the name. Over the next two years they produced versions of Machiavelli's *La Mandragola, Woyzeck, The Caucasian Chalk Circle* and *Antigone*; but the politics of the time could not be avoided. Welcome Duru, who was to play Azdak in *The Caucasian Chalk Circle,* was arrested – probably because of a pass book offence – days before the first performance and Fugard had to step in and take over. After that three more members were arrested, including Norman Ntshinga, who was scheduled for Haemon in *Antigone*. As Fugard was banned from New Brighton, where most of the players lived, this play was rehearsed in a kindergarten on the outskirts of Port Elizabeth. Despite these setbacks they continued their activities and began to work on improvisations concerned directly with issues in the townships. Examples were *Friday's Bread on Monday, The Last Bus* and *Sell-Out*, but the most important of these came about after Fugard attended the trial of Norman Ntshinga, where he gave evidence on behalf of the accused.

The First experiment

Richard Eyre, in his wide-ranging review of British Theatre in the Twentieth Century, *Changing Stages,* says that the Serpent Players' next major production, *The Coat,* was an adaptation of Gogol's short story while in fact its origins were specifically local. When Fugard went to Ntshinga's trial he took with him Norman's wife, Mabel, who was recognised at the court by an old man from New

Brighton who had just been sentenced. He gave Mabel his coat
and asked her to take it to his wife. With this incident as inspiration, the play was born and first produced at a public reading in
November 1966. As an indication of the strength of the 'Group'
ethos, the cast performing *The Coat* were identified by the names
of characters they had played in former Serpent Players productions such as Lavrenti (*The Caucasian Chalk Circle*) and Haemon
(*Antigone*). However, at one stage Fugard wanted to get away from
the cast simply telling the audience the story – the debate should
be widened to conjecture whether the wife might sell the coat.
From the *Notebooks*: 'It will certainly create more of Brecht's "ease"
and a chance to talk and think about it. The audience will participate.' [Nb, p 137] – as Brecht would no doubt have endorsed. The
Brechtian method of portraying the lives of urban blacks while
speaking directly to them appeared to suit the Serpent Players
who were providing fare totally different from the normal township melodramas of the likes of Gibson Kente. Fugard's view is
eloquently given in the *Notebooks*:

> To Sheila: 'The continuum of first-degree experience.
> What can I say, or write about today that could have
> even a hundredth part of the consequence of that coat
> going back. Even the greatest art communicates only
> second-degree experience. That coat is first degree, it is
> life itself. That man's family will take it back, smell him
> again, remember him again, it will be worn by a son or,
> tonight, will keep one of the small children warm in her
> blanket on the floor – move into her dreams, put her
> father back into her life. That coat withers me and my
> words.'   [Nb, p 125]

This experimental work is published in the Oxford University
Press edition of Fugard's plays under the heading *Township Plays*
and was revived in 1990 at the University of Witwatersrand
Theatre, Johannesburg directed by playwright Maishe Maponya.

It opens as the five actors walk onto a stage that is empty except
for five chairs. They sit. There are three men and two women.

Lavrenti speaks first. He introduces the group and explains they are a group of actors from New Brighton:

> That world where your servants go at the end of the day, that ugly scab of pondokkies and squalor that spoil the approach to Port Elizabeth.   **[p 123]**

He tries to tell the audience why they act and questions whether it is to understand the world they live in – or do they think they can, with theatre, change that world? It is while trying to achieve these goals that they come up with the story of the coat. The audience is then treated to a detailed account of the fate of this garment as the narrative is taken up by Marie (*Woyzeck*). The actors discuss, on stage, a number of hypotheses about the delivery of the coat to the owner's wife and how it might be used – to cover children sleeping on the floor when the nights are cold or the son using it for a job interview. In the next scene they try to determine whether the woman would sell the coat if money is needed for medicine for a sick daughter. She resists so they try to think up another scenario where she would sell because of a need to pay rent – or be evicted, and probably sent back to the Reserves. This prospect is too daunting and she uses the coat to raise enough to avoid having to leave the family house. Haemon, who plays the son in the play, suggests that the actors should then try to re-enact the courtroom scene when the coat-owner was sentenced to five years, but they exit the stage saying they might try that next time.

This was a brave concept. The story is told by actors playing the part of actors while representing other characters – a device Fugard was, to some extent, to use in his much later plays, *Valley Song, The Captain's Tiger* and *Exits and Entrances*.

Collaborators who did not jettison the writer

John Kani, who played Haemon in *The Coat* (and *Antigone*), introduced the group to a friend of his, Winston Ntshona, and this resulted in the birth of a remarkable theatrical partnership. John Kani was born in Port Elizabeth while Winston Ntshona came from King William's Town. After Ntshona left school in New Brighton, he worked as a factory janitor and then as a laboratory assistant. Kani was also a janitor at the Ford Motor Company and then moved to the assembly floor. They first performed together at The Space Theatre in Cape Town in a version of Camus' *The Just*, which was re-titled *The Terrorists* and which used township names and Xhosa songs. After this they both decided to give up their jobs and become full-time actors in a country where, for black people, this was a profession not recognised by the authorities; the only way this could be circumvented was for them to be registered as Fugard's driver and gardener, even though he did not own a car. This was a crucial moment in South African theatrical history, and within months the two workshop productions, *Sizwe Bansi is Dead* and *The Island*, became a reality.

Sizwe Bansi is Dead was first performed at The Space Theatre on 8th October 1972. It ran for about one hour and forty-five minutes, with the first three quarters of an hour taken up by a monologue delivered by Styles, a photographer, played by John Kani. This begins with Styles recalling a visit by Henry Ford the Second to the Ford factory where Styles worked before setting up as a photographer. The monologue is brought to an end when Sizwe Bansi, now calling himself Robert Zwelinzima, enters Styles' studio asking for a picture to be taken that he can send to his wife. After some exchanges between Styles and Robert, the photograph is taken with the camera flash freezing the action to reveal the illiterate Robert in the spotlight as he dictates, to the audience, a letter he will send to his wife with the photograph. This dictation leads into the remaining action of the play, beginning at Buntu's house in New Brighton. Buntu, also played by Kani, is about to receive Sizwe Bansi who has come to stay with him, even though this visitor does not have the necessary permit to remain in Port Elizabeth and he should return to his home in King William's Town. He does not want to do this, so Buntu takes him out for a night of drinking. On their way home they stumble on a dead man and, after much agonising, Sizwe agrees to change his identity and take the dead man's pass book that is in order; it contains a work-seeker's permit. The dead man is Robert Zwelinzima.

The Island, the second workshop collaboration is, within the political context, a natural bedfellow to *Sizwe Bansi is Dead,* as it shows the ultimate fate of those who rebel against the pass laws and other apartheid strictures. It was also first performed at the Space Theatre, on 2 July 1973. The play portrays life on Robben Island for two prisoners, John and Winston, and begins with a long, wordless period of useless labour, a theatre of the absurd, where they dig sand and then each struggles with his loaded wheel-barrow to fill the hole created by the other man's digging – even more Sisyphean than Boesman and Lena's wanderings. This mime is often extended to over fifteen minutes, or longer. Fugard has said that it is possible to portray what is happening in five minutes at the most but if drawn out the 'audience begins to experience the madness, the lunacy, the insidious nature of a pointless experience that just goes on and on until the audience wants to scream'. Peter Brook is uncomfortable with political theatre but *The Island* so impressed him that in 1999 he staged a revival at his Paris theatre, *Bouffes du Nord.* He also had some comments to make on the opening sequence:

> Not a word spoken, nothing on the stage, for 40 minutes – just two men [shifting sand] with imaginary wheelbar-rows, in an imaginary space. Gradually the audience went through a whole cycle. First amazement, then the begin-nings of irritation – 'We're an audience, we've come for something, what's going on here?' – then impatience.
>
> And then suddenly the whole audience was trans-formed by a deep feeling of shame for having dared to think to themselves, 'Come on, get on with it.'
>
> When one saw the reality of their sweat, the reality of the weight of the imaginary objects they were lifting, the audience dropped any expectation of the play 'starting'. They realised this was the play, and waited, with respect and absolute involvement, for whatever was coming next.   [Brook 2000, p 1]

Back in their rudimentary cell, the tired workers discuss a perform-ance of *Antigone* which they are to present to the warders and fellow prisoners. Before this occurs, John is told that his sentence has been reduced on appeal so that he will be released in three months' time while Winston still has seven years to go. The last scene is the performance of *Antigone* with John playing Creon and Winston Antigone.

Sizwe Bansi is Dead and *The Island* are published as being 'devised' by Fugard, Kani and Ntshona and in the introduction to the Oxford University Press edition Dennis Walder makes the point that the rights and royalties are shared. In the Introduction to *Statements,* an earlier volume that included these plays, Fugard wrote that they 'did not jettison the writer', but that the starting point was at least an image, which in the case of *Sizwe Bansi is Dead* was a photograph of a man with a cigarette in one hand and a pipe in the other. This collaborative enterprise had a booking to open at The Space Theatre on 8 October 1970 and yet, five weeks before that date, it had still not been agreed what improvisation would be presented. During the first rehearsal, after Fugard had fully committed himself to involvement with Kani and Ntshona, he tried to formulate a play by having them imagine the lounge of a local hotel with three or four tables crowded with self-satis-fied white students, whom John and Winston were to wait upon. Eventually Fugard had the two actors envisage only one table and one chair as a symbol of white hegemony, as was repeated ten years later in *'Master Harold'...and the boys.* From this experiment, plus the photograph and the memories of John and Winston, *Sizwe Bansi is Dead* was born.

As for *The Island,* this was principally based on notes and ideas that Fugard had accumulated over many years, and if *Sizwe Bansi is Dead* began with a single table and chair, *The Island's* first prop was a large blanket that Fugard spread on the ground outside his house and then called upon John and Winston to explore this space. The blanket was then folded several times until there was just enough room for them to stand on it, creating conditions of extreme confinement. Two weeks later they were on stage with *The*

Island in Cape Town and since then the play has been performed all over the world. In recent years there have been a number of revivals in London with the original cast, thirty years older and somewhat heavier. Fugard recounts that Mannie Manim has rather unkindly referred to recent productions as *'Sumo Island'*.

Since the first productions of these two plays, there have been some differences of view as to the respective contributions of the three practitioners involved. However, for the purpose of this analysis, it is contended that whatever credit belongs to Kani and Ntshona, these works contribute a valuable addition to the canon of Fugard political plays; his own words are well in evidence. During a revival of *The Island* at the Market Theatre, Mark Gevisser wrote in a review for the South African *Mail and Guardian* on 26 May 1995: 'despite the many temptations, neither Kani nor Ntshona steals the show and both allow the lyricism of Fugard – unmistakeable even in his "workshopped" scripts – to shine through'.

Sizwe Bansi is Dead differs from nearly all of Fugard's plays in that human relationships are not central: Styles has a practitioner/client affiliation with the visitors to his studio and a subservient/rebellious role at the Ford factory, while Buntu and Sizwe have only just met. This is deliberate: we are not given an inquiry into the strength of the blood knot between brothers, nor insights into an unlikely love affair between a pair of society's outcasts – no, in *Sizwe Bansi is Dead* and *The Island* the political dimension is paramount. To some extent an entry in the *Notebooks* shows that Fugard had a similar view: 'I've always rated *Sizwe* fairly low, a play which walked the tightrope between poetry and propaganda. Maybe I'm wrong.' [Nb, p 226] In view of the fact that these plays continue to be performed throughout the world – for instance *Sizwe Bansi is Dead* was at the New Vic Theatre, Newcastle-under-Lyme in October 2005 – would seem to indicate that he was wrong, even though the programme for that production was designed as a 'Reference Book'.

The Book of Life

Richard Hornby, in a 1990 article in *The Hudson Review,* described Fugard as 'the best political dramatist writing in English today' [Hornby 1990, p 123], and this political emphasis was in evidence in realistic terms when *Sizwe Bansi is Dead* was performed before a mixed audience at the Space Theatre. At the end of the play John Kani went around the audience to inspect passes, even of those members who were not required to carry them, which, in true Brechtian fashion, brought the message on stage across the footlights and into the auditorium, exposing the harsh reality of the South Africa outside the theatre. The play text we have for *Sizwe Bansi is Dead* specifically invites the audience to participate. When Buntu appears on stage exiting from Sky's place he 'discovers' the people in the theatre and reports directly to them on the good time they have enjoyed. Similarly, when Sizwe tears off his clothes, he asks a lady in the audience how many children her man has made for her.

No doubt Brecht would have approved, similarly Jerzy Grotowski who would have seen this performance as a primary example of 'Poor Theatre'. The influence of this Polish theatrical practitioner seen in *Orestes* becomes similarly significant in these two workshopped plays. *Sizwe Bansi is Dead* is a prime example of 'Poor Theatre' that would still constitute a striking instance of political drama without the opening monologue but, without the humorous and effective device of Styles' preface, world theatre would have been denied a character that stands shoulder to shoulder with some of Shakespeare's wisest fools. Fugard describes this monologue as 'an actor unaccompanied by orchestra, improvising on a theme'.

Styles appears in two costumes, the exploited Ford worker and the photographer. As he moves from paid employment as the factory worker to enter the private sector, some critics have suggested that he becomes a proto-capitalist who is exploiting his own people while providing them with pictorial evidence of their dreams, but for a profit. Styles is one of Fugard's most charismatic characters who, although firmly rooted in the black working class, is more enterprising than most and seems to have absorbed some socialist philosophy. He leaves the factory because he is being emasculated:

> Selling most of his time on this earth to another man.
>   '...if I could stand on my own two feet and not be somebody else's tool, I'd have some respect for myself. I'd be a man'. [p 156]

A closer examination of Fugard's text, and knowledge of the political history surrounding class formation at this time, provides one of the few arenas in these plays to explore how, by the 1980s, race discrimination had been partially subsumed into a class struggle. Even today, where the Government is pursuing a vigorous 'Black empowerment' programme and, on the surface, racism is still a constant subject for discussion in society, there is still a view that the divisions in South Africa are substantially about class and not colour.

There is another reason why this play is particularly appropriate for an examination of work, class and race; it is skilfully constructed so that not only are we given Styles in his two roles – worker and entrepreneur – but he is then recreated as Buntu who, although as enterprising as Styles, is second-generation black/urban working-class who, like Sizwe Bansi, is only too glad to be allowed to work – provided the racist authorities will allow:

> If I had to tell you the trouble I had before I could get the right stamps in my book, even though I was born in this area! The trouble I had before I could get a decent job...born in this area! The trouble I had to get this two-roomed house...born in this area. [p 174]

However, if Styles is to be seen as any form of capitalist, he is one with a heart, fully conscious of the sufferings of his customers. He wants to remember the 'simple people, who you never find mentioned in the history books, who never get statues erected to them...', or those:

...who would be forgotten, and their dreams with them,
if it wasn't for Styles. That's what I do, friends. Put
down, in my way, on paper the dreams and hopes of my
people so that even their children's children will remember a man... 'This was our Grandfather'...   **[p 159]**

One man is anxious to be photographed with the Standard Six
Certificate he has earned after seven years' part-time study. In
another case, twenty-seven people pose for the 'Family Card'.
Even though the 'Family Card' led to more sales, Styles the capitalist recalls the grandfather who dies before the photograph
is developed with words that display a compassion that would
appear to effectively counter the view that he is exploiting his
own:

... His grey hair was a sign of wisdom. His face weather-
beaten and lined with experience. Looking at it was like
paging the volume of his history, written by himself: He
was a living symbol of Life, of all it means and does to
a man. I adored him. He sat there – half smiling, half
serious – as if he had already seen the end of his road.

[p 161]

Reinforcing his place in the non-capitalist world, Styles then
provides a variation of the Marxist view that the worker owns
nothing except their ability to work, their labour power, when
he says:

... We own nothing except ourselves. This world and
its laws, allows us nothing, except ourselves. There is
nothing we can leave behind when we die, except the
memory of ourselves...   **[p 163]**

In this context these memories are the photographs that remain
after death – also seen to represent the dreams of the photographed. Capitalism thrives by selling dreams to the proletariat
– unrealistic illusions that a new washing powder will improve
your lot in life – but the dream world that Styles is involved in is

more honest than that. Although Morris and Zachariah equally own nothing except themselves, Morris is concerned that even their dreams might be mortgaged; Styles, on the other hand, is determined to protect this precious commodity – he has set up a 'strong room of dreams'. He does not ask stupid questions of his sitters – 'Start asking stupid questions and you destroy that dream' [p 160] – and when Sizwe first walks into the studio, Styles, in an aside to the audience, describes him as '"A Dream", with a capital D'.

Styles' limited private enterprise is contrasted with the world of capitalism, represented by the Ford motor plant, when he is reading aloud from the local newspaper at the opening of the play. One item refers to talks about an expansion at that plant: 'The talk ended in the bloody newspaper. Never in the pay packet.' The visit of Mr Henry Ford the Second to the factory where Styles worked provides an amusing interlude and an opportunity for further comment on exploitation when he acts as interpreter for Mr Baas Bradley: 'Gentleman, old Bradley says this Ford is a big bastard. He owns everything in this building which means you as well.' Mr Ford is described as a grandmother baas who will be 'wearing a mask of smiles', reminding us that Sizwe Bansi wears a mask himself as the play moves on to its defining message, projecting the contest between identity and survival. Morris abandoned the possibility of a change of identity when 'trying for white', his survival depended on the 'blood knot'; while Lena, who at the beginning of the play struggles to find out who she is, survives by establishing her identity in relationship to Boesman. Piet and Isabel survive with their identities fairly intact but the only way Sizwe Bansi can survive is to surrender his identity.

For the oppressed, such surrender may be of little import as they have no worthwhile identity to give up but, despite the vicissitudes experienced by the evidently 'worthless' people seen in Fugard's work, he consistently displays an acute regard for their value – he rebels against the dominant South African ideology that sees most of his characters as rubbish. In the case of Sizwe, the authorities would deal severely with the forgery that enabled him to assume another man's identity, but looked at *en masse*, it would not enter the minds of the oppressors that they needed to accord any identity to Fugard's men and women. Like Zachariah, Sizwe is invisible. Buntu confirms this when he explains to Sizwe what would happen if he went to the Labour Bureau: 'White man...takes the book, looks at it – doesn't look at you! – goes to the big machine and feeds in your number...' [p 172] However, he can use this non-recognition to his own advantage – even if he needs to 'live as another man's ghost'. Pragmatic Buntu tells Sizwe that with his identity intact he is only a ghost, but Sizwe is still reluctant, until silenced by Buntu's grip on reality:

> No? When the white man looked at you at the Labour
> Bureau what did he see? A man with dignity or a bloody
> passbook with an N.I. number? Isn't that a ghost? When
> the white man sees you walk down the street and calls
> out, 'Hey. John! Come here'...to you, Sizwe Bansi...isn't
> that a ghost? Or when his little child calls you 'Boy'...
> you a man, circumcised, with a wife and four children...
> isn't that a ghost? Stop fooling yourself. All I'm saying
> is be a real ghost, if that is what they want, what they've
> turned us into. Spook them into hell, man!   [p 185]

In Nadine Gordimer's 1994 novella, *Something Out There*, white suburbs of Johannesburg are haunted by the spectre of a something unknown 'out there', which turns out, in all probability, to be a baboon, but which acts as a metaphor for the menace of the black man in the changing times in South Africa:

> Since no one actually saw whoever or whatever was
> watching them – timid or threatening? – rumour began
> to go round that it was what...they called – not in their
> own language with its rich vocabulary recognising the
> supernatural, but adopting the childish Afrikaans word
> – a spook.   [Gordimer 1994, p 55]

This menace is not seen properly by anyone, resulting in that which has been ignored and has been invisible for so long becoming a possible reality. Buntu's advice is working.

Sizwe Bansi lived in the Ciskei where life was hard. In Sky's shebeen he is asked what he thinks of Ciskeian independence to which he replies:

> I must tell you, friend...when a car passes or the wind blows up the dust, Ciskeian Independence makes you cough. I'm telling you, friend...put a man in a pondok and call that Independence? My good friend let me tell you... Ciskeian Independence is shit!   [p 178]

These remarks were applied to the Transkei during a production of the play there in October 1976 and this led to the detention of John Kani and Winston Ntshona. They spent two weeks in solitary confinement, only being released and deported after protests were made around the world.

As a result of the harsh conditions in his homeland, Sizwe needs to find work in Port Elizabeth to feed his family, but streetwise Buntu, whom Styles describes as 'Always helping people. If that man was white they'd call him a liberal', explains to Sizwe, in agonising detail, that he does not have the right stamp in his passbook to enable him to stay and work. Sizwe suggests he might find a job as a garden-boy to which Buntu replies:

> I'll tell you what the little white ladies say: 'Domestic vacancies. I want a garden-boy with good manners and a wide knowledge of the seasons and flowers. Book in order.' Yours in order? Anyway what the hell do you know about seasons and flowers?   [p 172]

In other words, as far as Port Elizabeth is concerned, Sizwe does not exist: he has already lost his identity. However, the tragedy of the play, the whole thrust of what Fugard and his collaborators are presenting to the audience, is that it is one thing to accept the inevitability that the authorities do not recognise your existence, it is another thing for the individual to see no alternative but to give up his singularity and step into the shoes of a dead man and take over his identity. When a way out of Sizwe's predicament presents itself, and by surrendering his identity he can work in Port Elizabeth and feed his family, he is faced with an agonising decision: bread or dignity? For the black man in apartheid South Africa, it is an unequal contest.

The impact this contest has on the pride and dreams of the unfortunate is presented with graphic realism: 'Shit on our names and on our pride', says Buntu. He will give up everything that distinguishes him as a man in exchange for a piece of bread and a blanket, but even with such surrender, the book is still omnipotent: 'That passbook of his will talk'...in 'good English too' [p 180]. As Morris prayed for God's 'Kingdom to come as quickly as it can', Buntu warns that his people may not be as fortunate as Abou Ben Adhem: 'Be careful lest when the big day comes and the pages of the big book are turned, it is found that your name is missing' [p 180]. Sizwe is more vehement:

> They said: Book of life! Your friend! You'll never get lost!
> They told us lies.
> That bloody book...! People, do you know? No! Wherever you go...it's that bloody book. You go to school, it goes too. Go to work, it goes too. Go to church and pray and sing lovely hymns, it sits there with you. Go to hospital to die, it lies there too!   [pp 181–183]

Blame Me on History by Bloke Modisane, who played Shark in the first production of Fugard's *No-Good Friday*, has a Postscript on the reference book that vividly illustrates what a farcical horror this was:

> I see the South African law as the basis and the instrument of my oppression. I am black, the law is white.
> But the law is the law, they said. Well, this is the law.
> The 'Natives (Abolition of Passes and Co-ordination of Documents) Act' No. 67 of 1952 abolished the Pass

Laws, so instead of carrying a Pass I carry a Reference
Book No. 947067; it has ninety-six pages, is bound in
buckram and comes in two colours, the brown and the
green. It is divided into five sections...

In the last section is written:

*William is exempted from the Urban Service Contract
Regulations in terms of Section 3(4) of Act 67/52, having been
exempted under regulation 14 bis Proclamation 150/341*

Modisane continues:

The principle of the Exemption Pass is to exempt me
from carrying a Reference Book, as a result I carry
a Reference Book into which is written a certificate
exempting me from carrying a Reference Book.

[Modisane 1965, pp 306, 310–311]

Verbal racism and questions of identity are not the only themes
in *Sizwe Bansi is Dead* and *The Island* that are a repeat of those
encountered in other Fugard works. As in *Blood Knot*, clothes are
important. The incongruity of a man with a pipe in one hand and
a cigarette in the other is heightened by the too-large, obviously
new 'Sales House' suit, a prop in the change of identity, but no
defence against white autocracy – no defender of the black man's
pride. Buntu recalls an item of his father's clothing:

It's like my father's hat. Special hat, man! Carefully
wrapped in plastic on top of the wardrobe in his room.
God help the child who so much as touches it! Sunday
it goes on his head, and a man, full of dignity, a man I
respect, walks down the street. White man stops him:
'Come here, kaffir!' What does he do?
(*BUNTU whips the imaginary hat off his head and crumples
it in his hands as he adopts a fawning, servile pose in front of
the white man.*)

'What is it it, Baas?'

If that is what you call pride, then shit on it! Take
mine and give me food for my children.   [pp 190–191]

According to Brian Astbury, during performances at The Space
Theatre the crumpling of the hat was represented on stage by the
actor squeezing an orange.

Costume is important as a reflection of the society Fugard's
characters inhabit, but on the Island, John and Winston, like all of
the prisoners, wear identical shorts and shirts that take away any
semblance of individuality: they are not men, they are numbers
– if that, even. They have surrendered their identity as surely as
Sizwe Bansi, and the indignity of their costume is exacerbated
as they are required to drop these shorts for inspection. In *The
Island. A History of Robben Island 1488 to 1990*, edited by Harriet
Deacon, the details of this routine examination are described:

> Firstly, a daily feature of prison life was the tauza, which
> officials claimed was meant to prevent prisoners smug-
> gling objects on or in the body.
>
> In the tauza, the prisoner had to strip and once naked,
> jump around to dislodge any concealed object. He
> would end the 'dance' by bending over naked to expose
> his rectum to the warders.   [Deacon 1996, p 102]

Antigone *again*

In *The Island,* after the remarkable opening mime, the two prisoners are returned to their cell where they tend each other's wounds
and then, as they have done every night of their incarceration,
they play games of imagination to pass the time, much like Didi
and Gogo. Last night Winston had described a film they had both
seen and so tonight John imagines a telephone call to Scott, the
undertaker, where they also talk to an old friend Sky; places and
characters taken directly from *Sizwe Bansi is Dead.* This becomes a
mini play-within-a-play and serves as a *hors d'oeuvre* to the larger
in-house theatrical event yet to come. John, like Styles, impro-

vises his own script that has 'Winston squirming with excitement', but, unlike Antigone when Winston exits in triumph, this piece of theatre descends into anti-climax as they are brought back to reality when John recalls their experience that day of digging sand at the beach – a beach that was similar to the one he and his family visited with their 'buckets and spades' before being imprisoned: a devastating piece of irony contrasting the pain and degradation attached to the Robben Island sand with that used to fill the children's buckets. This apparently innocent amusement, invented by John and Winston to bring some sense of sanity into their insane world, provides a subtle overture to the events that crystallise the circulatory structure of *The Island*, wherein a play is presented in a theatre about a play being presented in a prison, but where the audiences for both plays are the same.

Playwrights have often employed the device of a play-within-a-play to provide an element of irony or metaphor to the drama. In many cases this draws attention to a particular point in the play, or a tension between characters, as they are shown another version of themselves played out in front of them. Most famously, in *Hamlet* the Prince decides: 'The play's the thing / Wherein I'll catch the conscience of the King'. Such references would have been familiar to some of the inmates of the island because, according to Anthony Sampson: 'If the Robben Islanders had a common culture it was not the Bible or the Koran, but Shakespeare' [Sampson 1999, p 233] – but it is unlikely that the conscience of the kings of the Apartheid State is caught by the use of this device in *The Island*.

However, mainly thanks to the opening mime, what Fugard and his co-authors have so strikingly achieved in this short dramatic work is to demonstrate how the theatre becomes the prison itself as the prison becomes a theatre. To prove this statement let us catalogue the experience of the audience as the play begins. As described in the quotation by Peter Brook, the playgoers settle into their comfortable seats in the stalls to be entertained, but what is on the stage? Nothing more than two identically and drably dressed black men engaged in wordless activity, conducted at breakneck speed. As a result, and in a short space of time, the actors are covered in sweat and the audience are steeped, firstly in impatience, then irritation and then bewilderment – followed, we hope, by the understanding that this repetitive dumb show *is* the play and that they, the spectators, are on the island and witnessing these fruitless labours. As described above, when John and Winston are back in the cell, they turn that confined space into an acting area as they dramatise for themselves what is to be seen and experienced outside of their confine. This gives them some comfort – it is part of their survival tactic – but then, as the play develops, the two prisoners turn the whole of the prison into a theatre for the staging of their version of *Antigone*; and, most crucially, they insinuate the audience in the theatre into the audience of guards and other prisoners that witness this show. The stage instruction at the beginning of Scene Four says that John '*addresses the audience*', both the real and the imaginary, as he begins: 'Captain Prinsloo, Hodoshe, Warders' and then pauses before adding '...and Gentlemen!', the latter group to include his fellow prisoners – and you in the stalls.

At the end of the play, the following stage instruction is given: *Tearing off his wig and confronting the audience as WINSTON, not Antigone.* Winston says to them, the audience in the theatre proper:

> Gods of our Fathers! My Land! My Home!
> Time waits no longer. I go now to my living death, because I honoured those things to which honour belongs.   **[p 227]**

But despite Winston's stirring words, we, the audience, are quickly taken back into the reality of the prison as the two men are, in mime, once more handcuffed together and returned to their imprisoned state, accompanied by a 'Greek' chorus of wailing sirens. The audience however is not imprisoned, but if the production they have seen has been true to the play's intent, they exit with some guilt and an understanding of the prison experience of which, for one and a half hours, they have been part.

Reverting to *Hamlet*:

> I have heard
> That guilty creatures sitting at a play
> Have by the very cunning of the scene
> Been struck so to the soul that presently
> They have proclaimed their malefactions.   [11.2 587]

The measure of guilt felt by the audience may depend on the extent to which they are fully cognisant with 'how and why' John and Winston came to be on Robben Island. Before the transportation to the prison, there would have been the arrest and trial, all completed according to the established apartheid legalities. The National Government, in an attempt to deal with internal disorder had, by stages, allowed the police to detain suspects without charging them, even in solitary confinement, for twelve days (1962), one hundred and eighty days (1965) and by 1976, for an unlimited period without recourse to any judicial authority. Once incarcerated in prison, the Prisons Act of 1959 made the unauthorised reporting of conditions in prisons an offence. As Fugard wrote: 'Sentenced to so many "years" of nothing... You are no more' [Nb, p 212], although history will reveal that Mandela and some of his fellow prisoners were destined to be very far from being 'no more'. Old Harry of the stone quarry, yet to be introduced, may not survive incarceration, but many did, to become the rulers of today.

As John and Winston recall how they came to Robben Island together, John asks Winston to remember the words that he said when they reached the jetty: 'Heavy words, Winston. You looked back at the mountains... "Farewell Africa!" I've never forgotten them. That was three years ago.' [p 215] From Robben Island one of the most beautiful cities in the world can be seen, so that day-by-day the prisoners can make the contrast between Cape Town and their habitat, much like those once incarcerated in Alcatraz, where the towers of San Francisco were in view. However, on release, American ex-prisoners could stay in that city, but not the South Africans; they would likely be endorsed out to return to their hometown district, as would have been the case for Sizwe Bansi.

The relationship we observe in *The Island* is as close as that of Morris and Zachariah and so, in addition to a treatise on prison cruelty, we are presented with a major subtext that defines the 'brotherhood' of John and Winston. The diabolical tasks inflicted on them by the warder, 'Hodoshe', the unending filling of holes in the sand dug by the other, so weighs upon the prisoners that at the end of the day they confess that they hate each other, but this dialogue is followed by a pertinent stage instruction: *'JOHN puts a hand on WINSTON's shoulder. The brotherhood is intact.'* However, following a familiar theme in Greek tragedy, this friendship is subjected to the severest of tests by an external authority, namely the news of John's early release. This is devastating for Winston, but it creates an equally devastating act of theatre. The anguish exhibited as Winston enacts the scenario of his cell companion's release to the delights of New Brighton, is aggravated as he concludes this recital by referring to old Harry who is serving life and who, in the quarry, has forgotten who he is. He has turned into the stone that he chisels and hammers day by day, just as Camus describes Sisyphus: 'A face that toils so close to stones is already stone itself'. However, Sisyphus, who scorns the gods, is aware of his wretched condition, while old Harry no longer recalls the gods of apartheid and is oblivious to what has been done to him. Nevertheless, Fugard rescues the scene of Winston's torment from total despair with an injection of hope – 'massively compassionate' – with a masterly stage direction that enthuses the actor to portray what is written. For the text reader, the hard work is already done:

> *JOHN has sunk to the floor, helpless in the face of the other man's torment and pain. WINSTON almost seems to bend under the weight of the life stretching ahead of him on the Island. For a few seconds he lives in silence with his reality, then slowly straightens up. He turns and looks at JOHN. When he speaks again, it is the voice of a man who has come to terms with his fate, massively compassionate.* **[p 221]**

This hope is reflected in Camus. After the sentence quoted above, Sisyphus has an hour of breathing space as he descends the hill:

> At each of those moments when he leaves the heights and gradually sinks towards the lairs of the gods, he is superior to his fate. He is stronger than his rock.

This highlights the underlying significance of *The Island*: the prisoners – as represented by John and Winston – are stronger than the rock that is the fortress of Robben Island, thanks to the brotherhood between them. They are shackled together, metaphorically and in fact, as surely as the blood knot that brought Morris back to the *pondok* in Korsten and his brother, but despite the gesture of independence in their staging of *Antigone,* the play ends with them shackled together again as at the beginning of the play: brothers in an absurd world but with a difference – some hope.

Fugard's interest in Greek drama had an early beginning when, in the mid-1950s, he had a minor role in André Huguenet's production of *Oedipus Rex.* This early exposure to classical drama manifested itself in the Serpent Players' production of *Antigone*, and his own works, *Orestes* and *Dimetos*; but, more importantly, with 'the play within the play' in *The Island.* The production of *Antigone* that was staged by the prisoners at Robben Island in real life had Mandela playing Creon. In *Long Walk to Freedom,* Mandela wrote: 'It was Antigone who symbolised our struggle; she was, in her own way, a freedom fighter, for she defied the law on the ground that it was unjust.' [Mandela 1999, p 541] No doubt this would have needed to follow Sophocles faithfully, but in Fugard's hands, the version we are given is directly relevant to twentieth century South Africa.

With splendid irony, the performance begins with Creon (John) addressing the prison authorities in the audience and calling upon them to see him, not as a King, but as their servant who measures the success of the state, over which he presides, by: 'the fatness and happiness of its people'. Antigone is found guilty because she has broken the law, which Creon insists is to 'protect you', but in South Africa the law only protects the privileged minority, the fat and the happy, and certainly not the prisoners of Robben Island. Winston, as Antigone, could easily represent a figure of ridicule, wearing false breasts, a wig made of rope and a prison blanket as a skirt, but as the play reaches its climax, she stands tall in classical mode, like Nelson Mandela at the Rivonia trial, and articulates her indignation at the oppression of the State. He/she counters the image of the all-powerful law of the State by reference to laws that are made by God, but these are no protection and she is found guilty and sent to the Island, described by Winston: '...to my grave, my everlasting prison, condemned alive to solitary death' [p 227].

SEVEN

Ancestral Voices

In Xanadu did Kubla Khan
A stately pleasure-dome decree

Samuel Taylor Coleridge

I n *A Lesson from Aloes*, the three voices heard during the play
emanate from *Xanadu*, described as 'a small house in Algoa
Park', a predominately Afrikaner working class area of Port
Elizabeth that is unlikely to contain any of the 'stately pleasure-
domes' referred to in Coleridge's poem. Even so, it is socially and
politically remote from where Morris and Zachariah dwell in the
'non-white location' of Korsten. These voices provide a variety of
South African ethnicities, and it is the ancestral origins of these
voices that provide the framework for this important play, even
if they are not 'prophesying war'. This chapter also deals with
'Master Harold'...and the boys that provides a captivating stage
picture of Fugard's own ancestry.

Whether the ancestry is from Afrikaner or English roots, or of
the Coloured variety, South African racism scars Harold and all
three of the people in *A Lesson from Aloes*. These three comprise
an Afrikaner with an impeccable pedigree, a representative of the
other white South Africa – a product of the English settlement
– and a Coloured man with similar antecedents to those of Morris
and Zachariah and Boesman and Lena. In this play, where more so
than in any of his others the psychological tensions are all-perva-
sive, the human relationships on display are once again of the
failed variety, as is the cause espoused by Piet and Steve, both in
their own worlds and in the political reality beyond *Xanadu*. The
flawed intercourse between these three unhappy and desperate

people, representing three of the faces of South Africa, is played
out against a backdrop of betrayal, both within the political arena
and the domestic one, a betrayal that is largely orchestrated by
the Apartheid State. In this case the State does not impose its
authority at a distance – as 'the eyes behind the back' – but by
direct and forceful intervention.

The play is presented in two acting areas, the backyard and
the bedroom of the house occupied by the Afrikaner Piet and his
wife Gladys. These two spaces, as becomes apparent as the action
unfolds and the character of the husband and wife is revealed, can
be construed as male and political for the backyard and female
and psychological for the bedroom. The time is 1963. Piet gave up
farming because of drought and moved to Port Elizabeth where
he found work as a bus driver, a job he lost when he became a
member of a protest group where he met a Coloured man, Steve
Daniels, a prominent member of that group. This experience was
a transformation – an epiphany, much like the change that miraculously converted Lena's life:

> It had nothing to do with me. Politics!... (*He smiles.*)
> until I drove my empty bus through that crowd walking
> to work. Hell, Gladys, it was a sight! Men, women, even
> schoolchildren, walking and laughing and full of defi-
> ance. Bitter and hard as I was inside, I felt emotions.
> At first I tried to ignore them. I said to myself the
> people were being stupid. Why make an issue of a
> penny? That's all the fares had increased by. But they
> didn't think that. They carried on walking and waving
> at me and my empty bus. Steve had a position on the
> corner of Standford and Kempston roads. I'd seen this
> man standing there handing out pamphlets or address-
> ing a little crowd. Then one morning the police moved
> in and arrested him... Next day he was back again. The
> comrades had bailed him out. That's when I thought:
> To hell with it. I want to hear what this little bugger is
> saying. And anyway my bus was empty as usual. So I
> stopped and got out. I got a little nervous with all of

them watching me as I walked over. I was the only white there. When I got to them I said I just wanted to listen. The next thing I knew is they were cheering and laughing and slapping me on the back and making a place for me in the front row. (*He pauses.*) I don't know how to describe it, Gladys...the effect that had on me. It was like rain after a long drought. Being welcomed by those people was the most moving thing that has ever happened to me.   [pp 241-242]

Steve is later arrested in earnest for defying a banning order and Piet is suspected of being the informer that led to Steve's detention. The security police also raided Piet's house and removed the personal diaries of Gladys. She experiences this trauma as a form of rape that is sufficient to require this highly-strung woman to be treated once again at Fort England, a mental hospital in Grahamstown. Fugard was familiar with this experience; his wife has suffered with nervous breakdowns in the past and his grandmother was in the Fort England Mental Home when she died.

In his retirement, Piet has taken to rearing aloes in jam tins in his backyard: as his wife describes it, 'Peter's new hobby, now that there's no politics left'. There may be no more politics for Piet outside his backyard but the aloe, restricted to tins rather than the open *veld*, can be compared to the majority of South Africans who, although not confined to tins, except when their shanties are constructed of corrugated iron – known generally in Africa as 'tin' – they are confined by the restrictions of apartheid. 'Tin' is referred to in *Woza Albert*, written by Percy Mtwa, Mbongeni Ngema and Barney Simon, and first performed in 1981. Outside of Fugard, this work was arguably South Africa's most successful anti- apartheid play:

MBONGENI: ...Where do we stay?
PERCY: In a tin!
MBONGENI: In a tin! Like sardine fish!
PERCY: In a tin, Morena.

> MBONGENI: Where do the bricks go to!? The bricks
> go to make a big house, six rooms, for two people.
>
> [Mtwa 1983, p 49]

When the play begins Piet is trying to identify one of his speci-
mens; there are many types of aloes and Piet intends to consult
the best expert:

> So... What I'll do is make some notes and go to the
> library and sit down with Gilbert Westacott Reynolds –
> *The Aloes of South Africa*. A formidable prospect! Five
> hundred and sixteen big pages of small print and that is
> not counting General Smuts's foreword.   [p 227]

Each plant has its own individuality, which cannot be said for
most of the citizens of the country where aloes grow – humanity in South Africa is only classified by race and the experts are
the successors of General Smuts. Piet works with his aloes while
waiting for the evening to arrive when Steve and his family are
expected for supper. The first Act emulates that sense of 'waiting'
to be found in Beckett and Pinter that powers the subsequent
events to such potent effect, even though a number of critics
considered it too long and too slow. As a result of the suspicion
that Piet betrayed Steve, their former friends have deserted them
and this is why the supper party for Steve and his family is such
an event. However, before they arrive, Piet tells Gladys that Steve
is coming to say farewell because he and his family are leaving
South Africa for England on a one-way-exit permit. In the event,
only Steve arrives for the party, where the question of Piet's guilt
is debated at the instigation of Gladys and, as Steve leaves, Gladys
tells Piet that she wishes to return to Fort England.

From entries in the *Notebooks,* it seems that this play had the
longest gestation of any in Fugard's *oeuvre*, with the first relevant
entry being made in 1961. For ten years he made a number of
attempts to realise the story, but by 1971 he had concluded this was
an abortive project. However, in 1977 the idea returned, with the
result that the play was quickly completed and first performed at

the Market Theatre in Johannesburg on the 30th November 1978. Subsequently, it was staged in Cape Town and Montreal before a limited run at the Yale Repertory Theatre from March 1980. It was then performed ninety-six times on Broadway and received the New York Drama Critics Circle Award for the best play of the season. As Frank Rich commented in *The New York Times* of November 18th 1980:

> Short of Beckett, it's hard to think of a contemporary playwright who so relentlessly and unsentimentally tracks down humanity in the midst of apocalypse.
>
> In a 'Lesson From Aloes', Mr. Fugard summons up the full agony and triumph of people who have lost everything except the gift of staying alive.

The Broadway run is also referred to in a 13 April 1982 review by Christopher Swan that appeared in *The Christian Science Monitor* :

> Like most of Fugard's plays, it deals with the bitterness and despair that can breed uncontrollably in a country where government policies authorize the human tragedy of racism and domination. But, like the rest of his works, it rides the political issue like an express train into the heart of the human tragedy.

Placing the three voices of the play in their political context reveals the insidious psychological impact of the police state fuelled, in part, by accusations of betrayal. South African racism has impacted on each of these three, to which they present three different reactions: firstly, resistance plus some measure of acquiescence by Piet; defeat and surrender for Gladys; and retreat and exile for Steve.

Piet

Like the aloe, Piet's ancestry determines that he can withstand the hazards of South Africa. The first Bezuidenhout, a Dutch man, arrived in South Africa in 1695, as did Fugard's forebears; his mother traced their origins on her father's side back to the earliest Dutch settlers, recognised *inter alia* by the playwright when he dedicated *A Lesson from Aloes* to his mother: 'In celebration of Elizabeth Magdalena Potgieter'. The stock whence Piet Bezuidenhout emerged had its origins in the earliest formation of the Afrikaners, stemming from the men who established the supply station at Cape Town for the Dutch East India Company. These men were not farmers, and for the first few years instead of supplying the vessels en-route to the East or Europe, these same vessels often needed to supplement the local agriculture for the garrison to survive. In an attempt to counteract this, a few of the Company's servants were given freehold smallholdings of about twenty acres, creating the first burghers of South Africa, but in time these farmers began to move from the coastal regions to further inland where they were deeded leaseholds over land extending to six thousand acres each. For the next hundred years or more the Boers, as they were called, were in conflict, of one sort or another, with the strictures of the Company, the indigenous population and the English administration, the British having taken final control of the Cape in 1806.

One recorded conflict concerned a Bezuidenhout. In April 1813, Cornelius Frederik (Freek) Bezuidenhout, who lived on the banks of the Baviaans River, refused to release a Khoikhoi labourer when his work contract expired. This was illegal under the labour regulations that the British had introduced in 1812 and when the labourer complained to the authorities, Bezuidenhout was required to appear in a local court. For a period of two years he stubbornly refused to do this, much as Piet refuses to answer questions about betrayal. Eventually, attempts were made to arrest Freek Bezuidenhout but he resisted the military detachment that came to do this and, after a battle lasting several hours, he was shot dead, by a Coloured sergeant.

In 1836 many of the Cape Boers took part in the Great Trek, moving further and further away from British control and influence, taking over the most desirable land in South Africa and in due course establishing the independent states of the Transvaal and the Orange Free State. From this history emerged the 'first white tribe' of South Africa who, from the end of the nineteenth century, developed their own culture and language which was used to firmly establish and maintain, for most of the twentieth century, their position of political supremacy.

Piet's Afrikaner ancestry is fully recognized by his wife. At the climax of the play when Piet is being confronted by Gladys and Steve about betrayal, she compares her husband to members of the Special Branch when she says to Steve: 'He looks like one of them, doesn't he? The same gross certainty in himself! He certainly sounds like them. He speaks English with a dreadful accent.' [p 266] This is a crucial speech within the play, emphasizing the 'otherness' Gladys perceives in her husband.

As the Afrikaners needed to create their own language, Piet, as a non-typical Afrikaner, pursues a contrary course with his frequent quotes from the poetry and literature of his wife's culture. He does this because he loves English verse; it has a richness not to be compared with anything in his background. In *Exits and Entrances,* Afrikaner André says: '...nothing of any significance has ever been written in that language' [p 12]. Piet is subconsciously trying to bridge the gap that separates him from his wife by adopting her language. Whatever, he appears unable to see the irony of this, particularly when his wife shocks him by swearing and goes on to say: 'I've learned how to use my dirty words. And just as well, because there's no other adequate vocabulary for this country.' [pp 237-238] In a properly ordered South African world, the Afrikaner would not be quoting English Romantic poetry and the genteel English women would not swear – but this is not a conventional household.

Gladys does not share a literary interest with her husband, except for the recollection of some lines by Thoreau which she used as the first entry in her diary, after the initial meeting before marriage with Piet. The Thoreau quotation is carefully chosen by Fugard: 'There is a purpose to life, and we will be measured by the extent to which we harness ourselves to it.' [p 234] The sad irony for Gladys is that these first words in the diaries that figure so prominently in the tragedy of her life are so stridently inappropriate. There is little purpose in her life and she has apparently not harnessed herself to any of the important purposes in the life of her husband. In another context, Piet's quotations from English literary culture might be seen as a form of prayer – a search for a faith in that backyard. The 'lesson' of the title of the play could be part of a church service – a reading of the lesson – as Piet uses *Romeo and Juliet* when declaring his identity and at the same time borrowing from the Christian marriage service:

> ... 'Then deny thy father and refuse thy name.' Hell! I don't know about those Italians, but that's a hard one for an Afrikaner. No. For better or for worse. I will remain positively identified as Petrus Jacobus Bezuidenhout; Species Afrikaner;...   [p 222]

Naming names is important in this play. At the outset, Piet is trying to identify a species of aloe – determining a name – as it was for Lena, who recites the names of the places where she and Boesman have lived in an attempt to try and establish an identity, not for a plant, but for herself. Even the name of the district where the Bezuidenhouts reside, Algoa Park, can be interpreted as indicating the different cultural and societal ancestry of the husband and wife: Algoa Bay, a wild place where the earliest European visitors landed – the Portuguese in 1487 – contrasted with the orderliness of an English Park where, in true colonialist fashion, the wilderness has been civilised. After Gladys and Piet have been discussing their own names, Piet says:

> ... What's the first thing we give a child when it's born? A name. Or when strangers meet, what is the first thing they do? Exchange names. According to the Bible, that was the very first thing Adam did in Eden. He named his world. 'And whatsoever Adam called every living creature, that was the name thereof.'   [pp 227–228]

No doubt Fugard was deliberate in choosing Adams as Gladys's maiden name but the people in this play are not living in any form of Eden. The 'separateness' that is ostensibly apartheid leads inevitably to names being imposed across the borders created by this policy, beyond the familiar 'one man's terrorist is another man's freedom fighter'. For instance, branding all dissidents as 'communists' was widespread in South Africa, never mind the string of epithets directed at the non-whites from 'kaffir' to 'John boy'. Piet, as farmer Baas Bezuidenhout, recalls how he was unable to articulate – to 'name' – his grief when asked to speak at the graveside of an African baby that had died: 'That hole with the little homemade coffin at the bottom defeated me' **[p 253]**. Gladys emphasizes her 'difference' by persisting in referring to her husband and his friend as Peter and Steven and, revealing a subconscious antipathy to her husband's friendship with Steve, she refuses to recall the names of the latter's children. However, at the end of the play when she has more or less purged herself of hate and sorrow, she uses the appellation 'Steve'. Sizwe Bansi gives up his name and significantly, at a crucial point in *'Master Harold'...and the boys,* Hally becomes Harold. In *Boesman and Lena*, Boesman's name is an insult to a Coloured man, having connotations of a Bushman of Khoisan descent, while for Piet, the trauma he goes through as a suspected informer results in the arch 'namer of names' meeting Steve and finding it difficult to make conversation, '...as if he was somebody whose name I had forgotten' **[p 244]**. It should also be recognized that, whether there is an informer in their midst or not, what an informer does is name names.

As the play opens, questions about the differences between husband and wife arise, even before a word is spoken, as the image is conveyed of Piet as the positive and Gladys as the negative. Gladys is passive but Piet is a man stripped for action. The stage instruction at the beginning of the play reads as follows:

> *PIET, seated at a garden table with an aloe in front of him, is studying a small field book on the plants. He is wearing spectacles, short trousers, no shirt and sandals without socks. GLADYS, behind sunglasses, sits very still on a garden bench.*

One critic compares this opening with that of *Endgame*, where Clov sits motionless, but in his case he is actively looking at

Hamm. Piet is not looking at his wife; he uses his spectacles in a constructive way, to pursue his hobby, while Gladys uses her sunglasses as a barrier to retreat behind. Piet is cataloguing his aloes, precisely repeating what is happening in his country where ethnicities are carefully and ruthlessly catalogued. This opening tableau is, in its own way, just as significant as the silence in *Blood Knot* and *Boesman and Lena* and as informative as the single un-stacked chair and table in *'Master Harold'...and the boys* and the three unoccupied chairs in *Hello and Goodbye*. Piet is superficially the archetypal Boer out-doors man, while Gladys had a mother who '...was so terrified that I was going to end up with a brown skin' [p 223]. Gladys represents the English South African white woman who protects herself from the harsh climate by the use of calamine lotion rather than the *Voortrekker* bonnet of the Afrikaner. Unlike the aloe, the English rose does not thrive in South Africa. The clothes are, again, important signifiers. Piet and Gladys dress to emphasize their contrasts – Piet the farmer; Gladys, the sensitive English lady – but this contrast is seen in starker, and yet paradoxical terms, when we reach the bedroom and discover that the macho-Afrikaner is not allowed to be present when his wife changes her clothes and before entering has to knock on his own bedroom door. Gladys, born in South Africa, can be seen to be perpetuating the etiquette of the nineteenth century English gentility in the 'English' space that is the bedroom.

Gladys

The second voice is that of Gladys. The content of Gladys's diaries that the Special Branch found interesting enough to justify confis-cation is not disclosed except for one revealing entry in the first set which was 'My mother died today. I haven't cried yet, and I don't think I'm going to' [p 235], echoing the famous opening lines of Camus' *The Outsider*: 'Mother died today. Or maybe it was yesterday, I don't know.' However, these diaries, a crucial item in Fugard's play, have two manifestations, the first being the ones removed by the Special Branch and the second set, where Gladys says she records 'the exciting life I've been living', that are entirely and significantly blank. Gladys herself is also portrayed in two separate and yet similar versions: one of them is the antithesis of Piet, where from childhood she has found South Africa alien; the second is the Gladys who was psychologically abused by the Special Branch when they metaphorically invaded her body by the reading and confiscation of her diaries. These binaries can also be seen in Gladys's role in the play: firstly as a subject used to show how an intrusion by the State can have just as much impact on the mind as on the body; and secondly, and perhaps more importantly, in the part she plays in the debate about betrayal. In the latter case, she becomes the grit in the oyster that provides us with the pearl of Piet's innocence. Piet and Steve are relatively easy to read, they are both 'good men', but Gladys is complex; in some ways she is the interloper in this Xanadu. The aloes are alien to her; they all look alike, as do most of the non-white South Africans that she meets. To quote William Golding: '...he spoke the great Caucasian sentence. "They all look the same to me."' [Golding 1979, p 67] However, the aloes do frighten her, as do 'alien' races. Her sensitivity, crossed with a disturbed mind, describes them as all thorns, bitterness and violence, a view she has about most of the population of South Africa:

> GLADYS: We've already had droughts, prickly pears
> and despair. I suppose we'll be into politics next
> and the black man's misery. I'm not exaggerating,
> Peter. That is what a conversation with you has
> become – a catalogue of South African disasters.
> And you never stop! You seem to have a perverse
> need to dwell on what is cruel and ugly about this
> country. Is there nothing gentle in your world?
> PIET: Is it really as bad as that?
> GLADYS: Yes, it is. And don't make me feel guilty for
> saying it. (*She gestures at the aloes.*) Look at them!
> Is that what you hope for? To be like one of them?
> That's not the only possibility in life, you know. If
> that's what your expectations have shrunk to, it's

your business, but God has not planted me in a
jam tin. He might have cursed you Afrikaners, but
not the whole human race. I want to live my life,
not just survive it. I know I'm in this backyard with
them, but that is not going happen to me.

PIET: I... (*He makes a helpless gesture.*) ... What can I
say? I'm sorry you don't like them.

GLADYS: Don't like them! It's worse than that, Peter.
(*He looks at her.*) I'm going to be very honest with
you. They frighten me. Yes, thorns and bitterness?
I'm afraid there's more than that to them. They're
turgid with violence, like everything else in this
country. And they're trying to pass it on to me.

[p 230]

The aloes are out to get her, but as she describes Piet's topics of
conversation, it can be questioned on this evidence whether he
is any more positive than Gladys, even if she is materially and
mentally just as desolate in her backyard as Lena is in hers. As
Boesman says: 'By the time you shut up we just a *vlenterbroek* and
his *meid* in the backyard of the world' [p 230].

Gladys doesn't believe, outside of her world, that the majority
of South Africans are suffering – 'I never thought things were as
bad as you made out' – but at the climax of the exchange with
Steve about whether Piet is a traitor, she intensifies these views
with the following speech, which encapsulates the nightmare her
life has become:

... I accept, Steven, that I am just a white face on the
outskirts of your terrible life, but I'm in the middle of
mine and yours is just a brown face on the outskirts of
that. Do you understand what I'm saying? I've got my
own story. I don't need yours. I've discovered hell for
myself. It might be hard for you to accept, Steven, but
you are not the only one who has been hurt. Politics and
black skins don't make the only victims in this country.

[p 267]

This speech reinforces one of the crucial messages presented by this play, namely that the cancer of apartheid spreads everywhere, and it can, and does, blight the lives of other South Africans besides those generally seen as the dispossessed. This is one reason why Fugard's drama in his country is in a class by itself, never mind worldwide. Although he is an apostle bearing witness on behalf of the oppressed, he is not dealing with myopic agit-prop theatre that believes that the South African tragedy is only reserved for the black and Coloured people. He is presenting a picture of a disturbed woman just as relevant to a scenario by Ibsen or Strindberg. Like Outa and Ethel, Gladys is a catalyst in this play, but unlike these more minor characters, she is not on the periphery of the action, she is both catalyst and victim – and the provider of Fugard's 'dark ambiguities'.

Steve

The third voice of the trio belongs to Steve, a member of the race that his father defines as 'a mistake'. He is the friend for whom Piet has betrayed his country, his Afrikaner roots. However, the other comrades suspect Piet is an informer and Steve is unsure. This doubt explains the comic and yet moving play-acting that opens Act Two; an interlude to hide Steve's embarrassment with a subtext on the role of the informer. During interrogation, Steve himself became an informer, and so, if he suspects Piet of the same transgression, is he looking for some form of sympathetic atonement from his friend and fellow sinner? The camaraderie between the two is shown by their pleasure in sharing a bottle of their country's wine – in contrast to Gladys who prefers sherry, an 'English' drink. By the time that Gladys joins them, the mood becomes more serious. Steve talks about his regret at leaving, and the trauma of packing up to go into exile from the land of his birth, even if, politically, his own birthright is denied him: '… It's a life lying around on that lounge floor like a pile of rubbish. That's what I'm trying to squeeze into a few old suitcases.' [p 257]

South African history has many examples of dissidents who have gone into exile with unhappy results, some of the most tragic examples being the refugees from *Drum* magazine in Sophiatown:

> Inside South Africa, the 1960s were inclement times for literature, especially literature that sought to remain obliquely political. Much of the decade's richest writing – including autobiographies of the exiled Sophiatown set – was penned abroad. Nakasa threw himself from a New York skyscraper; Arthur Nortje apparently killed himself in Oxford; Themba committed what amounted to alcoholic suicide in Swaziland. Modisane and the others lived on, doubly burdened by the isolation of exile and the knowledge that their books could be neither owned nor read inside South Africa. Nor, indeed, could anything the authors said be quoted. 'What is the use,' one of them asked, 'if the people you write about don't read what you're writing?' Very few of the Sophiatown diaspora could find the energy to produce thereafter.   [Nixon 1994, p 38]

Fugard has said that, amongst others, the fate of Nakasa and Nortje was inspirational in his portrait of Dawid – another exile like Steve – who features in *Sorrows and Rejoicings*, discussed in Chapter Ten.

Gladys believes that she has 'discovered hell' for herself, but her experience of the power of the Apartheid State apparatus has, on the surface, been benign compared with Steve's, where we are given two graphic examples – the savage impact of the Group Areas Act and of the interrogation technique of the Special Branch. Steve's father, with the Afrikaner-sounding name of Willem Gerhardus Daniels, is a skilled fisherman. The family lived near the sea at Fairview but this area was designated for whites only and the family were removed:

> STEVE: They kicked us out, Gladys. Separate Group Areas. Fairview was declared white and that was the end of us...

But that finished Willem Gerhardus. He hadn't just
lost his house and his savings, they also took away
the sea. I mean...how the hell do you get from Salt
Lake to Maitland on a bicycle?! He tried the river a
few times, but that wasn't for him.
I'll never forget one day in the backyard there
at Salt Lake. I had started to get a bit conscious
about things, and I was going on about our rights
and what have you. He just listened. When I was
finished he shook his head and said: 'Ons geslag
is verkeerd.' Hell, that made me angry! And I told
him we have only ourselves to blame if we let them
walk over us. He just shook his head and repeated
himself: 'Ons geslag is verkeerd.'
Sorry, Gladys. That means...how would you say it
nice in English, Piet?
PIET: Our generation...our race is a mistake.

[pp 259–260]

The subservient 'other' sees themselves as 'mistakes' with little
prompting from their masters: a triumphant victory for the apartheid ideology. Fugard, as pessimist, wrote in 1973 that Steve's
father's view applied to all South Africans:

For the moment I can't see past the appalling wreckage
of human lives that our society is creating. A dumb and
despairing rage at what we are doing.
    'We, all of us, are a mistake.'   [Nb, p 206]

The injurious impact of the Group Areas Act is then followed by
a description of what finally forced Steve into exile. The loss of
the house and the sea finished Steve's father but it was the loss
of Steve's manhood on the fifth floor of police headquarters that
delivered the *coup de grâce*. At the beginning of Donald Woods'
book *Biko* there is a section entitled: 'In Memoriam' that begins
with this grim statement:

The following South Africans are known to have died in detention in the hands of the Nationalist government's Security Police. All were imprisoned without trial, charge, prosecution or evidence. All were denied legal representation and access to friends or relatives. The causes of death alleged by the Security Police are given in brackets.   [Woods 1979, p 9]

There then follow forty-four names – and one 'Unnamed person' – with the causes of death ranging from 'suicide by hanging' and 'slipped in the shower' to 'fell seven floors during interrogation'. Steve Biko, who is included in the list, is said to have died as a result of 'injuries sustained in a scuffle'. Maishe Maponya's forceful play of 1984, *Gangsters*, is said to be based on this incident.

Steve Daniels could have been one of these:

... I was scared Piet. I knew where I was going. Anyway, up there on the fifth floor the questions really started. And Steve Daniels replied: 'I've got nothing to say.' (*He laughs again.*) You want to know how they made me change my mind? There's a room up there on the fifth floor...they call it the waiting room. All it's got is a chair by an open window. Every time I said that... 'Nothing to say!'...and I kept it up for a long time, Piet!...they put me in there and left me alone. Every half hour or so a couple of them would stick their heads in, look at me...and laugh. I got no bruises to show you. That's all they ever did to me. Just laugh. But they kept it up. One night back in my cell, after another day of that, I knew that if they put me in there once more... I'd jump. And I wasn't thinking of escape from five floors up. Ja! They had laughed at my manhood and every reason I had for diving out of that window. When they came to fetch me the next morning I was crying like a baby. And they comforted me like I was one. When they started their questions again, I wiped my eyes and answered...for the

first time. I told them everything. Every bloody thing I
knew.   [pp 265–266]

In between the recital of these two examples of apartheid's evils,
Gladys, with great prescience, remarks, 'Oh dear, is the party
over?' [p 262]. Steve is left in no doubt that, as a result of the
power of the State apparatus, he must agree with Gladys that 'the
party is over'.

Betrayal

In *The Meaning of Treason*, Rebecca West says, 'Loyalty is, in
essence, a beautiful contract' [West 1949 p vi], and this accurately
describes Piet's friendship with Steve – they have a beautiful
contract – which makes the suspicion that Steve has been betrayed
by Piet even more poignant and wounding. Piet's meeting with
Steve on the streets of Port Elizabeth came as a revelation in his
life, but when the germ of suspicion enters the bloodstream, it
becomes insidious – everyone can be suspected. When Gladys
says that before she went away, presumably an earlier visit to Fort
England, there was talk amongst their group of an informer, she
asks Piet if she is not right that this was how Steve was discovered
breaking his banning order. He confirms this but when she asks
who the informer might have been he replies: 'I discovered that
if I tried hard enough I could find a good reason for suspect-
ing everyone. I wouldn't have had any friends left if I carried on.'
[p 246]

However, by the end of the play Piet can no longer stop himself
thinking about this mystery as Gladys, acting as *agent provocateur,*
tells Steve that Piet is guilty, which results in a confrontation where
he has to answer the direct question – but does not. Although it
is difficult to see why Piet, if he is innocent, is reluctant to say
so to Steve, Fugard's interpretation is that Piet cannot answer
such a question from the person, other than his wife, whom he
loves the most. Steve has been responsible for the conversion that
transforms his life, and because of the bond that has grown up
between them, it seems that he can only remain silent; he cannot

deny or confirm which, if somewhat inexplicable, does lead to an absorbing piece of theatre. However, Gladys then stops playing her game and tells Steve the truth:

> STEVE: Please, Gladys! What's going on? Are you
>   playing games?
> GLADYS: You wouldn't be doubting him if you were. I
>   doubt everything now. But not him. When you come
>   to think of it, it's almost stupid. He's lost a farm, his
>   friends…you!…the great purpose in his life, and
>   he's going to lose a lot more before its all over, but
>   his faith in himself refuses to be shaken. Of course
>   he didn't do it! What's happened to you, Steven?
>   He isn't an informer. It must have been one of your
>   other trusted comrades. Go back to Mavis and start
>   all over again, because it wasn't him.   **[p 267]**

We believe in Piet, but according to Athol Fugard, many people cannot deal with Piet's silence and as the audience leaves the theatre, doubts begin to fester, just what the apartheid system wants – doubts, distrust, betrayal, divide and rule. The result of an informer in any group is to weaken the unity of that group. Once the seed is sown the State does not have to tend this garden of sorrows, the comrades, like Morris and Zachariah, are doing the authorities' job for them and policing themselves. The act of betrayal in society has a long history, with Judas as the paradigm figure. *My Children! My Africa!* is based on the murder in the Eastern Cape of a schoolteacher by youths who believed him to be a police collaborator and it was also an informer that led the authorities to the farm in Rivonia where Nelson Mandela and his colleagues were arrested.

Apartheid is in itself a betrayal of the majority of South Africa's population, but there are other betrayals on view in this play: Piet of his Afrikaner roots; and in Gladys' case, she feels that society and Piet have betrayed her. She has not been allowed to hide behind her sunglasses, but she does not blame the State for this betrayal – she accuses Piet. If he had not joined the comrades, the Special Branch would not have invaded her territory and her mind and she might not have finished up in Fort England, where, as she bitterly quotes: 'They've burned my brain as brown as yours, Steven'. After she has had the violent confrontation with Steve over Piet's guilt or innocence, she berates Piet:

> GLADYS: (*Turning on him with equal violence.*) I don't
> need you! I don't need you to protect me any more!
> You never did anyway. When they took away my
> diaries you did nothing. When the others took away
> my false teeth and held me down and blew my mind
> to pieces, you weren't even there! I called for you,
> Peter, but you weren't there.   [p 267]

Survival and the Liberals

For most of the apartheid era, the failure of the liberal opposition constituted a further betrayal, and nowhere in Fugard's work is the dilemma of liberalism in South Africa more potently displayed than in *A Lesson from Aloes*. Whatever their differences, both in colour and attitude – one being the stoic and the other accepting exile as inevitable – and though they both appear to generally adopt a left-wing stance, Steve and Piet are liberals drawn in the image of Fugard himself. They emphasise, as does he, the value of the individual, removed from any policy of violence. In the interview with Andrew Foley, referred to later in this chapter, Fugard said:

> Oh the label 'liberal', is one with which I'm very happy.
> In political and philosophical terms, the values of liber-
> alism are the cornerstone values of my life, the values
> I believe in: education, a certain concept of freedom, a
> certain concept of society, an emphasis on the individual
> above group identities. Yes, I'm absolutely happy with
> the label 'liberal'.   [Foley 1994, p 64]

Although the collective action involved in the bus boycott appears to demonstrate a genuine left-wing belief, signs of their incipient liberalism are to be observed in the following extract from Piet's long speech on the bus boycott:

> ... The really important thing was that those two weeks of boycott had raised the political consciousness of the people. They had acted politically, some of them maybe for the first time in their lives. My first lesson from Steve, and the most important one. An evil system isn't a natural disaster. There's nothing you can do to stop a drought, but bad laws and social injustice are man-made and can be unmade by man. It's as simple as that. We can make this a better world to live in.   **[p 242]**

Fugard has never been a member of a political party, but if Sam, as discussed later, is seen as a natural intellectual, Fugard is clearly a natural liberal, and as such was just as aware as others more politically involved of the failure of the liberals in the political arena. By 1982 he is reported as saying: 'Paranoia is a potent factor in white South African psychology. It is a psychology of fear. And the white liberal has become a joke. Eventually, he will be caught in a cross fire between Afrikaner nationalism and black South Africa.' [Gussow 1982, p 79] In the OUP volume *Township Plays*, Dennis Walder says: 'The near-total hegemony of the white minority created by apartheid has meant that white liberals and other dissidents such as Fugard participate in the structures of domination which they attack...' [p xi] This is difficult to refute. Fugard cannot wholly abdicate his white liberal skin, but if he is inevitably participating in 'the structures of domination', his pen shows how he abominates what these structures have done to those with non-white skins.

If the liberal, both in South Africa and in Fugard's plays, is doomed, are there any survivors in this play, liberals or otherwise? Gladys dismisses the aloes as turgid and ugly; she says that she wants to live her life and not just survive it, but after the crucial role she performs within the drama, she returns to a state of passivity. Steve retreats but, as with others amongst Fugard's sad and unhappy characters, there is some hope in the portrayal of Piet.

Gladys does not think there will be many survivors, particularly if the end of the world is nigh, One of the few visitors she receives is a representative of the Watchtower Society, who has a date worked out for the end of the world: 'It's not far off, either'. However, she believes Piet will be one of the survivors. Early in the play she tells her husband – with some irony on the question of how many survivors there will be:

> ... If I haven't got the radio on or a car isn't passing in the street, it's hard sometimes to believe there is a world out there full of other people. Just you and me. That's all that's left. The streets are empty and I imagine you wandering around looking for another survivor. If you ever find one, Peter, you must bring him home.   **[p 232]**

The play inclines us to believe that as Piet sits: '*in the backyard,... with the unidentified aloe*' (the last stage instruction of the play), he is not totally defeated. James Fenton believes the message of the play contains some reason to be optimistic:

> Mr. Fugard's great strength in this work derives from an intimate knowledge of defeat and the consequences of defeat. At least it seems to me that those who really know what defeat is are in a better position to lead their companions to victory.
>
> At one stage the Afrikaner hero makes a plain distinction between a natural disaster, like drought, and a man made catastrophe, like the political system in South Africa. Nothing can be done about the first. Everything can, and must, be done about the second. The optimistic credo is plainly set forth, and then tested against the experience of the three characters.   **[Fenton 1980, p 40]**

The gloom that invades all three characters in the play mirrors the mood of the country in 1963, the play's time frame, and 1978, the date of the first production; but despite this, the ultimate message appears to be that even away from the veld, Piet, like his aloes, will survive.

> PIET: (*Looking around at his collection.*) This is not fair
> to them. An aloe isn't seen to its best advantage in
> a jam tin in a little backyard. They need space. The
> open veld with purple mountains in the distance...
> That veld is a hard world. They and the thorn trees
> were just about the only things still alive in it when I
> finally packed up the old truck and left the farm...
> GLADYS: Is that the price of survival in this country?
> Thorns and bitterness.
> PIET: For the aloe it is. Maybe there's some sort of
> lesson for us there.   [pp 228–229]

The clear conclusion by the end of the play is that if the aloe is a metaphor for something that survives, whatever South Africa subjects it to, then it only goes to show that people are not aloes. The oppressed, unlike aloes, do not all have the same characteristics; Gladys may be spiky and bitter and Piet thornless but capable of survival, but in Fugard's plays, his dispossessed deal with the drought in their lives in a variety of different ways; they do not all have the same botanical roots. On the other hand, even if Piet does survive, Fugard envisaged a bleak future for him as far back as 1966:

> At last. An image which defines a human predicament
> and Piet. Thinking back to the drought, he cries out, 'I
> am frightened of being useless!' The logos behind his
> humanity, his politics. He escaped the horror of his
> impatience on the parched, dying land, by a life of action
> among men. And then the second drought – and again
> alone – just himself, empty handed, useless. Piet face to
> face with himself – the absurdity of himself, *alone*.
> 'A man's scenery is other men'.   [Nb, p 140]

Steve may survive, even though many who went into exile did not live happily ever after; but Piet sits with only his unidentified aloe as scenery, with not another man in sight. As for Gladys, she was damned whatever happened; not suited to the climate, meteorological or political. She is unable to combat the psychosis that apartheid created in many South Africans, but in the recesses of her mind, she may find some form of rest and comfort from thoughts of *Sunset in Somerset,* the picture she so admires at Fort England; even though it is hung in the room where patients wait their turn for electric shock treatment. As Fugard has failed to provide for her a way out of the quagmire of apartheid, she retreats to Fort England to escape the political reality. Her fate can be seen to constitute South Africa's ultimate act of betrayal.

Violence and his most personal play

'Master Harold'...and the boys is a work of Fugard's mature years; he is reported as saying: 'In spite of the pain involved, it has at a technical level been one of the happiest writing experiences I've ever had.' **[Benson 1997, p 123]** It was first performed in 1982 and was the first full-length play he chose for an initial showing outside South Africa; it opened at New Haven in the USA on 12 March 1982, was transferred to New York in May and then to Johannesburg, first presented at the Market Theatre on 22 March 1983.

The uninterrupted action of the play – there is no interval – takes place in a real-life location, the tea room at St George's Park in Port Elizabeth. There are only three characters: a seventeen year-old boy Harold (shortened to Hally – Harold Athol Lannigan Fugard was known as 'Hally' when a boy) and two black servants, Sam and Willie. They look after the tea room during Hally's mother's absence and had previously worked at the Jubilee Boarding House, another enterprise run by Hally's mother in the past. When the play opens, Sam and Willie are found alone discussing ballroom dancing while Hally's mother is at the hospital visiting her husband. Hally comes in from school to finish his homework and reveals, initially, the friendly and yet somewhat condescending relationship he has with these two, particularly Sam. They recall one particularly happy moment in the past when he had made a kite for Hally. However, the news that his father is to be released from hospital changes all that, and there is an angry confrontation leading to Hally spitting in Sam's face, which replicated what had happened when Fugard himself, at the age of ten, spat in the face of his mother's servant, Sam Semela.

In the play this event becomes one of theatre's most disturbing moments, on a par, at one level, with the plucking out of Gloucester's eyes in *King Lear*. In Brecht's *In the Jungle of Cities*, one result of a bizarre quarrel between the two main characters is when one of them calls upon his opponent to spit in the face of a Salvation Army preacher – which he does. Shylock's Jewish gabardine is spat upon in the Rialto and Anne responds to Richard III's unwanted wooing by spitting at him; but in context, these examples begin to verge on the insignificant compared with Fugard's shocking occurrence. He commented on the incident, quoting Oscar Wilde: 'In "The Ballad of Reading Gaol," Wilde says that each man kills the thing he loves – some do it with a word, some do it with a sword. And there's one little boy who did it with spit.' [Gussow 1982, p 88]

Sam is a surrogate father to Hally and *'Master Harold'...and the boys* is principally concerned with the damage done to this young man by the conflict within himself over his two fathers, the natural one and Sam. It is a 'Tale of Two Fathers' revealing, as in Dickens, 'the best of times and the worst of times'. This play is set in 1950 when, for the dispossessed in South Africa, the times were more often of the worst variety, but in this play there are some moments that are of the best variety, particularly when the singular affinity between Sam and Hally is observed. However, before the curtain falls, this relationship is destroyed by an insensitive act of violence of such impact that when the play was previewing in Philadelphia in 1982, and during the scene where Sam asks Willie if he should hit Hally for spitting in his face, a group of young black audience members in the balcony screamed out 'Hit him, hit him'. This sentiment was echoed in the New York black newspaper, *New Amsterdam News*, which expressed disgust about the apparent unconcern by Fugard, a white writer, for the racist climax that 'set up a situation in which a black man's dignity is so assaulted by a little boy that he had the impulse to hit him...and didn't.'

In an interview with Andrew Foley, Fugard provides a vigorous response to these attitudes:

> And a lot of critics in America, especially black critics in America, said, 'Why didn't you have Sam beat the living shit out of Hally at that moment?' Now, that would obviously have satisfied them, that would really have made the play in their eyes a contribution to the 'cause'. Right?... If any moments of my writing define me as a liberal, it is those moments when violence is there as a potential choice, when a character says 'I can either destroy or I can try to use this to take myself one step higher.' In my opinion Sam makes the right choice and goes one step higher, because hitting Hally would have achieved – what? What would it have achieved? It would have achieved in my opinion absolutely nothing. An act of destruction, an act of violence, is blind and only creates darkness. I believe most passionately that of all the things men and women resort to in terms of their dialogue with other human beings, the most stupid, the most pointless, the most tragic, the most misguided, is violence. Because it only perpetuates itself.
>
> [Foley 1994, p 65]

Fugard has consistently seen South African theatre as an instrument for change, an alternative to violence. The demise of apartheid was principally achieved through non-violent action and this is reflected in his work where physical aggression on the stage is rare, but in *'Master Harold'...and the boys* the spitting incident is so unexpected as to constitute the most violent of actions in any of Fugard's plays. And it is still so. It is reported that a student at the University of the Western Cape who was taken to see this play in the year 2000, 'actually screamed with shock' at the spitting incident. Of even more significance, it is not brother or sister against brother or a Coloured man beating a black man – this is an attack by a white boy on a man who has been a substitute father to him, but who is black.

Hally's unexpected action is not the only hostility on display. The one act of violence that might be justified, Sam hitting out in response to the degradation inflicted by Hally, does not take place, but the play illustrates, particularly during the deterioration in the relationship between the spitter and the spat-upon, how insidious was violence in South Africa. The state's authority was predicated on its preparedness to employ physical violence, whether on the streets or in the interview room, but in the majority of instances, citizens experience the oppressive arm of authority either as the threat of violence, or in its psychological or symbolic form. Fugard's later play *Playland* is concerned with memories of violence – the white character of atrocities in Namibia and the black man of a murder he has committed. In Fugard's own words:

> Useful comparison with the innocence of the two brothers in *The Blood Knot*. Morrie and Zach face the *threat* of violence. Martinus and Gideon live with the *consequences* of violence...which in a sense is the story of South Africa during the 35 years of my writing career.
>
> **[Barbera 1993, p 534]**

Unless in the possession of a valid pass with valid stamps, most of the population walked the streets of South Africa with the fear that force might be inflicted upon them at any time. Even when legally allowed to occupy the white man's pavement, the pass holder could have been subject to overt verbal violence, insensitivity or the hurt inflicted by being ignored and unrecognised. When the intolerant Hally calls Sam a bigot for not appreciating the importance of Charles Darwin, Sam, as a result of years of oppression, does not react any more than he does when Hally says he doesn't want 'any more nonsense in here', even though all the nonsense has been caused by Hally's reaction to the possibility of his father's release from hospital **[p 28]**. As the action proceeds, the temperature in the tea room rises and Hally *'gives WILLIE a vicious whack'* with his ruler **[p 30]**. This leads to Sam being named as a servant who is getting too familiar (and who should now address Hally as 'Master Harold') and then on to the spitting incident. Sam does not physically respond – the stage direction at this juncture reads: '(*His violence ebbing away into defeat as quickly as it flooded.*)' – but his verbal reaction sums up how violence inflicted on the oppressed is tolerated to the extent that it is. Sam says to Hally, 'you think you're safe in your fair skin' **[p 46]** and indubitably it is the protection provided by race, universal in the perpetration of South African violence, that is instinctively accepted as the norm.

Using differences in colour as an excuse for violence, and other indignities, is part of the central racial issue exposed in these Fugard plays, but this is one of the only ones where there is a direct representation on stage of one of the primary elements in the real world of apartheid – the confrontation between white and black. In *'Master Harold'... and the boys* the political context is up front and open: Hally in the white corner and Sam in the black. It is not, however, as elementary as this. The relationship between Sam and Hally is too complex to be confined to the roped enclosure of an apartheid boxing ring, but what the juxtaposition of a black Sam and a white Hally in this play does do is to open up an opportunity to compare this relationship with the black and white reality in South Africa, either in 1950, when the play is set, or in the early 1980s, when it was first staged: to compare what happened on that wet and windy afternoon with the social, economic and political fates in store for the myriad white Hallys and black Sams. According to a review by Joseph Lelyveld in *The New York Times* of 24 March 1983, when *'Master Harold'...and the boys* was presented in Johannesburg, Archbishop Desmond Tutu, who was in the audience, said: 'It holds a mirror up to our reality. It shows what we have become.' Careful analysis of this important play shows how justified is this remark.

The Man of Magnitude and the Dancing Lesson

Sam, the surrogate father, will have received very little formal education, but over some years his close relationship with Hally has meant that their schooling has paralleled and perhaps equalled each other. However, there is one subject at least where Sam is higher in the class than Hally, and that is revealed when they discuss Napoleon and the 'equal opportunities for all' that he is said to have espoused. In a light-hearted way, but with serious undertones, Sam tells Hally, 'I'm all right on oppression' [p 14], an assertion made no doubt from first-hand experience. Hally might feel he is oppressed by some of his teachers and to some extent by his father, due to his own ambivalent feelings, but Sam is oppressed in many arenas – park benches for one example. Although not as puerile as the comic books left for Hally's father, the scholastic exchange between Sam and Hally, where they discuss candidates for men of magnitude and compare Wilberforce to Tolstoy and Jesus to Mohammed, is somewhat trite if not ironic in the context of South Africa: these ethical men might well find their beliefs very difficult to promote in Port Elizabeth. Darwin and Tolstoy are two of Hally's choices. The former can be seen as supporting the superiority of the white race in South Africa – the survival of the fittest – and endorsing Hally's incipient racism, but Tolstoy's Christian desire to free the serfs runs directly contrary to the boy's avowed atheism – and the politics of the country.

However, there is a deeper meaning to all this; the most eminent candidate for the title of a 'Man of Magnitude' could be Sam himself, even if he has little 'magnitude', little importance, in this South African world. Sam is no fool and if more education had been available to him, could he have been the social reformer referred to in the play who was going to rescue his people – the leader of 'The Struggle for an Existence'? [p 15]

Fugard has described Sam Semela as the man in whom he had discovered 'the presence of dignity, pride, compassion and wisdom' [Benson 1997, p 123], and as the fictional Sam is drawn, he undoubtedly possesses such a high degree of understanding, humanity and common sense that he might be seen as one of nature's intellectuals. Fugard demonstrates Sam's sense of pity and understanding of Hally's relationship with his father as he encourages the boy to recall his younger days and the Jubilee Boarding House where he visited Sam and Willie in the servants' quarters, leading to the building of the kite and the pleasure it gave: 'I was running, waiting for it to crash to the ground, but instead suddenly there was something alive behind me at the end of the string, tugging at it as if it wanted to be free' [p 24]. Sam, the kite's architect, might also wish to be free, but he is not. As Hally is told later, Sam leaves him sitting on a bench in the park with the kite because he does not want to spoil the occasion by telling Hally that he is not allowed to sit on the same bench.

This is one of the few direct references in the play to an apartheid regulation. At this time the government had been challenged in the courts over the separation of public facilities, facilities that the appellants claimed should be equal. However, in 1953, the government removed the opportunity to contest this inequality by enacting the Reservation of Separate Amenities Act covering public premises and transport, which enabled provincial authorities to extend this legislation to such things as park benches.

Although the revelation by Sam of this prejudice is an essential ingredient in understanding his relationship with Hally, what is more telling is the explanation, eventually given to Hally, as to why Sam had made the kite in the first place. After the spitting incident has taken place, Sam reminds Hally of the time he had helped to carry his drunken father home from the Central Hotel Bar (where Hally had first needed to obtain permission for Sam to enter the premises), and of the aftermath and its place in the kite-building exercise:

> After we got him to bed you came back with me to my room and sat in a corner and carried on just looking down at the ground. And for days after that! You hadn't done anything wrong, but you went around as if you owed the world an apology for being alive. I didn't like seeing that! That's not the way a boy grows up to be a man!

... But the one person who should have been teaching
you what that means was the cause of your shame. If you
really want to know, that's why I made you that kite. I
wanted you to look up, be proud of something, of yourself...   [pp 46-47]

This whole episode is suffused with Sam's wisdom and honesty but
the sense of freedom and the gratitude of Hally are all destroyed,
as if the kite had suddenly plunged to earth, by the telephone call
from his mother saying that his father might be allowed home.
However, before Hally becomes the typical white racist, Sam,
by bringing to life the forthcoming Eastern Province Ballroom
Dancing Competition, recaptures the mood of lightness and
optimism seen at the beginning of the play. Sam's message, as he
describes this competition, is blatantly escapist. The black man
and woman can flee from the drudgery of their everyday existence to the ballroom, but the paradox is that at the black man
and woman's haven that is the dance floor, the steps of the dance,
the waltz, the foxtrot and the quickstep, are European – not even
like Lena's steps, as she says to Outa: 'not like your dances. No
war dances for us'. Lena's perception on Outa's dance reflects the
standard image of the 'native' as portrayed in much of Western
popular culture – scantily-clad warriors stamping the ground
around the camp fire. To some extent this view was thrown back
into Western faces with the story told concerning UK journalists covering the celebration of Nigerian Independence in 1960.
They had needed to file their articles three hours before the
midnight lowering of the Imperial flag, articles that referred to
happy Nigerians dancing in the streets. As these journalists drove
through the streets of Lagos at midnight they found only orderly
groups of citizens wending their way home, whereupon one journalist shouted from his car: 'Dance, Dammit, you're meant to be
dancing.' [Crowder 1987, p 21]
    Nevertheless, Sam and Willie find comfort from appropriating
an artefact of the white cultural hegemony, an appropriation that
was apparently widespread. In Joyce Cary's novel *Mister Johnson*,

at Mister Johnson's last party, there were 'two thickset Yoruba girls, dancing an American fox-trot together' [Cary 1976, p 209]. Fugard also uses the ballroom symbolically to suggest that if the harmony, manners and courtesies observed there could be translated to South African society as a whole, a lot of collisions could be avoided, collisions that occur every day between the oppressor and the oppressed.

Fugard and his sister were ballroom dancing champions when young, but for black people in South Africa it was a communal activity that perhaps, for an hour or two, gives some meaning to their lives. Sam further explains to Hally:

> SAM: There's no collisions out there, Hally...like being in a dream about a world in which accidents don't happen.
> HALLY: (*Genuinely moved by Sam's image.*) Jesus, Sam! That's beautiful!

Hally warms to these ideas and moves the dream onto the international stage:

> HALLY: ... You know, Sam, when you come to think of it, that's what the United Nations boils down to...a dancing school for politicians!
> SAM: And let's hope they learn.   [pp 36–37]

Tragically, Hally has not absorbed the lesson, nor can he see how Sam is teaching him to understand the world differently, and for the better. His father cannot dance, he is on crutches, but Hally is about to bump violently into Sam, who can dance but who is unable to avoid the tragic collision to come. Avoiding collisions, like proper dialogue, involves a mutuality that, as this play tragically reveals, is not available to Sam and Hally. Despite his best intentions, apartheid cripples Sam and as Hally says: '...the cripples are...also out there tripping up everybody...' [p 41] – just as they did for Johnnie and Hester.

A Tale of two fathers

The contrast and contest (at least in Hally's psychology) between the two fathers is fascinating when the character of each is considered within the South African political context. On the surface Sam is severely handicapped in this competition, not only is he black but his identity in the tea room is that of a servant. Despite this, the play demonstrates how, up until that particular afternoon, Sam had been successful in his role as a substitute father. For a son of his own, Sam would have been using a different set of norms in the education of a younger male, but in the case of Hally, Sam has instinctively provided support for Hally as the reverse side of the coin that displays the defects in the character of his racist biological father. There is also another obstacle for Sam to overcome in this contest – and only the playgoer is fully aware that there is a contest; Sam did not view it that way, and as for the real father, it would not, for the merest instant, have entered his mind. That is the element of love.

There has clearly been a great deal of affection between Sam and Hally but when it comes to the crunch and Sam remembers how they carried his father back from the Central Hotel Bar, Hally's reaction is to say (with a stage instruction of *'Great pain'*), 'I love him, Sam' **[p 46]**. Hally's uncertainty is painful in the extreme. As was the case with Fugard, Sam may have been the only friend of Hally's boyhood, but any recollections of this nature are subsumed by the prospect of returning home and finding his demanding father there. He allows these conflicting emotions to explode to the surface as he tries to show that he has a good relationship with his father by repeating one of his racist sayings:

> ... Want to know what our favourite joke is? He gives out a big groan, you see, and says: 'It's not fair, is it, Hally?' Then I have to ask: 'What chum?' And then he says: 'A kaffir's arse'...and we both have a good laugh.

Sam's riposte to this is to drop his trousers and show: 'A real Basuto arse...' **[pp 44–45]** which pushes Hally to the final degradation of spitting in Sam's face. He uses Sam as a scapegoat to exorcise his guilt over this ambivalence towards his father.

This section of the play can also be seen as Hally's coming of age. To quote Rob Amato:

> It seems to me that Hally cannot stay in the world of the tearoom, has lost that magic afternoon world, cannot accept Sam's several attempts after the spitting to save the situation, because the resurrection of the trauma makes him, again, at seventeen, perceive of himself as guilty of the one crime which South Africans who are white simply can't commit. The central commandment of the hegemony of apartheid may be 'Show not thy weakness to thy neighbour race, to the helots.'
>
> [Amato 1984, p 212]

In this context, Hally has revealed his weaknesses over many years, one example being that, contrary to the norm, he has acknowledged that the two servants were probably the only friends of his childhood years. However, the final weakness, the resort to shameful violence, has destroyed the generally non-racial relationship he had hitherto enjoyed in a world that might have transcended the racial reality, but now Hally has to get into step with his racist brothers. When Sam is explaining that there is no bumping into each other on the dance floor, Hally responds with the words 'You've got a vision, Sam!', that are accompanied with the stage instruction, '*Deep and sincere admiration of the man*' [p 37]. With this admiration, and by overtly accepting Sam's friendship and guidance, Hally has broken Amato's commandment – such friendships between the races are a sign of weakness. This is no accident, but Doris Lessing's view still applies – Hally has brought down the whip:

> ...when a white man in Africa by accident looks into the eyes of a native and sees the human being (which it is his chief preoccupation to avoid), his sense of guilt, which

he denies, fumes up in resentment and he brings down
the whip.   [Lessing 1994, p 144]

Just as other dissidents in South Africa have been punished without
trial, so this confused white representative of the ruling class
considers that the native has gone too far and Sam is 'whipped',
precisely as Doris Lessing suggests. Hally cannot tolerate the
goodness in Sam and tragically displays all of the worst characteristics of the white racist State. With what can perhaps be seen
as the naivety of youth, Hally accepts Sam's friendship and sees
the humanity in this 'native', but the drama Fugard provides is to
show how this can be so comprehensively shattered by events that
are triggered both by Hally's personal circumstances and temper-
ament, but also due to the need to bring himself back within the
inviolable code of black/white relationships in South Africa.

Sam eschews violence but racial prejudice can destroy the
strongest of friendships. When cracks in a relationship occur
between brothers in *Blood Knot* and the couples in *Boesman and
Lena* and *A Lesson from Aloes,* what real chance is there for a black
man of forty-five years of age to have a lasting friendship with a
seventeen year-old white boy, highlighting the irony in the title of
the play? The person who is referred to as 'Master' is a teenager,
but the inverted commas indicate that there is some ambivalence.
Is he the Master in authority or is he only a 'Little *white* boy' as
Willie refers to him? Against that, the boys are unquestionably
mature men. In South Africa the term 'boy' as a form of address
was universal whatever the age of the black man, as referred to in
Blood Knot:

> ZACHARIAH: What's this 'old fellow' thing you got
>   hold of tonight?
> MORRIS: Just a figure of speaking, Zach. The
>   Englishman would say 'old boy' but we don't like
>   that 'boy' business, hey?
> ZACHARIAH: *Ja.* They call a man a boy...   [p 74]

The last scene is underscored by Hally's final words, 'I don't know anything any more', and Sam's response, a final attempt at reconciliation, which Hally ignores and leaves. The final chorus is not chosen at random:

> 'Johnny won your marbles,
> Tell you what we'll do;
> Dad will get you new ones right away;
> Better go to sleep now,
> Little man you've had a busy day.'   [pp 48–49]

It has been a busy day in Hally's growing up but his dad is not going to be putting anything right. Once more at the end of a Fugard play there is a sense of isolation in an unhappy world. Sam and Willie might be considered fortunate amongst the dispossessed of South Africa; they have jobs and a relatively considerate employer, but fundamentally they are just as disadvantaged as the remainder of the non-white populace of their country. We can conjecture that Sam harbours more expectations from life than a Boesman or a Lena, but the cruelty of Hally's treatment traps Sam just as certainly as Winston and John are trapped on Robben Island. In *The Island*, the white warders are not physically present in the drama, but in Hally's case he is the oppressor centre-stage and when offered the alternative of walking away from the South African racist norm, he simply exits the sorry scene. As Doris Lessing emphasizes, his recognition of humanity in a black man has led, perhaps inevitably, to him abandoning a friendship across the racial divide – a friendship that could have been a precious jewel in that barren world.

He does not know what will happen next. Sam appeals to him to gain something from the events of the afternoon and advises him to turn his back on apartheid and racism: 'You know what that bench means now, and you can leave it any time you choose. All you've got to do is to stand up and walk away from it.' [p 48] – discard prejudice and emulate Nelson Mandela by taking the 'Long Walk to Freedom' – but he does not. 'Master Harold' exacerbates the racial prejudice by taking the few coins left in the cash register, in contrast to 'the boys' who use their bus fare, their remaining coins, for a tune from the jukebox, the last dance. They then close up the tea room and begin their long walk through the rain to New Brighton – but Sam cannot take the action he has advocated for Hally; the bench is still there for him, and he and Willie cannot turn their backs on the reality of apartheid – they cannot 'stand up and walk away from it'. Like the kite tied to the 'whites-only' bench, they are inevitably tied to their segregated spaces in the world they inhabit, a world that Fugard has dramatically brought into the tea room to such effect as to make tangible to the audience the reality of that bench, and the kite that symbolises a freedom not available to its maker – it is tied down.

EIGHT

Art and Rebellion

Rebellion starts, Miss Helen, with just one man or woman standing up and saying, 'No. Enough!' Albert Camus. French writer.

The Road to Mecca

ugard's theatre is a hotbed of a rebellion – but not red-hot. Insurgence may not always be outspoken and obvious – he is too skilled a playwright for that – but Piet and Miss Helen and Hester unassumingly, but significantly, oppose the established order. Some of his work is also directly concerned with art: firstly where he himself is reflected as the artist in plays such as *The Captain's Tiger*, *Valley Song* and *Exits and Entrances* and secondly in his characterisations of such as Miss Helen with her cement and broken glass and Mr M with his words; but the first play in this chapter is concerned with a problematic artist called Dimetos. In this case the artistic view is more that of spectator than practitioner, but attempting to determine the accuracy of such a statement is only one of the questions posed in this aberrant play. Fugard projects himself into his work, both overtly and covertly, and it is an intriguing exercise to compare the writer with his dark creation, Dimetos. They are both craftsmen but Dimetos is more master than worker. His skills allow him to supervise – to direct – others, exactly what a playwright does. The villagers over time learn to trust Dimetos – 'They've started knocking on my door when the need arises' **[p 120]**, much like the founder members of the Serpent Players knocked on Fugard's door in 1963. There is however an essential difference between them that is displayed from the first action of the play. For Dimetos, the rescue of the horse involves no feeling, only mechanics, but with Fugard, although the mechanics of playmaking are essential, the projection of feelings is paramount.

Looking for answers to the abstruse questions raised in this work are not made any easier when the critic is faced with the contrived setting of the play. As if Fugard wanted to underline the universality of his themes, *Dimetos* is set nowhere – or anywhere – and at no identifiable time. It could in part be seen to be centred on a dark medieval world where the people believe in witches and evil omens, contrasting in Act Two with a utopian idyll where the sun always shines.

Fugard's Dimetos

The play's text states that Act One is located 'In a remote Province' and Act Two, 'Beside the Ocean'. After the first performance at the Edinburgh Festival, Fugard revised the play and, according to his *Notebooks,* changed the settings – in his imagination – so that the first Act was moved to Nieu Bethesda (Further references will use the English spelling), and the other to Gaukamma Beach – a desolate location in the Eastern Cape near Mossel Bay [Nb, p 219]. Applying some specificity, at least it in his mind, may have helped in the revised composition of the play, but the finished article provides none of the reality of place – and time – as is found in *The Road to Mecca* and *Valley Song.* However, the undetermined and somewhat alien world of *Dimetos* suits the complexities of this recondite work where, typical of Fugard, there is little action on view but he does provide the audience with more than enough to ponder on.

Dimetos, a skilled and much respected engineer, has left the metropolis to live in the remote community where the play opens. With him is a housekeeper, Sophia, who arrived in his life when he was ten years old and she seventeen. The third member of the household is Lydia, his young niece. The play opens when, using his engineering expertise and with Lydia involved in the action, Dimetos is instrumental in rescuing a horse that has fallen down a deep well. Lydia is exhilarated by this, a sensation that is prolonged when, on the same day as the horse raising incident, a young man named Danilo arrives. His quest is to persuade Dimetos to return to the city where his particular skills are urgently required. The request is refused, but Lydia persuades Danilo to try again and, for reasons that become apparent later, Dimetos suggests that the young man should stay a little longer so that the decision can be reconsidered. After five days have passed, and when the two young people are together, Danilo kisses the girl and then cannot control himself. The stage instructions at this point, and the use of the word 'eventually', allows the director to determine how close this encounter becomes to a scene of rape – or nearly so:

> (*He kisses her gently. At first LYDIA responds but as DANILO goes further she begins to resist him. He can't control himself. The struggle becomes violent. Her dress gets torn. She eventually manages to break free and runs away. DANILO is left alone.*)   **[p 145]**

At the end of Act One, Lydia hangs herself. During Act Two, many years later, there is a short visit by Danilo on Dimetos and Sophia, who now live in a small cottage by the sea, but other than that, this second and shorter Act is mostly given over to revealing the guilt they both have over the death of Lydia.

In most cases Fugard's plays have sparse, or even non-existent, sets and there is a revealing indication of this when he recorded in the *Notebooks* how *Boesman and Lena* was staged in Durban in 1970:

> ... on stage all that the actors will need – props, the material for the pondok, clothing...
>
> When the audience is in, without dimming house lights, actors come on – barefoot, rehearsal clothes – and in front of audience put on their 'character' clothes. Outa takes a box and sits at the back of the stage, his back to audience. Boesman and Lena load up their bundles and walk...round and round the stage. Lena falls behind.

> ...When Lena sees Outa for the first time, the actor
> must turn to face the audience......Lena and Boesman
> never leave the stage.   [Nb, p 185]

Dimetos is no exception. In Act One, for the action at the well, by
the pool, in the garden and in the house and Lydia's bedroom,
there is no scenery. In Act Two, at a beach and a small cottage, there
is no sea and only a handful of sand – and no walls or windows.
The stage is as bare as that in *Valley Song*. However, in this unusual
play, Fugard, the consummate man of the theatre, introduces into
this barren universe a frightened horse trapped at the bottom of a
deep well that presents a theatrical challenge that in its own way
is as difficult to deal with as, for instance, providing an adequate
staging of the revelation of Banquo at Macbeth's feast. Fugard's
coup de théâtre is not just a whim or a fancy. The horse, and particularly the details of the rescue and its consequences, is essential
to the play. It creates a sensational first scene. Fugard's intention
from the outset was for the animal to be represented by a bench
that Lydia can straddle where she attaches straps to the make-
believe horse, to which ropes are fastened and with the vertical
movement at the well being represented by Dimetos pulling in the
ropes, now untied, through a series of pulleys. The bench would
be static. Recollections of a revival at the Gate Theatre in London
in 2003 are that the elongated shape of the open stage, where
sections of wall had been introduced, produced a tunnel effect
– a horizontal well-shaft – which allowed the bench to be moved.
Seeing Lydia on the bench being drawn towards Dimetos added
another dimension to Fugard's thrilling opening sequence.

Shakespeare's plots come from a myriad of written sources
but, as we have seen before, for the South African playwright the
origins of his works are invariably to be found in someone he
knows or has met, a fortuitous encounter, an image or a chance
remark, but rarely from something written. A number of his plays
are clearly autobiographical – and *The Guest* is partly biographi-
cal – but only *Dimetos* is based, however loosely, on the work of
another writer. Fugard had been commissioned to provide a piece

for the Edinburgh Festival of 1975 and he took this opportunity to use something he had read in the *Carnets* of Albert Camus:

> The story of Dimetos in Camus's *Carnets*: falling in love with a beautiful but dead young woman washed up by the sea, and having to watch the decay and corruption of what he loves. Camus: 'This is the symbol of a condition we must try to define.'
> When I first read his note on Dimetos I was excited and immediately thought of it as the germinal idea of a play. Yesterday I re-remembered it.
> Dimetos goes mad watching the decay of her body.
>
> **[Nb, p 107]**

Most of the reviews of the Edinburgh staging were dismissive – the play was not generally understood – and many critics could not take on board that this was a Fugard play that had no apparent reference, geographically or politically, to South Africa. One German critic wrote: 'Even from a (white) South African one cannot, if you please, constantly expect apartheid plays. But does it *have* to be such mytho-mishmash?' **[Wertheim 2000 p 101]** There was a better reception when it was presented the following year, in a re-worked version, at the Nottingham Playhouse with Paul Scofield as Dimetos, Ben Kingsley as Danilo and Yvonne Bryceland repeating her Edinburgh appearance as Sophia. In 1981, Marius Weyers, who twenty years later was to be so important in the staging of *Sorrows and Rejoicings*, played Dimetos in the play's first local performance – in Cape Town.

Frustrated love

In the introduction to this book it is reported that Fugard said: 'I always write out of love.' He also writes about love, indeed love is one of the fundamental threads that run through all of his work – in some instances more strongly than in others; *Boesman and Lena* being a prime example where it is an over-arching focus. Elsewhere, in *'Master Harold'...and the boys* it is the destruction of the love between Sam and Hally that becomes the leitmotiv for that play and later the reader will be introduced to Marta, in *Sorrows and Rejoicings*, who exhibits this emotion as profoundly as anyone in Fugard's parade. But in *Dimetos*, there is another dimension altogether; love that is tainted and illicit and unconsummated. The two Fugardian-fraught people who inhabit the abstract nowhere of the play's landscape are lovers – but not the loved. Sophia is astutely aware of the difference as she advises Lydia:

> ... A pretty little thing like you will have to cope with a lot more passion before she's old. But in your prayers tonight make sure you ask that it be the other person's and not your own. To love is a position of weakness, to be loved a position of power. I was careless about my prayers when I was your age.   [p 146]

A profound observation in the context of this play. Sophia is in love with Dimetos. He may recognise this but does not reciprocate and she gains little from her passion other than his company over many years. In another story it might have been different and master and housekeeper happily married, but Dimetos loves his niece – he is sexually attracted to her – and is racked with guilt as a result. In the field of romance, normality, even convention, is to be seen in Lydia's relationships. She loves and admires Dimetos as an unusual man and as her uncle and guardian. With Sophia, she treats her as an elder sister and friendly confidante, but her feeling for Danilo is a new and unusual emotion for her. This affection is returned by him but after having too much to drink his regard for her is transformed into a lust that he cannot control. Lydia may well have been able to recover from Danilo's assault until she discovers that Dimetos, who would have liked to have been in Danilo's place, is implicated in the act; he has become a voyeur observing the scene from the nearby lemon orchard from where he could have intervened and rescued his niece, but did not. It is this that impels Lydia to commit suicide. Sophia also has a part to play in this tragedy. In Act Two she confesses:

...She would still be alive today if I hadn't abandoned her to... You are not God! If I had so much as put my arm around her when she sat there wilting...one gentle touch, and I had it in my soul. But I was jealous and I knew, that left to your own devices, you were going to hurt her. So I went for a walk, for a long walk...   [p 156]

Dimetos is theatre that may be better appreciated in the reading than as a member of the audience. The language or, more accurately, the meaning behind the language, is complex. One of the principal reasons for this is because the guilt-ridden couple, Dimetos and Sophia, have been together for so long they are unable to openly express their true feelings. The stoical Sophia might better have been named 'Patience', like the black women in *The Road to Mecca*. In Act One there is a dialogue between them that sums up the situation:

> DIMETOS: What are we guilty of?
> SOPHIA: Our lives, if nothing else.
> DIMETOS: All we've done is live them.
> SOPHIA: Speak for yourself. A dedicated servant ends up without a life of her own.
> DIMETOS: Where does that word come from suddenly?
> SOPHIA: Which one?
> DIMETOS: You know the one I mean. I never called you or thought of you as that.
> SOPHIA: But it's true, isn't it? If I'm not a servant what am I? Mother? Sister? I'm not old enough for the first and I never thought of myself as the second. There's also 'friend', 'companion'...if the others are too personal. How do *you* see me, Dimetos? Who am I?
> DIMETOS: Sophia.
> SOPHIA: Faithful, loyal, trustworthy Sophia!
> DIMETOS: You have been all of those.

SOPHIA: They are the virtues of a good servant.

[pp 138–139]

A further excursion into Sophia's psyche is given when she thinks for a moment that the assault on Lydia might have been made by Dimetos:

> SOPHIA: (*Terrified of her question and its possible answer,*
> *but unable to resist asking it.*) Who...who was it?
> (*Sinking to her knees beside LYDIA.*) Lydia, please
> help me. Who was it? (*Her pain turns to violence. She*
> *scrambles to her feet and assaults LYDIA physically.*) For
> God's sake, tell me. Who was it?
> LYDIA: Danilo.   [pp 145–146]

Dimetos is, equally, unsure and introverted. Lydia accuses him of hiding his feelings, but with him there is another emotion on display – caring – or more importantly, not caring. He describes himself as an artisan and not an artist but he is being disingenuous. He is passionate about craftsmanship but, if we are to believe what he says, he left the city because that passion had waned – he no longer cared. He is a very convoluted man. He believes in the '...mysterious distance between head and hands...' [p 124] but Sophia's insights are more meaningful; she brings the heart into the equation. Perhaps Dimetos is best defined as an 'onlooker' – as he proved to be in the lemon orchard – and not the achiever. He recalls a man named Jerome who was a potter and a Daniel who was a master at wielding a four-pound hammer, but he reserves his most intense admiration for a fairground juggler, a striking image for this play where none of the characters, except perhaps for Danilo, are able to juggle their confused lives with any skill.

Danilo is the catalyst that intervenes into their uneasy and hitherto uneventful existence and changes everything. As Lydia says: 'It won't ever be the same... Dimetos, Sophia, and myself. Something has happened.' [p 143] Even so he is only indirectly concerned with Lydia's death. The explanation for her pointless

end is contained in ten words spoken during the last scene of Act
One:

> ...You didn't stop him.

Dimetos replies by launching into a description of the solstice but
Lydia ignores this and says:

> Go. (*Exit DIMETOS. LYDIA is alone.*)
>
> I know your story now.   [pp 146–147]

This is all confirmed when Danilo visits Dimetos five years later
at the seaside:

> Because you see, Dimetos, I eventually worked out what
> really happened during those five days with you. You
> do understand, don't you, that her death was on *my*
> conscience. She committed suicide because of what *I*
> had done. When *I* eventually realised that it belonged
> on yours...! (*Pause.*) You had a guilty love for her, didn't
> you? When I discovered that, everything fell into place.
> ... Those five days must rank as one of your more
> ingenious pieces of engineering. You used us like tools
> and with such consummate mastery because of your
> passion for your niece.   [p 154]

This speech encapsulates the core of the play. Lydia says she
knows the story of Dimetos, but is it that easy for the viewer or
the reader? Questions abound and answers are hard to find. Is it
simply more of Sartre's anguish? Are we prepared to accept the
futility of Lydia's death and in any case, would she really have
taken her life because she discovers her uncle's forbidden passion?
Act Two is no more helpful in interpreting this problematic play.
Dimetos retreats from the reality of the situation just as patheti-
cally as does Gladys in *A Lesson from Aloes*. Any pretension he had
as an artist has gone – it is the death of the artist and the death of
the man that is on view. Sophia describes it as such:

> Throwing stones and playing games. You know what
> that sounds like, don't you? Dimetos's hands have come
> to an end.   [p 150]

There is an end of sorts. After a succession of powerful confrontations between Dimetos and Sophia – and an intervention by the spirit of Lydia – the play ends with the apparent madness of a wretched Dimetos and the supposed, and inevitable, continuation of Sophia's unhappy and frustrated existence.

A chorus of anguish

The Afrikaner ancestry of Piet Bezuidenhout is dealt with in *A Lesson from Aloes*. Piet was driven from the farm after four years of drought, but his early family could well have replicated the family unit seen in *The Guest*. In this film a typical rural Afrikaner family is shown side by side with an individual who was one of South Africa's most eminent intellectuals, albeit a flawed one. It is a fascinating mixture: the sophisticate and the men of the soil, roots contrasting with homelessness.

The published text says that this film was devised by Athol Fugard and Ross Devenish and the incident portrayed is taken from a biography of Eugène Marais by Leon Rousseau entitled *Die Groot Verlange*. Marais was seen as one of the founding fathers of the Afrikaans language and made a major contribution to Afrikaans literature, particularly in the field of poetry. In his poem *Die Lied van Suid-Afrika* (*The Song of South Africa*), he saw South Africa as a callous woman, unmoved by the suffering of her children, in stark contrast to the patriotic hyperbole of C J Langenhoven's *Die Stem van Suid-Afrika* that was used for the country's first National Anthem.

Marais was also an important scientist, often described as being far ahead of his time. His most significant work in this area was concerned with the white ant and the chacma baboon and as a result of these studies he opined that natural selection was not, as according to Darwin, the survival of the fittest, but rather the line of least resistance; for termites their survival depended on instinct while for the baboons, they had causal memory. He was born in 1871 and, after working as the editor of an Afrikaans newspaper, went to London to study law. His young wife, Aletta – the same name given to the wife of Marius in *The Road to Mecca* – died in childbirth and around this time he turned to morphine, to which he became addicted. This addiction is the principal subject of this film, which was shown on the BBC in March 1977 and which that April was awarded prizes at the Locarno Film Festival for direction and for Fugard's performance as Marais.

According to the script, his doctor, A G Visser, another renowned South African poet, has lodged his patient with the Doors family on their farm at Steenkampskraal in the Heidelberg district of the Transvaal. The purpose of this is to attempt to reduce Marais's addiction to cocaine. The film initially shows the deterioration in Marais's condition – and his desperation as he seeks to obtain more drugs than the doctor prescribes – and in due course, an improvement in his health; but at the close he obtains an illicit supply using Stuurie, the Doors African employee, and lapses into an uncontrolled condition. He turns to *Othello*:

> MARAIS: (*Off-screen.*) The evil is undone. With hands washed pure from blood, you can enjoy her most subtle perfection. She lives! Iago has not distilled his poison. Start again. Take up your candle, Othello. (*On-screen.*) If I quench thee, thou flaming minister, I can thy former light restore.   [p 213]

At this point Dr Visser removes him from the Doors homestead.

The portrait of this clever, unhappy man is shown against a background of the Doors family: father and mother, two grown-up sons and daughter, Little Corrie, nine years of age. For security reasons – and because the homestead is not over-large – Marais sleeps, at least initially, in the same bedroom as the two boys but he develops the closest relationship with the young girl, a marriage of the simple mind of the young and innocent with the mind of a man unhinged by drugs.

There are some similarities between this film and *Dimetos*. The locations of both are remote and the plots are concerned with exile, although the reasons for this are more tangible for Marais than the disillusioned engineer. On the other hand there are few long speeches in *The Guest*; the theatre is more receptive to Dimetos's philosophical monologues than the cinema, although in many ways this is an ideal subject for the camera, able to depict the remoteness of the farm and the arid landscape of the Highveld and compare these with the oppressive confinement of the bedroom where Marais spends most of his time during the film.

The factual setting allows Fugard to allude to history, particularly the Boer War. Marais tells Oom Doors that he needs the pills prescribed by the doctor for his malaria, caught during the war, when in fact his addiction began ten years before the conflict. There is no such distortion of the facts in Oom Doors' wartime memories:

> Ja, in the end, you know, we ended up counting our bullets more carefully than I've ever counted the money in my pocket. It almost hurt to take aim at a rooinek and pull the trigger. [p 180]

His wife has her own recollections of the times as she tells Marais about their arrival at what is now the family farm:

> Just remembering what it looked like when we first came. Nineteen hundred and five: homestead burned down. Bare veld. We outspanned and put up our tents there where the kraal is now. Bitter hearts. The two boys still small; myself out of the concentration camp; Doors as long a prisoner of war. We have nothing when we started...except that bitterness.

She goes on to tell him about the concentration camps. During the Boer War the British established these camps to house the Afrikaner families they had rounded up, including nearly an equal number of the Africans. Many died, leaving within the Afrikaner a deep sense of bitterness:

> Turffontein. The race course. Ja. Two years. The longest two of my life. Not even the drought in nineteen ten and nineteen eleven seemed to last as long. It wasn't the Almighty's mercy we were waiting for, but an end to man's stupidity. Don't talk to me about the English! Those first few years, Doors and the two boys worked like kaffirs on this land, Mr Marais. (*Pause; looks at MARAIS.*) Don't judge us harshly. Life hasn't been easy for us...droughts, locusts, the English. I know my men aren't gentle...   [p 196]

Fugard has never avoided difficult subjects, only those that he considers commonplace. This episode in the life of an unhappy man is no exception. Marais finds so much to interest him in nature, in contrast to his own humanity. Shortly before he receives the extra drugs from Stuurie he muses:

> From the very beginnings of life we hear a chorus of anguish. Pain is a condition of existence. Escape from pain is the purpose in all striving.   [p 212]

He does not manage it. Ten years later, still trying to beat the drug addiction, he shot himself.

> MARAIS: (*Off-screen.*) Put out the light and then again put out the light. If I quench thee, thou flaming minister, I can thy former light restore if I repent me. But once put out thy light. Poor Othello. Doubt, darkness and death.   [p 214]

Helen the wizard and Little Elsie

As demonstrated, Fugard's people are conceptions of an imagination that is fed from a variety of sources, but on rare occasions his characters had a fame in their own world – in real life – before becoming an inspiration for his dramas. The piece he wrote for television, *Mille Miglia*, concerned racing driver Stirling Moss and, as already described, *The Guest* is about the Afrikaner poet and scientist Eugène Marais. Perhaps *My Life* should also be included amongst these works as it is an autobiography of five girls who, in the play, perform their own lives. Other than these, and the extent to which the playwright himself is a member of the cast for '*Master Harold*'...*and the boys, Valley Song, The Captain's Tiger* and *Exits and Entrances*, there is one notable celebrity reconstructed for his stage and appearing in one of his major plays – and that is Helen Martins.

In the Indian town of Chandigarh, which in the 1940s was being planned as a modern Utopia by the architect Le Corbusier, there lived a road inspector working for the Public Works Department. His name was Nek Chand and he had a strange hobby. During his road inspections, but in his spare time, he collected material from demolition sites and over a period of years recycled this to construct pottery covered concrete sculptures of musicians, dancers and animals. He hid these creatures in a forest outside the city and they remained secret for eighteen years – until discovered by the authorities in 1975. By that time there were hundreds of his extraordinary statues covering a twelve acre site that is now a major tourist attraction, named the Rock Garden of Chandigarh, and visited by over five thousand people every day.

More than ten years before Nek Chand began his work, and across the world in South Africa, the father of Helen Martins died. She lived in the small village of New Bethesda, set in a valley of the Sneeuburg Mountains in the Great Karoo. Helen had trained as a teacher and worked in various parts of the country. In the 1930s she returned to her birthplace to care for her ailing parents; her mother died in 1941 and her father in 1945. Shortly after her father's death she began a similar journey to that taken by the eccentric Indian, albeit on a much smaller scale, and started to decorate the interior of the small house where she had lived for many years. This decoration used ground glass that transformed all the rooms in this nondescript property but, even more remarkably, she built outside the house an assortment of amazing statu-

ary in what she referred to as the 'Camel Yard'. Partly influenced
by the *Rubaiyat* of Omar Khayyam, there were pyramids and
sphinxes, wise men, a pool of healing, mermaids and the Moon
Gate, plus a corner of debauchery and many other wonders. At
first the local inhabitants were astonished with what was happening within – and without – this typical village property, but this
soon grew into suspicion and antagonism so that Helen became
more and more a recluse. Her health deteriorated and in 1976
she committed suicide by drinking caustic soda. Her legacy, now
known as the Owl House, is visited by more than ten thousand
tourists every year.

Fugard was born in this region and owns a house in New
Bethesda, and so perhaps it was inevitable that he would see
the story of Helen Martins as a prime subject for his pen, but
in typical fashion the resulting play, *The Road to Mecca*, does not
have as its main focus the vision of this extraordinary woman – or
the artistic results of that vision. He has used these as a backdrop,
but the emphasis is on the relationship she had with two people: a
schoolteacher in her late twenties and an Afrikaner pastor, Marius
Byleveld, the same age as Helen. There is a history to the reason
for this. An actress, who had performed in *Boesman and Lena* and
A Lesson from Aloes, pointed out to Fugard that although he had
created some marvellous roles for women, there had not been one
of his plays with two women together.

This was a challenge, and when he later discovered that there
had been a friendship between the real Miss Helen and a young
social worker from Cape Town, he decided to remedy this omis-
sion in *The Road to Mecca*. As a result, Fugard's small-cast motif
is repeated with only three characters on view: Helen, Marius
and the teacher, Elsa Barlow. Fugard is careful about the names
he gives to his characters. When this play was written the South
African conglomerate Barlow Rand, begun by Major Billy Barlow
in Durban in 1902, employed over two hundred thousand people
all over the world. Elsa Barlow was of the same English stock
– or did Fugard, keen cricket fan that he is, have Eddie Barlow
in mind (if not for the isolation of South African sport, this all-

rounder could have entered the annals as one of the best cricketers of all time).

Act One begins to reveal the history, and character, of the two ladies – and of their friendship – and then in Act Two, all three of the performers are together, where more revelations are made. As to the setting, the stage instruction given at the beginning of the script is so relevant to what is about to be performed, it is worthy of being repeated in full:

The lounge and, leading off it, the bedroom alcove of a house in the small Karoo village of New Bethesda. An extraordinary room by virtue of the attempt to use as much light and colour as is humanly possible. The walls – mirrors on all of them – are all of different colours, while on the ceiling and floor are solid, multi coloured geometric patterns. Yet the final effect is not bizarre but rather one of light and extravagant fantasy. Just what the room is really about will be revealed later when its candles and lamps – again, a multitude of them of every size, shape and colour – are lit. The late afternoon light does, however, give some hint of the magic to come.   [p 15]

The time is the autumn of 1974.

The play was first staged at the Yale Repertory Theatre on 5 May 1984 and then in November at the Market Theatre in Johannesburg. The first performance in the UK was at the National Theatre, opening on 22 December 1985, before touring to Bath, where the UK premiere of Fugard's latest play, *Victory*, took place in 2007.

The first meeting with Helen came about when Elsa, for reasons not explained, was on a trip to New Bethesda:

...walking down a dusty, deserted little street in a God-forsaken village in the middle of the Karoo, bored to death by the heat and flies and silence, and then to be stopped in your tracks – and I mean stopped! – by all of that out there. And then, having barely recovered from that, to come inside and find *this*! Believe me Helen,

> when I saw your 'Mecca' for the first time, I just stood
> there and gaped.   [p 33]

From this encounter, an unlikely friendship develops. Elsa's
singular admiration was crucial, as Helen had been afflicted with
an artistic block that meant she had been unable to continue with
her statues and decorating for nearly a year: 'Because all those
years of being laughed at and thought a mad old woman had
taken their toll...' [p 35] As a result of Elsa's attitude, diametrically
opposite that of Helen's neighbours, the creative urge was rein-
vigorated and by the time of the next visit, Helen had produced a
stern-faced Buddha where 'The cement was still wet' [p 35].

The stage Helen, whom Elsa refers to as a 'little wizard', has
lived in New Bethesda all of her life. She had married as a young
woman and for many years had been the dutiful church-going
wife; but when her husband died things changed, as she reveals
to Elsa and Marius in a long and passionate speech near the end
of the play:

> All those years...it was all a terrible, terrible lie. I tried
> hard, Marius, but your sermons, the prayers, the hymns,
> they had all become just words. And there came a time
> when even they lost their meaning.
>
> Do you know what the word 'God' looks like when
> you've lost your faith? It looks like a little stone, a cold,
> round, little stone. 'Heaven' is another one, but it's
> got an awkward, useless shape, while 'Hell' is flat and
> smooth. All of them – damnation, grace, salvation – a
> handful of stones.
>
> You brought me home from the cemetery, remember,
> and...pulled the curtains and closed the shutters. Such a
> small thing, and I know that you meant well by it... but
> in doing that it felt as if you were putting away my life
> as surely as the undertaker had done to Stefanus a little
> earlier when he closed the coffin lid.

When Marius left that night he lit a candle. As Helen sat there
waiting for it to go out, something happened:

> ...that small, uncertain little light seemed to find its
> courage again. It started to get brighter and brighter. I
> didn't know whether I was awake any longer or dream-
> ing because a strange feeling came over me... that it was
> leading me...leading me far away to a place I had never
> been to before.   [pp 70–72]

That place was Mecca, and it was the vision that came to Helen
that night that lit the spark of her creativity.

The play opens as Helen, described in the stage instructions as
'*a frail, bird-like little woman*', is absorbing the fact that her friend
has arrived at the house unexpectedly after an eight hundred mile
car journey from Cape Town. The reason for this is an extremely
disturbing letter received from Helen that the writer now wishes
she had never sent. This attitude prompts Elsa to read it out
aloud:

> 'My very own and dearest little Elsie,
>   Have you finally also deserted me? This is my fourth
> letter to you and still no reply. Have I done something
> wrong? This must surely be the darkest night of my soul.
> I thought I had lived through that fifteen years ago, but I
> was wrong. This is worse. Infinitely worse. I had nothing
> to lose that night. Nothing in my life was precious or
> worth holding on to. Now there is so much and I am
> losing it all...you, the house, my work, my Mecca. I can't
> fight them alone, little Elsie. I need you. Don't you care
> about me any more? It is only through your eyes that I
> now see my Mecca. I need you, Elsie. My eyesight is so
> bad that I can barely see the words I am writing. And
> my hands can hardly hold the pen. Help me, little Elsie.
> Everything is ending and I am alone in the dark. There
> is no light left. I would rather do away with myself than
> carry on like this.

Your ever-loving and anguished
Helen.'   [PP 38–39]

During the early action two secrets are exposed, one by Helen and
the other by Elsa. Helen asks about the boyfriend, David, and as
she is told that the relationship is at an end, it is also revealed that
he was in fact a married man with a devoted wife and daughter.
Helen then responds to Elsa's question about losing her house,
as raised in the letter, by telling that the Church Council believes
she can no longer look after herself and they want her to move
to the 'Sunshine Home for the Aged' in Graaff-Reinet run by the
church – a church she no longer attends. There are however two
more serious and intimate secrets that they keep to themselves
until the climax of the play, namely that as a result of an accident with a candle, Helen nearly set fire to the house and that two
weeks after splitting up with David, Elsa found she was pregnant
and has had an abortion. At the end of the play, Elsa intuits that
there is a further secret; Marius is in love with Helen, and has
been for the last twenty years.

As a result we realise that despite other themes in this play
that deal with art and convention, trust, the Afrikaner mentality
and even the plight of the Coloureds, this is another Fugard play
primarily about love. A female relationship is the nexus of the
drama: this allows the playwright to introduce the cause of femi-
nism, a subject not really dealt with elsewhere in his work. His
portraits of strong women have already been referred to, but in
this play Elsa is inspired by Helen and vice versa. They comple-
ment each other. Her vision, her journey to her Mecca, has given
Helen the sort of freedom that would be welcomed by anyone,
but for a seventy-year-old Afrikaner woman living in the South
African platteland it is a prize beyond price. Fugard is not a great
admirer of Ibsen – during a personal interview in November
2002 he said: 'There are not many writers who are poets to the
extent Beckett is, to the extent Tennessee Williams is... Ibsen is
no goddam poet at all' – and Helen's Owl House is not another
A Doll's House. Helen stoically complies with the norms while

locked for many years in a marriage to a man she does not love, but hers is a very different cause to those of Nora. The Afrikaner world Helen lived in was more restrictive than that of Victorian times, which renders her eventual rebellion even more striking. She does not leave and slam the door, as the Nora does, but stays, against much pressure, and completes her destiny, her journey to Mecca. Her future thereafter is more difficult to predict. We know in real life that suicide provided the answer but on the stage there is rather more optimism than that:

> You see, I meant what I said to Marius. This is as far as I can go. My Mecca is finished and with it – (*Pause.*) I must try to say it, mustn't I? – the only real purpose my life has ever had.
> (*She blows out a candle.*)
> I was wrong to think I could banish darkness, Elsa. Just as I taught myself how to light candles, and what that means, I must teach myself now how to blow them out... and what that means.   [p 78]

To bring together two Fugardian women on the same stage, the playwright has taken the most difficult of roads to achieve this in placing, side by side with a seventy-year-old Afrikaner, an athletic English-speaking schoolteacher more than forty years her junior, who describes herself as a bit 'of a blue-stocking'. Not only are they seemingly poles apart, their histories are completely different. For example, Elsa's recent life in Cape Town, outside of her affair with a married man, is revealed to the audience as she brings Helen up-to-date with her news:

> ELSA: Right. The *Elsa Barlow Advertiser*! Hot off the presses! What do you want to start with? Financial, crime or sports page?
> HELEN: The front-page headline.
> ELSA: How's this? 'Barlow to appear before School Board for possible disciplinary action.'
> HELEN: Not again!

ELSA: Yep.

HELEN: Oh dear! What was it this time?

ELSA: Wait for the story. 'Elsa Barlow, a twenty-eight-year-old English language teacher, is to appear before a Board of Enquiry of the Cape Town School Board. She faces the possibility of strict disciplinary action. The enquiry follows a number of complaints from the parents of pupils in Miss Barlow's Standard Nine class. It is alleged that in April this year Miss Barlow asked the class, as a homework exercise, to write a five-hundred word letter to the State President on the subject of racial inequality. Miss Barlow teachers at a Coloured School.'

HELEN: So what is going to happen?

ELSA: Depends on me I suppose. If I appear before them contrite and apologetic, a stern reprimand. But if I behave the way I really feel, I suppose I could lose my job.

HELEN: Do you want my advice?

ELSA: No.

HELEN: Well, I'm going to give it to you all the same. Say you're sorry and that you won't do it again.

ELSA: Both of those are lies, Miss Helen.

HELEN: Only little white ones.

ELSA: God, I'd give anything to be able to walk in and tell that School Board exactly what I think of them and their educational system. But you're right, there are the pupils as well, and for as long as I'm in the classroom a little subversion is possible. Rebellion starts, Miss Helen, with just one man or woman standing up and saying, 'No. Enough!' Albert Camus. French writer.   [pp. 27–28]

For her part, Helen relates the recent minor happenings in her life and in the community. The husband of seventeen-year-old Katrina, a Coloured girl who is virtually Helen's only friend in the village, has started drinking again and, on a similar subject, one of the Afrikaner residents has applied for a licence to open a liquor store. Elsa applauds this, particularly as the village is very upset – including Pastor Marius whose last sermon was on the dangers of drink – and this gossip gives rise to another example of her views that differ from those of the locals. When Elsa suggests that the Coloured inhabitants of New Bethesda should be asked what they think about a liquor store licence, Helen's response is to say that they do not do things like that, it is not like Cape Town. Elsa's riposte, in vintage Fugard style, is:

> Well, it can't cut itself off from the twentieth century for ever. Honestly, coming here is like stepping into the middle of a Chekhov play. While the rest of the world is hoping the bomb won't drop today, you people are arguing about who owns the Cherry Orchard.   [p 25]

Near to the end of Act One, Elsa tells Helen, with some irritation, that she cannot postpone a decision on whether to move as the Church Council wants: she must make up her mind, one way or the other, that night. The tension between the two friends is unresolved as Marius makes his appearance, in a perfect act of theatre, just as the curtain is about to fall. The move into Act Two is more or less continuous. Until then, Marius has figured in their conversation but now he is here in person. He has brought a basket of vegetables for Helen, dug from his garden that afternoon, and he treats the two ladies to a sermon on the virtues of this produce, potatoes, beets and tomatoes. Two root vegetables brought from the darkness of the Karoo soil in contrast to the light provided by Helen.

Marius

The introduction of the Pastor allows Fugard to paint a more detailed picture of the two women with Marius acting as a perfect mirror that reflects the true picture of them both, particularly Helen. According to the stage instruction Marius: '*speaks with simple sincerity and charm*' and as we listen as the scene proceeds to its emotional, but upbeat ending, this instruction appears to be fully justified. He does not understand Helen but his concerns for her are genuine.

His wife had died just before he came as the Dominee to New Bethesda, twenty years ago. He has a genuine affection for the Karoo, unlike Elsa who only visits because of Helen. She describes it as 'dry and desolate' and 'a landscape of extremes'; the sort of desert defined by Balzac as 'God without mankind' [pp 50–51]. This obviously provokes Marius and she follows this up by asking if the Coloured population feel the same way about this harsh environment. He deflects her argument by suggesting that, unlike Helen and him, she is an outsider who doesn't understand. This may be condescending – she is after all a teacher at a Coloured school – but again he truly believes what he says. He exerts no pressure when discussing the application form for the Sunshine Home for the Aged but he cannot avoid the reality of such a move when he comments: 'There's plenty of space for personal possessions and a few of your...ornaments' [p 58]. When Elsa learns of the accident with the candle and that her friend made no attempt to retreat from the flames, she is understandably angry and advises that the form be signed. However, Elsa's attitude finally convinces Helen which brings about a confrontation between the teacher and the Pastor that precipitates a wave of self-revelation from them both. Elsa realises that the real reason why the village, and Marius, want to move Helen away is because they are frightened and jealous of her. And why? Because she dares to be different and as a result achieves the priceless gift of freedom. Elsa is exhilarated when she realises this:

> Those statues out there *are* monsters. And they are that for the simple reason that they express Helen's freedom. Yes, I never thought it was a word you would like. I'm sure it ranks as a cardinal sin in these parts. A free women! God forgive us!
>
> Have you ever wondered why I come up here?

She challenges me, Dominee. She challenges me into an awareness of myself and my life, of my responsibilities to both that I never had until I met her. There's a hell of a lot of talk about freedom, and all sorts of it, in the world where I come from. But it is mostly talk, Dominee, easy talk and nothing else. Not with Helen. She's lived it.

...the first truly free spirit I have ever known.

[pp 66–67]

Marius tries to fight back by comparing Helen's statues to idols, but she is gaining strength all the time and this comes into full flow as she '*speaks with authority*' and instructs Elsa to light the candles. The symbolism is not lost on the audience. As the true splendour of this room is revealed all three people on stage are seeing things in a different light. Helen is regaining her former self. She recalls the early days when she started to build her statues and decorate the house: 'My hands will never let me forget' [p 73] – like Dimetos who believed in the 'mysterious distance between head and hands'. At the same time Marius sees the object of his affections, perhaps for the first time, in her true persona. He leaves, saying goodbye for the last time, and as he does he kindly tells Helen to be sure to put out the candles before going to bed. His exit line is: 'There is more light in you than in all your candles put together' [p 74]. Elsa sees the same thing:

... And he's right. You are radiant. You can't be that naive and innocent, Helen!

It's a very moving story. Twenty years of loving you in the disguise of friendship and professional concern for your soul.

And you did more than just say no to him. You affirmed your right, as a woman.   [p 75]

Elsa asks her friend if she loves Marius the way he loves her. Helen thinks before replying in the negative which prompts Elsa to conjecture that if the answer had been yes, there would have been an even better story: 'The two of you in this Godforsaken little village, each loving the other in secret!' **[p 75]**

The other women

There are two other women in this play, both off-stage – it would hardly be a Fugard play without such a presence. The first of these is Katrina, whom Elsa has helped with clothes for the baby – and a warning for the husband not to beat her anymore. The contrast in political thought between Elsa and Helen is evident throughout the play and the subject of Katrina provides another opportunity to show this. Elsa wonders why this young girl, whose husband refuses to accept that the baby is his, doesn't leave him – a suggestion that horrifies Helen: 'She can't do that, Elsie they're married.' Elsa attributes this remark to Helen's Afrikanerism – her view is that 'There is nothing sacred about a marriage that abuses the woman' **[p 23]**. This attitude is to be expected from Elsa, but her relationship with the other off-stage female is less straightforward.

The image that brought forth Lena, the woman met on the road to Cradock, obviously had a lasting impact on Fugard as he recreates her in this play. When Elsa first arrives at the house she is out of spirits, principally because of the letter from Helen, but she is also distracted about an African woman she gave a lift to, someone who was walking to Cradock. Helen understands the kindness involved but the tension between them, because of their secrets, makes her question the tone of voice Elsa used in telling this story – as if she didn't care:

> Of course I cared. I cared enough to stop and pick her up, to give her money and food. But I also don't want to fool myself. That was a sop to my conscience and nothing more. It wasn't a real contribution to her life and what she is up against.   **[p 22]**

Another reason for Elsa's irritation about this woman is explained at the end of the play when she tells Helen about the abortion. Hester in *Hello and Goodbye* also had an abortion, but her child was not conceived in love, as was Elsa's. The Afrikaner is not concerned as to her fate when, as Johnnie puts it, 'the time comes to face your maker...' [p 177]; but Elsa agonises over her decision. She confesses that strangely enough she is jealous of Helen and even of Marius, she feels lonely and even envies the woman met on the road – because she had a baby:

> There is a little sequel to my story about giving that woman a lift.
> ... I asked her who she was. She said: 'My English name is Patience.' She hitched up the baby, tightened her *doek*, picked up her little plastic shopping bag and started walking. As I watched her walk away, measuring out the next eighty miles of her life in small steps, I wanted to scream.
> I think I lost control of myself. I screamed louder and longer than I have ever done in my life. I can't describe it, Helen. I hated her, I hated the baby, I hated you for dragging me all the way up here... and most of all I hated myself. That baby is mine, Helen. Patience is my sister, you are our mother... and I still feel fucking lonely.
>
> [pp 76–77]

Helen recommends she stops screaming and tries crying, which she does. This releases the emotions that enable her to become part of the optimistic finale. They decide upon a cup of tea before bed which Elsa suggests be supplemented with a Valium tablet – and is highly amused, as is the audience, when Helen naively, or mischievously, asks if they are 'artificial sweeteners'.

The artistic imagination

Up to now the analysis of this important and moving play has, quite correctly, concentrated on the theme of love. The combination of love stories is masterly. However strange, that between Elsa and Helen is out in the open, demonstrating the adage that opposites often attract each other. Helen loves Elsa because of her understanding and, in the other direction, Elsa admires the courage of Helen. The other story is secret and agonising. Marius cannot subdue his feelings but they have to be undeclared because of Helen's Mecca. They have both lost their spouses – and are free to re-marry – but his love, even if recognised by Helen, is not reciprocated and he does not have her courage. The conservative Afrikaner mind-set must overrule the heart. However, the glaze over this love story, just like that used to decorate Helen's walls and statues, concerns the genius involved in true art – and the nature of art and the artist.

The play highlights the necessary isolation of the artist – and in Helen's case she is a more isolated than most. Fugard and other writers can talk about the loneliness of the writing desk and a blank sheet of white paper but this extraordinary woman had no one, until Elsa came along, to share her artistic aspirations with. Just the opposite. She was surrounded by resentment and scepticism. The epigraph for this play, from Emily Dickinson, is carefully chosen:

> The soul selects her own society –
> Then – shuts the door –
> On her divine majority –
> Present no more.

Helen cannot avoid doing what she does. That 'small uncertain light' of a re-born candle on the night of her husband's burial began her apprenticeship. It became the beacon of her artistic genius, but sadly that light has now gone out. We believe she is going to be able to deal with this:

> Just as I taught myself how to light candles, and what that means, I must teach myself now how to blow them out...and at what that means.
> (*She attempts a brave smile.*)
> The last phase of my apprenticeship...and if I can get through it, I'll be a master!   [p 78]

This is a neat solution on stage but in real life, is it so easy? The solution for the real Helen Martins was to take her own life, although she may have done this because of ill-health rather than because she could not continue her career as an artist.

How would Miss Helen's creator cope? He recognised this as an important feature of his play, but would he be able to deal with the loss of creative energy as well as his heroine. He wrote in 1993:

> I have some sort of creative energy... I know that I am propelled, obsessed, driven to make things.
>
> The story of Helen Martins gave me an opportunity to try and understand this demon that has possessed me all of my life.
>
> What am I going to do with myself if I can't write any more? What am I going to do with myself if suddenly the appointment book is empty – if it doesn't come? This is a real dilemma, because I have fashioned my life around the fact that I am a storyteller.
>
> What would happen to me if the stories stopped coming? *The Road to Mecca* showed Helen Martin's fear of darkness and her discovery of the miracle that lighting a candle means. Her life gave me the opportunity to use that symbol of what creative energy tries to do, light a candle. What happens when there are no more candles left to light?   [Barbera 1993, p 387]

Fortunately for the sake of world theatre, Fugard is still finding candles to light.

A small village somewhere in the author's imagination

Orestes, Fugard's most experimental work, and *Dimetos*, at least on the surface, differ from all of his other plays; but in *A Place with the Pigs* we are in a different world altogether. Dimetos is to some extent running away, but the protagonist in this play takes escape to a farcical extreme. Fugard has not to date written a fully-fledged comedy but in a play that features a pathetic figure of a man, sometimes dressed as a woman, and who lives in a pigsty – with the pigs and their excrement – the elements have to lean more towards the comical than any other mode. If it were otherwise, would this be a somewhat pointless item of theatre? The audience needs to smile because at first sight there is little else in the content of this unusual piece to arouse their interest. A message might be discovered, but for the moment it is sufficient to say that in this play the trademark symbols of love, hope, truth and ambiguity seem to be buried under the aforesaid pig waste.

Fugard agonises over the creation of all of his plays, even those that are often referred to as 'aberrant' and however out of the norm *A Place with the Pigs* is, it had, in his view, a place in his scheme of things. This is clearly revealed in the Epilogue to his partial memoir, *Cousins*:

> Looking back now over the thirty-five years that I have been writing I can see something in the way of a ten year cycle to my work, each turn of the wheel being marked by the writing of an aberrant play. There have been three of these 'aberrations' to date: *Orestes, Dimetos* and most recently, *Pigs*. Writing each of them was an exceptionally hard and painful process accompanied by huge emotional disturbance – so much so that I think of these three plays as my 'literary breakdowns'. The reason for their overload of trauma and angst is the fact that they all marked the start of a regenerative process and that, by its very nature, is bound to be painful. This also happens to be the central theme of *Pigs*, which made the experience doubly harrowing – having first had to write the damned thing, I was now up there on stage six nights a week acting it out! The hell of it all was given a further boost, not that it needed it, by the fact that this was only my second play since I stopped drinking. The first one was *The Road to Mecca*, and as had been the case with that, I was again floundering helplessly in a quagmire of self-doubt and panic. That little voice inside me

was very insistent, telling me all the time that my creativity needed a certain percentage of alcohol in my bloodstream in order to function.   [Fugard 1994, pp 89–90]

Alcohol is alluded to in Chapter Two of this book, but in Fugard's case, he had his father as an example – and possibly this, and the pressure he worked under while producing plays with a message that most of the other white citizens in his country did not agree with, or would not accept, pushed him into using alcohol to keep his artistry alive and active. The worldwide success of his plays since the first non-alcoholic one, *Road to Mecca*, seems to have proved that his creativity did not need to be so oiled.

However, the most interesting point that emerges from the extract from *Cousins* given above is the concept of the need to stop the wheel every so often to regenerate the next phase of his writing life. The facts speak for themselves. Ignoring the Sophiatown duo, four major plays were presented from *Blood Knot* in 1961 to *Boesman and Lena* in 1969 followed by *Orestes*. The next shorter phase covered *Statements after an Arrest under the Immorality Act* and the collaborative plays – a period of only four years – from *Boesman and Lena* to *The Island* in 1973. This phase was followed by *Dimetos*. After the collaborative period there was a void in his writing progress when he grappled to return to his normal style of teasing out the situation, and the words, while seated at his lonely desk but this barren interlude then gave birth, in 1978, to one of his most thoughtful works, *A Lesson from Aloes*. If this phase is measured from *Dimetos* in 1975 to *The Road to Mecca* in 1985, the ten year cycle he refers to is precisely accurate and a requirement for another aberration was to be answered by *A Place with the Pigs*. After that he emerged, two years later in 1989, with one of his major successes, *My Children! My Africa!* and has moved on since then, turning out a major new work every two years.

But, back to the pigs. The play script contains the following as an introduction, taken from a report in the *New York Times* of 27 May 1985:

The writing of this play was provoked by the true story of Pavel Ivanovich Navrotsky, a deserter from the Soviet army in the Second World War, who spent forty-one years of self-imposed exile in a pigsty.

Mandela was only incarcerated for twenty-seven years.

Fugard's interpretation of the story is told in four scenes, each of which, unusually, is titled. They are: *The Anniversary of the Great Victory, Beauty and the Beast, The Midnight Walk* and *Orders from the Commissar.* There are two characters, beside the pigs, and Fugard uses their real names. Pavel is the deserter and his wife, Praskovya, who keeps her husband hidden in the pigsty for all of those years. The play was first staged at the Yale Repertory Theatre in March 1987 with Fugard playing Pavel.

The first scene takes place, in the pigsty of course, ten years after Pavel deserted. He is rehearsing the speech he intends to make when he reveals himself at the imminent village meeting being held to commemorate the defeat of the Germans by the Russians in the 'Great Victory' of 1944. He means to attend this function dressed in his military uniform but this is now in tatters – as is, we are soon to observe, his resolve to leave the pigsty. Despite the passionate speech he has ready, he cannot bring himself to take that fateful step and leave his hiding place and he therefore instructs his wife, attired in her black mourning dress, to attend and report. She protests that she rarely goes anywhere these days – she is as much a prisoner as he is – but Pavel insists and she returns with spirits uplifted. Her husband has been awarded a medal, his bravery is lauded by all and on her way home she is proposed to by one of the neighbours:

> At least that is what I think he was doing. 'The joyful vision of my pigs and his cows under the same roof'... is how he put it. He said it would be a happy ending to the sad story of Widow Navrotsky. I couldn't get rid of him! He's coming back next week for an answer.   [p 71]

A situation worthy of Feydeau! The first husband is not hidden in an adjoining bedroom but lodged with the assets the suitor covets. After this revelation, Pavel laments his fate and wonders if his soul is now nothing more than a pigsty. His wife's delicious response to this is: 'That sounds like a theological question, Pavel. I don't think I know enough to take it on', which leads Pavel into sarcasm:

> ... So, my life is going to go on! How wonderful! Just think of all the challenging possibilities that lie ahead of me in here. The fact that the pigs will be my only company makes the prospect even more exciting, doesn't it? (*Rubbing his hands together in mock relish.*) So what should it be? Something in the line of religion? I'm being serious! Maybe there are souls worth saving inside those little mountains of lard.
>
> Then what about politics? Yes, that's a possibility as well. This pigsty is a very political situation. **[p 72]**

The pigs in *Animal Farm* are very political, but these Russian ones, hardly!

In the next scene the beauty is an unusual visitor to the pigsty, a butterfly, and the viewer can choose whether the beast is a pig or, more realistically, Pavel. Halfway through the play he leaves his hideaway for the first time in forty years for a midnight stroll, dressed as a woman. By this time he has deteriorated dramatically – he cries a lot and needs a table for support as the disguise is fitted – but even so there is an element of farce. This pitiable Widow Twanky calls for a mirror to view himself and then asks his wife if she can add 'a little brooch or something...' **[p 83]**. During this excursion he experiences: 'Strange and powerful urges' and pleads with his wife that they do not return home but 'follow the road into the Future' **[p 86]**. Practical Praskovya refuses and turns her back on him as she retraces her steps and, after some prevarication, he follows – back to the pigsty. The play ends as Pavel, at the end of his tether, lets the pigs out of the pen – he would have accompanied them except for his nakedness. When Praskovya appears and experiences for the first time a total silence in the pigsty she rejoices – they are free at last – and Pavel can dress in his wedding suit and hand himself over to the military authorities: but will they be very interested in him?

The ludicrous life of Pavel is self-inflicted and that is what the author wanted to communicate. Some of the other South African pigpens Fugard has shown us cannot be escaped from. Gladys in *A Lesson from Aloes* is only released from hers at Xanadu by moving to another at Fort Elizabeth. Morris and Zachariah in *Blood Knot* are as locked into their Korsten *pondok* as is Boesman and Lena in their pointless itinerary but some of his people get dressed, like Pavel, and leave – or defy. Miss Helen escapes the pigsty of her marriage; Isabel in *My Children! My Africa!* is enlarged by her friendship with Mr M; and Piet survives. Nevertheless, whether the effort expended on *A Place with the Pigs* was worthwhile, for the author it was a personal parable that he needed to relate. He wrote that he made his pigsty out of a bottle of Jack Daniel's whiskey. Pavel's circumstance is not a punishment by God – any more than is alcoholism. Fugard wrote:

> I wrote the play because I had an experience. The experience was that I had left the pigsty. I had discovered that to get out of a pigsty you just have to stand up and get out of it.
>
> Suddenly he realises his hell is self-inflicted. It's not God's punishment. He just has to leave it. I wrote the play for that reason.   **[Barbera 1993, p 388]**

In *A Lesson from Aloes*, Piet Bezuidenhout says:

> An evil system isn't a natural disaster. There's nothing you can do to stop a drought, but bad laws and social injustice are man-made and can be unmade by men.
>
> **[p 242]**

Pavel's situation is not natural – he can walk away from his hell with the pigs just as Fugard can give up the bottle.

NINE

Between me and my country

The future is still ours, Mr M.

My Children! My Africa!

The lessons to be found in *'Master Harold'...and the boys* and *A Lesson from Aloes* are presented in domestic arenas, but with *My Children! My Africa!* we observe education in an actual classroom. For Africans and Coloureds, until the advent of the National Government in 1948, education had generally been in the hands of Christian missionaries, and by 1935 there were over three hundred and forty thousand African pupils in these schools. However, nearly all of the teachers in the majority of mission schools were Africans who were themselves not particularly well educated, and they were teaching a syllabus prepared to suit the education of white children. In particular, the view of South African history was that of the white man. However, the majority of African children during the apartheid era were concerned with finding any reasonable form of education, whatever the bias. In 1946, the government was spending twenty times more per head on the education of white children than of black. As the policy of the new National Government crystallised, Verwoerd was reluctant to leave the education of black children in the hands of the missions who, in any case, could not cope with the rising demand from a larger African population. In addition, as the economy expanded, there was more demand for black workers who were at least semi-educated and literate so, by the Bantu Education Act of 1953, the central government took over all public African education. In 1960 this was extended to Coloured and Asian children. This education was expanded but tightly controlled and still

strictly segregated: by 1979, three and a half million black children were at school. Even with this expansion, however, expendi-
ture for whites was still ten times more per capita than for the
black child. The object of the Bantu Education system was to
stifle ambition and ensure that the only training available was for
entry to an unskilled or labouring class. When introducing the
act in 1953, Dr Verwoerd's blunt message included these words:

> I just want to remind the Honourable Members of
> Parliament that if the native in South Africa is being
> taught to expect that he will lead his adult life under
> the policy of equal rights, he is making a big mistake.
> The native must not be subject to a school system which
> draws him away from his own community, and misleads
> him by showing him the green pastures of European
> society in which he is not allowed to graze.
>
> [Goddard 1992, p 35]

The Political Schoolroom

The disparities in education, and the results of this policy, are
fully evident in *My Children! My Africa!* where, unlike the opening
silences of *Blood Knot* and *Boesman and Lena* or the passivity when
we first view the Bezuidenhouts' backyard, this play opens to
noise: 'Everybody is speaking at the same time'. This is appropriate as the classroom at the Zolile High School, the main setting
for this play, has become a chamber where a vigorous debate on
gender politics is in progress. Isabel, captain of the visiting team
from the whites-only Camdeboo Girls High School, is opposing
the motion: *'That in view of the essential physical and psychological
differences between men and women, there should be correspondingly
different educational syllabuses for the two sexes.'* Her opposite number
is Thami, captain of the Zolile team, who is the prize pupil and
favourite of the third character on stage, the schoolmaster referred
to as Mr M. All of the school voting audience is comprised of
black pupils, but much to Mr M's delight, Isabel wins the day.
This leads to him entering her and Thami into an inter-school

literary competition, but before the date for this is reached, Zolile High School is subjected to a student boycott. Mr M does not support this action and so, to try and bring this to an end, he gives the police the names of the political action committee that he believes is organising the unrest. As a result, and despite the best efforts of Thami to save him, Mr M is murdered by the mob, Isabel is left with a mixture of bewildered despair and hope, while Thami leaves the country to join 'the movement'.

The play was first performed on 27 June 1989 at the Market Theatre in Johannesburg but it is set in 1984, inspired by an actual incident in the Eastern Cape where a school teacher, who was thought to be an informer, was killed, necklaced by a burning car tyre. The first Cape Town run began at the Baxter Theatre on 4 October and later that year it was presented in New York and in 1990 at the National Theatre in London. On both overseas occasions Fugard's daughter Lisa played Isabel. A review in *The Eastern Province Herald* by Kin Bentley on the London debut of Lisa Fugard provides one source for this play:

> Fugard said the play was largely inspired by his daughter. 'I think to a large extent it came from watching Lisa dealing with the problems of growing up in South Africa – the question of white guilt, the accident of a different colour skin and the whole dilemma of the country...'

However, what is more likely to have been the main inspiration for this drama was the realization, in the late 1980s, that the end of apartheid might be in sight and that this end might be accompanied by continuing acts of violence. In the Foreword to the selection of plays including *My Children! My Africa!* (used for this chapter), Fugard wrote:

> ...*My Children! My Africa!* was written out of the darkest decade in my country's history. It was a time when the prophecies of a bloodbath seemed to be coming true, when to have any hope in the future seemed the height of idiocy.

Or, in the words of Mr M:

> Yes! The clocks are ticking, my friends. History has got a
> strict timetable. If we're not careful we might be remem-
> bered as the country where everybody arrived too late.
> [p 184]

Politics are in the fabric of all Fugard's principal works, but
nowhere is the weave as dense as in *My Children! My Africa!* This
play represents a turning point in his writing, as he directly
contributes to the campaign to try and avert South Africa from
arriving 'too late'. Critic and academic Ian Steadman, in a 1989
newspaper article, describes this moment as follows:

> It has been fashionable in recent years to distinguish
> between cultural work which domesticates (showing
> how people should cope with things as they are) and
> cultural work which liberates (showing people how
> things can and should be changed). Much of Fugard's
> previous work has been (somewhat unfairly) pigeon-
> holed in the former category. With this play he takes his
> audience forcefully into a symbolic debate which is not
> merely liberal but liberating.   [Steadman 1989, p 22]

Steadman suggests that for Fugard, *My Children! My Africa!* was
a departure from the past, and it is clear that this play provided
a more noticeably stronger 'liberating' voice than in any of his
previous works; but the cultural debate with audiences on the
subject of the evils of apartheid is there in earlier dramas, even if
the discussion is less heated than in this play. In all of Fugard's
apartheid plays there are elements of a liberating force and most
of the characters are aware of what should be changed, even if
powerless to do anything about it. Lena and Isabel find some form
of release but this force may not prevail for Hally and Gladys.
Nevertheless, Steadman's point is well made and pertinent to the
more didactic Fugard at work in this play.

The recent political history that prompted Fugard to be writing
in this vein was principally concerned with the last blows in a

conflict that had been going on, in one form or another, for decades. Unlike other freedom struggles elsewhere in the world, in South Africa's case never has a more powerful modern industrialised state been overthrown from within, or at least mostly from within – a case of self-emancipation. External pressures and economic sanctions clearly had a major impact, the calling in of the Chase Manhattan loan in 1985 being one instance, but in the main the apartheid regime was finally defeated by non-violent action within the country, action in which culture played its part. From a purely political viewpoint, it can now be seen with hindsight that non-violent action, a passive revolution, was the only internal option that had any real chance of success. There was little possibility that urban terrorism would have succeeded and, indeed, the sabotage that did take place, particularly in the 1960s, was aimed at targets to create most publicity rather than to kill white people. The most effective elements within the campaign of non-violent action were strikes and boycotts. The two-day general strike in 1974 appears to have terrified the Government as it brought the nation to a virtual standstill: eight hundred thousand people refused to go to work and four hundred thousand students boycotted classes. Rent boycotts were also extremely effective: by September 1986 it was estimated that 60 per cent of the black population was not paying rent.

These strikes and other demonstrations, labelled by the National Government as 'unrest', were hidden, as far as possible. The government attempted to impose a blanket of silence over the whole affair, which in many cases meant that the literature of the time, where there was only a limited censorship, was the only source of information available to the white population. André Brink expresses it well:

> ...a volcanic explosion of creativity in the country. Painters, sculptors, photographers, poets, dramatists, fiction writers, singers, dancers, all of them were drawn into a massive cultural movement that mobilised the masses into resistance by writing the history of their time in the form of fiction.   [Brink 1996, p 138]

Recognising this background, Fugard has structured and styled *My Children! My Africa!* in a very different way to his earlier political plays in an attempt to enhance the more polemical nature of this work as he wrote his version of 'the history of their time'. In the other plays, with the exception of the Styles' monologue, the characters reveal themselves through the medium of the play's dialogue, but in *My Children! My Africa!* the background and thought processes of the *dramatis personae* are mainly explicated through a series of self-revelations projected directly at the audience; what Fugard refers to as 'confidences' rather than soliloquies. Some critics suggest that most of Fugard's considerable theatrical art is devoted to the monologues to the detriment of the rest of the play, and Gerald Weales considered that this work (and *Playland,* first performed in 1992) 'seem less substantial, less complex than earlier ones' **[Weales 1993, p 513]**. To some extent this criticism is justified. Certainly this play does not have the subtlety of *A Lesson from Aloes* nor the careful sequential passage to a climax that is seen in *'Master Harold'...and the boys,* but the structure Fugard has adopted suits this more didactic work, resulting in one of his most powerful plays, a play that reveals a deep concern for the tragedy involved in the provision of education for the oppressed and for the events of the 1980s that saw an escalation of 'black-on-black' violence.

Between me and my country

As one of his most explicitly political plays, Fugard decided that unlike *'Master Harold'...and the boys,* *My Children! My Africa!* must first be shown in his own country – hence his words (that appeared in the *Time* magazine of 10 July 1989) 'This one is between me and my country.' To quote Stephen Gray:

> Nevertheless, Fugard the man of provocative stances meant it: South African audiences should have this play first...and for sound, practical reasons. Apart from the fact that *My Children! My Africa!* will not play quite the same way out of here, Fugard knows there is

a hard, tough core in the South African skull that loves
a hefty moral pummelling, and that night after night
guilt-ridden, unrepentant masses will stream in to their
community cockpit for something they're not getting in
the world outside. And like any good Calvinist preacher,
Fugard knows just how to dole out the punishment accurately. He also knows that South Africans are no longer
impressed by *their* plays appearing at the National or on
Broadway first.   [Gray 1990, p 25]

Although the play was created in the late eighties, the context of
the work reflects events during the school boycotts of 1984. Mary
Benson wrote:

> Athol forged *My Children! My Africa!* from within the
> cauldron of the violence in the Eastern Cape. 'Despite
> its huge success at the Market,' he said in a letter, 'I still
> wake up in the middle of the night and lie in the dark
> agonizing as to whether I gave Mr M, Thami and Isabel
> the life they deserve.'
>
> At the core of the story was the bitter conflict
> between black youths with their enraged demand for
> LIBERATION BEFORE EDUCATION and a black
> schoolmaster who warned them to 'Be careful!' He
> symbolised Athol's passionately held credo: 'Don't scorn
> words. They are sacred! Magical!'   [Benson 1997, p 134]

Black schools provided arenas for agitation of considerable political importance in the anti-apartheid struggle, particularly in the
1980s. With Sam and Hally 'there was a hell of a lot of teaching
going on', but this is not the case in *My Children! My Africa!* The
knowledge that is being disseminated in Classroom Number One
at Zolile High School is principally concerned with the self-educa-
tion course each of the three characters embarks upon, so that,
rather than a seat of learning, this classroom becomes the arena
for debating, not the equality of the sexes, but the efficacy of the
word versus the gun. It also represents a battleground where each

of the three protagonists is fighting their own separate and yet complementary wars, searching to understand what is happening to each of them as the play moves on to its tragic and yet quietly optimistic ending. All of their battles concern the political realities of the time: Isabel's to try and understand, Thami's to rebel and for Mr M to reconcile his passionate and romantic liberal character with what is going on outside his classroom

Whatever the fate of the characters on stage in this play, more than with any of his others, Fugard is occupied in presenting a learning process directly to the audience. The crucial monologues are delivered across the footlights, the stage directions say Isabel *'speaks'* and Mr M *'talks'* and – stage directions again – there is a *'Wild round of applause from the audience'* when Thami stands to make his closing remarks during the debate. Isabel, on the other hand, receives *'polite applause'*.

In some productions pre-recorded applause must have been used, but Fugard clearly intends that where possible Mr M should organise the audience so that they do respond and enter into the action. According to Stephen Gray:

> Votes are taken. The audience is forced to take sides too, for Fugard uses the Market Theatre ushers – strapping youths in shorts too short and striped ties stopping at the sternum – as unruly hecklers, Thami's classmates. Their interjections from all corners heat up the battle to violent pitch.
>
> What is this but every South African's nightmare? Being caught up in the crossfire of your own most basic choices.   [Gray 1990, p 28]

Another view on audience reaction when the play premiered at the Market Theatre is given in a critical essay by Nicholas Visser:

> Standing ovations are customarily directed towards playwrights and are usually reserved for opening nights. Subsequent standing ovations, if there are any, are typically directed towards the actors. Neither convention

accounts for the impassioned standing ovations that nightly accompanied the first South African runs of *My Children! My Africa!* In a curious way these ovations were directed toward the audience itself: those applauding so enthusiastically were responding to what they saw to be an affirmation of their own social and political positions and values, which had come under increasing pressure through all the 1980s.

He goes on to say, in a somewhat superficial jibe, that after this opening, reviews of the play were generally very favourable and that:

> The playwright, the audience, and the reviewers all seemed to share in a ritual celebration of their own intrepid righteousness. In short, the play made them feel good about themselves.   **[Barbera 1993, p 486]**

Nicholas Visser did not believe that the first Market Theatre audience were genuinely engaged in any debate with the playwright, symbolically or otherwise; but Fugard's objectives were to provide three examples of self-revelation, three characters discovering themselves on stage, reflecting both the influence of Brecht and that the audience was in fact a Brechtian one, acknowledging *My Children! My Africa!* as a 'Learning Play'. In an introductory note to *The Measures Taken and other Lehrstücke*, Brecht wrote:

> Briefly the aristotelian play is essentially static; its task is to show the world as it is. The learning play (*Lehrstück*) is essentially dynamic; its task is to show the world as it changes (and also how it may be changed).
>
> **[Brecht 2001]**

Precisely the point made by Ian Steadman in 1989. The world is changing for all three of Fugard's characters, but the extent to which they can and do influence these changes is seriously limited.

Isabel

The political reality has so invaded Zolile High School that no really worthwhile teaching is going on, even though the three people on stage are learning lessons. The ones that Thami is subjected to are hard ones, and for Mr M they are tragic, but it could be said that it is Isabel who learns most during her personal crusade. Although she is from a sheltered white liberal background, early on in the play she demonstrates that she is aware of the racial inequality in South Africa when she uses this point as the clinching argument during the inter-school debate, but the true early sense of 'who she is' is provided by the monologue that comprises the whole of Scene Two. Zolile High School is in what most everyone calls 'the location' but this does have a name, an evocative and calculated choice, Brakwater: not a particularly 'sweet' spot! As far as the white people are concerned, they would like to 'relocate' the location, 'moving it to where it can't be seen'. For her, the location is on the 'edge of her life' – not something she has thought about – but now her involvement with Thami and Mr M is going to require her to think about it, and the battle to extend her horizons beyond the restrictions imposed by her white liberal background is about to begin; Brakwater and its people are no longer on the edge of her life. When she visits the Zolile High School, she starts to realise that not everywhere is as 'safe' as her own environment:

> When I stood up in front of those black matric. pupils in Number One Classroom it was a very different story. I wasn't at home or in my dad's shop or in my school or any of the other safe places in my life. I was in Brakwater! It was their school. It was their world. I was the outsider and I was being asked to prove myself. Standing there in front of them like that I felt... exposed!...in a way that has never happened to me before.

She continues:

You see I finally worked out what happened to me in
the classroom. I discovered a new world! I've always
thought about the location as just a sort of embarrass-
ing back yard to our neat and proper little white world,
where our maids and our gardeners and our delivery
boys went at the end of the day. But it's not. It's a whole
world of its own with its own life that has nothing to do
with us.

But it is also a little...what's the word?...disconcert-
ing! You see, it means that what I thought was out there
for me... No, it's worse than that! It's what I was made
to believe was out there for me...the ideas, the chances,
the people...'specially the people!...all of that is only a
small fraction of what it could be.   [pp 172–173]

This is an important speech that reveals Isabel as a thoughtful
exception to the hidebound individuals in her world. As the action
progresses, the changes in Isabel are manifested in the respect she
has for Mr M; after his death she refers to him as '...one of the
most beautiful human beings I have ever known and his death is
the ugliest thing I have ever known'. But more important is her
relationship with Thami.

Despite being of the same age, Isabel is not an Ethel. At eighteen, the phantom figure in *Blood Knot* becomes engaged to Stoffel,
who works at Boetie's garage and plays in her brother's team – at
fullback. Isabel is still at school with no hint in the play of any
boyfriends – except Thami. There is however a more major difference between these two girls. Ethel, as far as can be ascertained, is
an Afrikaner of the 1960s, a time when their hegemony appeared
politically unassailable. Isabel is an intelligent third-generation
English schoolgirl of middle-class stock, reaching adolescence in
the 1980s when the ascendancy of the white battalions in South
Africa was no longer so assured, and it is these facts that add such
poignancy to her association with Thami. However, there is no
obvious inference in the play about the powder keg that could be

exploded if their association was to become other than between friends.

Sexual relationships between black men and white women formed one of apartheid's most sacred shibboleths. In an article, 'Athol Fugard and the Liberal Dilemma', Derek Cohen raises this subject:

> Not once, even in the fulsome soliloquies, is the sexual relationship between them brought up. Isabel could as well be a boy as a girl. So single-mindedly does Fugard direct his drama to its crashing finale, that he omits what is truly the most explosive and devastating and obvious issue which the relationship includes by definition.
>
> [Cohen 1991,p.13]

Frank Rich, in *The New York Times,* suggests that in this regard Fugard is acting as a chaperone: 'afraid to leave the two kids alone in a room, for fear they might get out of his tight control'. [Rich 1989] Clearly a strong friendship develops between Thami and Isabel, and there are hints that, in other circumstances, this friendship could have blossomed into something more intimate. When Isabel asks Thami to meet her family he says: 'Me. Why? Are they starting to get nervous?' [p 199] The picture given of Isabel's parents, the small town chemist and the nervous mother, makes it unlikely that they envisage their daughter in a sexual relationship with this unknown black boy, but this remark shows that Thami clearly knows what is at stake. In addition, Isabel herself recognises a possible problem when she tells Mr M: 'being eighteen years old today is a pretty complicated business as far as we're concerned' [p 187]. However, if there is an underlying sexual tension in the relationship between Isabel and Thami, and one of the crucial and optimistic themes of the play is that normal intercourse between black and white is possible in a future South Africa, then it seems reasonable to attempt to determine whether there is any sexual chemistry at work that might have coloured the eventual fates of Isabel and Thami.

Ultimately Isabel achieves the understanding she battles for. Her liberal stance may be naive but her new experiences have made false the Saturday chats with her father's assistant, Samuel, and her final promise to the memory of Mr M can be seen as truly genuine, reflecting what she has understood about his sacrifice and the problems that Thami has faced all his life:

> I am going to make Anela Myalatya a promise. You gave me a little lecture once about wasted lives...how much of it you'd seen, how much you hated it, how much you didn't want that to happen to Thami and me. I sort of understood what you meant at the time. Now, I most certainly do. Your death has seen to that. My promise to you is that I am going to try as hard as I can, in every way that I can, to see that it doesn't happen to me. I am going to try my best to make my life useful in the way yours was. I want you to be proud of me. After all, I am one of your children, you know... The future is still ours, Mr M. [pp 237–238]

Thami

Compared with Isabel, Thami's schooling is very different. Her privileged background means that she is more than one step ahead of him as they seek to achieve their aspirations but, in addition, because of the inequality of resources directed at black education, Thami needs to work harder than Isabel to realise his ambitions. During his early years he had an insatiable appetite for learning, but that has changed because, according to Thami, the classroom has been invaded by politics. As he explains to her:

> I've told you before: sitting in a classroom doesn't mean the same thing to me that it does to you. That classroom is a political reality in my life...it's a part of the whole political system we're up against... [p 202]

At a later stage in the play when he is debating different concepts of freedom, Thami says: 'There is no comparison between that and the total denial of our freedom by the white government. They have been forcing on us an inferior education to keep us permanently suppressed.' [p 215]

The history of black and Coloured education amply justifies Thami's contention, and this background needs to be appreciated when considering the character of Thami as presented in the play. Frank Rich, writing in the *New York Times,* considers that this script is under-written when the characters on stage speak to each other, but he applauds Thami's speech, that comprises the whole of Act One Scene Six, as the most ambitious piece of writing in the play that, just like Styles' monologue, could almost be performed in isolation from the rest of the play. [Rich 1989, p 19] Thami's monologue is in stark contrast with the somewhat muted portrait that is presented when he is a member of the ensemble. He makes a good show of leading the debate for his school, but this is really not an important issue for him and he can afford to be light-hearted and flippant. His concerns are with the plight of the black people in his country, not about the equality or otherwise of the sexes. However, he does bring the banal exchange of literary quotes with Isabel back to reality when they are discussing 'Ozymandias'. The early socialist in Thami is revealed when he recalls a picture in a book of Bible stories showing the building of the pyramids by thousands of slaves. Fugard may well have read Brecht's poem, *Questions from a worker who reads.*

> Who built Thebes of the seven gates?
> In the books you will find the names of kings.
> Did the kings haul up the lumps of rock?

Isabel light-heartedly asks if Thami is attempting 'to stir up a little unrest in the time of the Pharaohs' to which he replies:

> Don't joke about it, Miss Dyson. There are quite a few Ozymandiases in this country waiting to be toppled. And you'll see it happen. We won't leave it to time to bring them down.   [p 196]

This exchange with Isabel finally erupts into anger as a prelude to his monologue: 'Don't tell me what I need, Isabel! And stop telling me what to do! You don't know what my life is about, so keep your advice to yourself.' [p 203]

Thami epitomises the hunger of so many African parents for education for their children as revealed in his initial appetite for learning; not for him Shakespeare's 'whining schoolboy [...] creeping like a snail unwillingly to school'. As a child he was standing at the school gates before the caretaker arrived but by the time he reaches high school, this enthusiastic flame has been extinguished:

> That little world of the classroom where I used to be happy...that little room of wonderful promises where I used to feel so safe has become a place I don't trust any more. Now I sit at my desk like an animal that has smelt danger, heard something moving in the bushes and knows it must be very careful.   [p 206]

There is another character in this play that only appears through the medium of Thami and he is Mr Dawid Grobbelaar, the Inspector of Bantu Schools in the Cape Midlands Region, who visits the school every year for a 'pep-talk'. Thami recalls the last one: 'We have educated you because we want you to become major shareholders of this wonderful Republic of ours. In fact we want *all* the peoples of South Africa to share in that future...'. Thami's response to this is to meditate:

> I look around me in the location at the men and women who went out into that 'wonderful future' before me. What do I see? Happy and contented shareholders in this exciting enterprise called the Republic of South Africa? No. I see a generation of tired, defeated men and women crawling back to their miserable little pondoks at the end of a day's work for the white *baas* or madam.
>
> [p 207]

All of which leads to a final political response and the resort to militancy.

The flawed and marvellous Mr M

The characters of Isabel and Thami are relatively uncomplicated, but this cannot be said for Mr M, one of the playwright's favourite creations. Due to an apparently emotional involvement with the beliefs and ethos of the schoolmaster, Fugard has provided us with a deeply contradictory individual, part saint, part fool. There is ambivalence on display in the portraits of Hally and Morris and Boesman, but with Mr M, what appears to be a splendid tragic hero turns out to be Fugard's prime example of paradox.

Contradiction in literature's leading men and women is not an unusual device. To take one example: an article in the *Times Literary Supplement* of 3 September 2004 on a new introduction by James Wood to Graham Greene's *The Heart of the Matter* refers to a review at the time of the novel's original publication by George Orwell. This includes: 'Scobie is incredible because the two halves of him do not fit together' – any more than they do with Mr M. Wood then looks at the contradictions he sees in Scobie (the leading figure in the novel who eventually kills himself), 'more acutely'. Although the precision, in logic and theology, of Wood's conclusion can be questioned, he suggests that if Scobie can allow 'human love' to rob him of the love of God 'for all eternity', then he was never a very passionate Christian; but if he is not the latter, why then his Christian passion? In Scobie's case, these contradictions arise because of the power of his Catholic faith; but in the case of Fugard's contradictory creature, the power is the Apartheid State.

Although Mr M in effect commits suicide, there is no way that he or Boesman or others like them can renounce the power of the State, while escape from a passionate faith is possible: it can be agnosticized.

Described by his creator as that 'flawed, beautiful Mr M and his passion for learning', the schoolmaster is a liberal idealist in a far from perfect world. On the surface he may appear as the romanticised schoolmaster, but he is not prepared to accept the school boycott and tolerate his pupils joining in, and would he have forgiven the Germans as the hero of *Goodbye Mr Chips* did? Mr M's stubborn zealotry rendered him irrelevant and yet pitiable in the historical context of the turbulent mid-1980s. He was killed because he acted as an informer but it could be shown that, however laudable his intentions, he had been acting for the oppressor all his working life. While preaching the liturgy of the supremacy of the English language, he was acting as an ambassador of the apartheid authorities who were perfectly content for the oppressed to learn the works of Wordsworth if this diverted them from thoughts of a violent overthrow of the oppressor. For the unfortunate Mr M, language betrays him just as much as he has betrayed his pupils. The irony is that Mr M's love of the English language and his reverence towards words is in direct contrast with one of the causes of the unrest, the imposition of Afrikaans for some lessons.

Undoubtedly the climax of the play is in the *coup de théâtre* when Mr M compares the weapon of aggression – the stone – with the dictionary – the word – epitomising tolerance and peaceful negotiation. Fugard gives the best lines in the play on the sanctity of the word to Mr M:

> Be careful, Thami. Be careful! Be careful! Don't scorn words. They are sacred! Magical! Yes, they are. Do you know that without words a man can't think? Yes, it's true. Take that thought back with you as a present from the despised Mr M and share it with the Comrades.... If the struggle needs weapons, give it words, Thami. Stones and petrol bombs can't get inside those police armoured cars. Words can. They can do something even more devastating than that...they can get inside the heads of those inside those armoured cars. I speak to you like this because if I have faith in anything, it is faith in the power of the word.   [p 217]

In this instance Mr M sees the positive value of words entering into the heads of the policemen rather than the insidious
Orwellian control of the dreams and thoughts of *Blood Knot*'s
Zachariah, that so concern his brother. As described later, the text
reveals that the crux of this play is the relationship between Mr M
and Thami, but the powerful subtext is the correlation between
the word and the stone. It would be simplistic to consider that
Mr M represents one and Thami the other; they both present to
the audience and the reader only a partial perspective. Thami is
wrong to reject the word – the campaign to regain 'consciousness'
for his people needed the word – as exemplified by Steve Biko,
who was a prolific wordsmith. Equally, Mr M cannot be so unrealistic as to believe that in the highly-charged political situation
of the 1980s, the authorities would listen to reason; they will not
accept words as instruments of insubordination or insurrection
any more than they will permit their opponents to use weapons to
forward their cause.

Mr M represents the antithesis of the Black Consciousness
Movement that was no longer prepared to compromise and co-
operate with the white man. As Thami tells Isabel: 'The Comrades
don't want any mixing with whites'. Mr M's way is no longer relevant and his failure to change with the times, plus the deliberate choice to act as an informer, leads to his death. He can be
compared to Piet Bezuidenhout who also loved English poetry
(and who might have been an informer), but where in Piet's world
of the 1960s he can retire and log his aloes, for the schoolteacher
in the 1980s, the consequences of betrayal, as he well knows, are
rather more dire than a future as a lonely aloes cataloguer. Mr M
tells Isabel that 'knowledge has banished fear', but in the end it
proves little protection for him. Thami sums him up the best:

> He is out of touch with what is really happening to us
> blacks and the way we feel about things. He thinks the
> world is still the way it was when he was young. It's not!
> It's different now, but he's too blind to see it. He doesn't

open his eyes and ears and see what is happening around
him or listen to what people are saying.   [p 200]

There are characteristics that Mr M and Fugard have in common;
they are both liberal humanitarians and the love Mr M has for
Thami is reflected in the camaraderie and sympathy Fugard has
with the black and Coloured people of his country, both in his
personal friendships and in the sentiments we have seen on his
stages. However, where Fugard may well agree that the liberal
approach in his plays has not always been accepted by audiences
as fully successful, what we are given in this play is a portrait of
Mr M who, except for the impact he has on Isabel's future, can
be seen as a full-blooded failure (in view of his fate, perhaps an
inappropriate adjective).

The English word has also failed because in effect it is this word
that Thami rebels against. He has absorbed romantic poetry at
the feet of Mr M, but he cannot accept the liberal ideology that
his teacher represents, and although his radicalism is directed
at the Bantu Education Act and the Afrikaans language, it can
also be seen that English culture and the English language, even
if only whispered, has kept the likes of Thami in his place. Mr
M compares the efficacy of the dictionary, the book, against the
stone, but they are both objects of subjugation. The stone represents the authorities' tactics of force used against the more mili-
tant politics of the Black Consciousness Movement while with the
book, Thami, but not Mr M, comes to recognise this as another
weapon used in the control of the oppressed – as it was for Sizwe
Bansi who says about his out-of-order reference book: 'My pass-
book talks good English too...big words that Sizwe can't read...
Sizwe wants to stay here in New Brighton and find a job; pass-
book says, "No! Report back"'. Thami tells Mr M that in the
circumstances of today, his lessons are not relevant:

Yours were lessons in whispering. There are men now
who are teaching us to shout. Those little tricks and
jokes of yours in the classroom liberated nothing. The

struggle doesn't need the big English words you taught
me how to spell.   [p 216]

Before his final exit, Mr M tells the audience why he decides to
become an informer:

> I sat here before going to the police station saying to
> myself that it was my duty, to my conscience, to you, to
> the whole community to do whatever I could to put an
> end to this madness of boycotts and arson, mob violence
> and lawlessness...and maybe that is true...but only
> maybe...because Thami, the truth is that I was so lonely!
> You had deserted me. I was jealous of those who had
> taken you away.   [p 225]

This confession leads directly to the kernel of the play, namely
the relationship between Thami and the worthy Mr M with the
high ideals that he is prepared to sacrifice because, if we are to
accept at face value what he says to the audience, he feels deserted
and is jealous of the fact that Thami is prepared to put the cause
before any affection or regard he has for his teacher. For all of the
real-life political context forming the substance of this work, and
however important the themes of self-revelation are, particularly
for Isabel, Fugard has once again provided a romance, but this
time the love story has the most tragic of endings. Mr M longs for
a role like that of Sam as surrogate father to Thami, but while this
might have been possible in the 1950s, even between black and
white, by 1984 such a relationship between the conservative Mr
M and the nascent rebel Thami is impossible.

After Mr M reveals that he is an informer and Thami tries to
save him, these two stubborn and yet articulate people are unable
to put into words what the real issue is. When Mr M queries
Thami as to whether he would lie to save him, Thami says yes but
when Mr M asks why, there are two crucial stage directions:

> MR M: (*Desperate to hear the truth.*) Why?
>   (*THAMI can't speak.*)   [p 228]

Mr M wants Thami to admit that the reason is because he loves his schoolmaster but this fact is avoided; Thami prevaricates and agrees that his only motive is the 'Cause'. As a result Mr M says he does not need to hide behind Thami's lies and he goes out to face the mob. When Isabel and Thami meet three weeks later, just before Thami leaves the location, he finally reveals that he did love Mr M.

Mr M's death provides a dramatic deceit, more sentimental in nature than Fugard has indulged in before, and the audience might wonder how credible is Mr M's action and whether his creator realises that the character of the 'beautiful and flawed' Mr M is surely more flawed than anything else. Was the schoolmaster really prepared to accept the violence that would have been inflicted upon the boycott leaders as a result of his treachery, just because he was lonely? The horrible death Mr M suffers is melodrama of the highest order that is totally absent in the other Fugard plays. Mr M's death is entirely his own fault, brought about due to what, outside the high drama of the play, appear spurious if not totally unbelievable reasons.

TEN

Truth and Reconciliation

The wind is old and still at play
While I must hurry upon my way
For I am running to paradise.

WB Yeats, 'Responsibilities 1914 – Running to Paradise'

P oet Dawid in *Sorrows and Rejoicings* is fond of Yeats, but the South African poet runs away, into exile from his country, with disastrous results. Hester and Gladys also retreat and in happier days Master Harold ran down the hill with his kite, but for Boesman and Lena, their fate is in walking and not running. However, whether running or walking, few of Fugard's people found any form of paradise until after the release of Nelson Mandela in 1990, when prospects became somewhat brighter for the playwright's newer creations, as it was hoped they would do for the majority of the citizens of the country. Certainly *Playland*, his first play of the 1990s, which contains many of the usual ingredients, presents, against a background of the two character's visions of hell, a perceptible hint of optimism, even if not exactly paradisiacal.

Playland is Happyland!

Playland has two separate stories, about very different incidents, but with similar consequences. One is told by a black man, Martinus Zoeloe. The other belongs to an Afrikaner, Gideon le Roux, which refers directly to a particular passage of South African history – the military action in Namibia and Angola.

Namibia, formerly South West Africa, was part of the German African Empire until the First World War. In 1914 South African troops invaded the country and in less than a year the German garrison of eight thousand was forced to surrender. After the Paris peace talks of 1919, South Africa was mandated a to administer the country and in due course this authority was renewed by the United Nations. However, as South Africa attracted more and more opprobrium over its apartheid policies, the mandate was revoked in 1966 and South Africa was required to leave the territory. They refused to do this as they were at the time intent on controlling as many neighbouring countries as possible to prevent them from being used as bases from which attacks might be made against them. The people of South West Africa then began a campaign for self-government and a number of alternative plans were proposed, but none of these succeeded and this lead to a long-term armed confrontation between the guerrillas of the South West Africa People's Organisation (SWAPO), which was emerging as the prominent political force, and the South African Defence Force (SADF). The guerrillas mainly operated out of neighbouring Angola to where the SADF took the conflict under a policy known as 'hot pursuit'.

This bitter engagement, which was known as the Border War and continued from 1966 to 1989, was between two unequal opponents, despite SWAPO being supported by Cuban troops and Russian armaments: the South African National Government at that time had the most powerful army and security force on the continent of Africa. By the early 1980s, there were one hundred and eighty thousand men fully operational, with a reserve force of half a million troops from the all-embracing conscription requirement for white South African males. This impressive display of manpower was backed up by a considerable armoury of military equipment. In the Border War the SADF pursued a ruthless policy. A former South African lance corporal in a BBC interview said that their task was: 'To take an area and to clear it. We killed everything...we killed cattle, we killed goats and we killed people.' [Saunders 1988, p 463] There were heavy losses on both sides and it was to became known as South Africa's 'Vietnam'.

Playland is about memory and this conflict is the background to one half of the remembering that occurs in the play. Fugard was not however the first playwright to use the experiences of the SADF as material. Anthony Ackerman, who served as a conscript in the Army as an eighteen year old, wrote *Somewhere on the Border* in 1982. This was more directly concerned with what in *Playland* is only described by Gideon. Instead of a fairground, the two locations in Ackerman's play are at a training camp somewhere in South Africa and in an operational area on the border of Namibia and Angola. There was printed in the programme, when this play was first staged, a photograph and some comments by the author:

> Going into the army was part of growing up in white South Africa. It was the first hurdle you had to clear after leaving school... Most of us thought it was a waste of time. But in the back of your mind you knew you could always be used to maintain the status quo. Now the boys are sent to the border... On 4 May 1978 South African forces attacked a village 260 km inside Angola. The village was populated by Namibian refugees who had fled from the South African army occupying their country. During the attack 160 men, 295 women and 300 children were killed. The wounded who died in the days after the attack brought the death toll to over 1000. The village is called Cassinga. The photograph is of a mass grave.   [Gray 1993, pp 2–3]

Gideon has his own grave story

Playland is dedicated to Yvonne Bryceland but it is one of Fugard's few major works that does not feature a female character. It is also somewhat unusual in that the two characters on stage are strangers to each other – they have no relationship in common as in so many of the earlier plays – but in *Playland* these two, a black man and an Afrikaner, even if their meeting is at the nadir of apartheid, form an unusual partnership. The Afrikaner wants to find a confessor and looks to the taciturn night watchman to fill this role, but Martinus has his own pain that needs to be dealt with. In reality, even in 1989, it is unlikely that an Afrikaner would choose an elderly black man as an instrument to attempt an assuaging of guilt, but on stage, and in Fugard's skilful hands, this combination makes for intriguing theatre.

It was first presented at the Market Theatre in July 1992 and later in that year it was performed in the USA. It came to the Donmar Warehouse in London in February 1993 with the original cast of John Kani as Martinus, Sean Taylor as Gideon and Bill Flynn as the voice of 'Barking Barney'.

For the last fifteen years Martinus has been employed as a watchman and handyman at a travelling amusement park known as 'Playland'. Gideon, who was discharged from the Army ten months earlier, is visiting the park looking for it to deliver some escape from the torment he is suffering. Playland is encamped outside a small Karoo town and it is New Year's Eve 1989, a memorable date: in less than two months time Nelson Mandela was to be released from prison. At the end of the evening the proprietor of the funfair, 'Barking Barney' Bakkhuizen – we never meet him but he is part of the play as an offstage voice – complains that business has not been very good and the fair will not be back next year if a better site is not provided. However, for 'Apartheidland' there is no such uncertainty; it is about to close down for ever and the play perceptively reflects this.

Martinus is sarcastically sceptical about the happiness quotient delivered by this fun fair. He has seen, at locations throughout the Great Karoo, that a ride on the Big Wheel does not deliver any relief from man's anxieties – because he cannot forget his and believes that all sins are recorded by God in the 'Big Book'. Buntu, in *Sizwe Bansi is Dead*, warns against finding your name is missing from this book, but in Martinus's case he knows, only too well, the nature of his crime – breaking the Sixth Commandment – will be written therein. At heart Gideon believes he is similarly guilty of 'Number Six' but scoffs at the night watchman and says that he is not like the other Karoo zombies, 'grazing on candy floss' [p 27]. He tries to justify his killings:

...What about self-defense?
(*MARTINUS shakes his head.*)
Or protecting women and children?
(*MARTINUS shakes his head again.*)
What about Defending Your Country Against
Communism?   [pp 14–15]

Despite these protestations, he recognizes deep inside that his guilt cannot be erased by such arguments.

The revelation that both of the characters on stage are killers provides an opportunity to expose their separate hells; firstly the one that is so often found in South Africa alongside the fact of having a black skin; and secondly the equal torment that Gideon is going through as a result of being a white man conscripted into an army waging a debilitating guerrilla war. This is what they have in common. Where they differ is that Martinus does not look for repentance; he will not apologise to God, or man, for his sin, but Gideon is desperate to find some form of release from his memories. Martinus murdered a white man, Andries Jacobus de Lange, who raped his girlfriend and only escaped hanging when, at the last moment, the wife of his victim told the authorities that her husband was accustomed to bedding their black female servants. On Gideon's part, he cannot shed the guilt he feels for the SWAPO soldiers he killed – and buried.

As well as two stories there are two habitats. Playland itself is represented by:

> *A large sign with the name PLAYLAND prominently positioned. There is also an array of other gaudy signs advertising the various sideshows and the rides – the Big Wheel, the Wall of Death, the Ghost Train and so on. They are all festooned with coloured lights which will be switched on when the night gets under way.*

However, the meeting between Martinus and Gideon takes place within the black man's space:

...the night watchman's camp: a broken car from one of the
rides with a square of canvas stretched over it to provide shelter
from sun and rain, and a paraffin tin brazier.   **[p 5]**

Fugard is at the height of his powers. He is writing at a time of
great change in his country when, to use his own words from the
2001 play, the sorrows of the past are hopefully to be given up
for the rejoicings of the future. It is therefore theatrically adroit
that his introduction to this new dawn features a partnership – of
sorts – between the two main antagonists in the apartheid war. If
he had substituted Martinus with another Afrikaner, or someone
like Elsa in *The Road to Mecca*, the impact would have been very
different.

The action takes place on the black man's territory, even if this
is within boundaries held at the command of the white man. It
represents a border land between the past and the future, wholly
appropriate for this encounter. An added dimension is how
unlooked for – and unlikely – this meeting is. Gideon did not
leave his mother at home in front of the TV with the intention of
finding someone to whom he could unburden himself, but that
happens. Their meeting is by chance – serendipity – much as
in Edward Albee's *Zoo Story* where the sane member of the duo
on the park bench is static, like Martinus. Gideon is mixed up,
but hardly schizophrenic like the man in Albee's play; but the
comparison has some relevance. In both cases there is an apparently inconsequential and unplanned meeting that leads to an
important climax.

What is not explained is why at this unplanned meeting Gideon
chooses this particular person to hear his confession. Martinus
has come to terms with his crime, although the evening's events,
and his role in them, do bring about some change in this attitude
– but the principal purpose of the play is to enable Gideon to
come to terms with what happened, 'on the border', and take his
life forward. His conscience is there to represent that of the South
African nation as a whole and he needs to accept, and adapt, to
the new order over the horizon in the New Year. He tells Martinus,

with what is described as 'hollow laughter': '... I promise you my friend that in 1990 you will be a happy man' [p 23].

The happening in the past that causes Gideon's suffering was when, after a major operation, he and another soldier were detailed to bury the SWAPO dead. This was not an isolated occurrence – he had been on grave detail before – but this time the number was much larger than usual; twenty-seven corpses. The enormity of what he is invoved in makes him recall how he used to help his father count the cabbages in their backyard:

> When it was all over – the shooting and screaming... I would take a deep breath, say to myself 'You're alive Gid,' then walk around and count. I always wanted to know how many there were, you see... You could take your time you see, walk around slowly and carefully and do it properly like my pa used to do when he counted his cabbages in the backyard...that's how I learned to count. Even before I was in school man I knew how to count my blessings. But now it wasn't cabbages anymore, it was 'One Swapo, two Swapo, three Swapo...' My very first time I counted there was eight of them... Then for a long time it looked as if fifteen was going to be the record until that follow-up when we ambushed a whole bloody unit...and when it came time to count...! Twenty-fucking-seven of them! I couldn't believe it man. A new record! 'Twenty seven Swapo cabbages in the garden daddy!'   [PP 37–38]

While these corpses were being dumped into a hole, Gideon notices an old woman come out of the bush and watch them. He conjectures whether they are manhandling her husband – or her son? For some reason this reminds him of how, when a small boy, he had cut open a fish from which had spilled hundreds of unborn progeny. He equates this memory to what he is doing now but the dead men are not fish and this reduces him to tears. He goes to look for the old woman to seek forgiveness, but she has disappeared and now back home, he looks for her every night in his dreams – but without success. As the play reaches its climax, this woman can be seen to have the role of witness – a part Fugard often played – to the specific sins of Gideon and Martinus and the political system that has directly, or indirectly, traumatised these two disparate South Africans.

As he tells his story to Martinus he begins to understand the real reason for this New Year Eve encounter: Gideon wants the night watchman to stand in for the unknown woman and grant him absolution. Martinus refuses because if he forgives Gideon, he will need to grant the same mercy to the man he killed and ask God to forgive him also. He has learnt to live with his hate but this night with a white man, the same race as the man he killed, may result in a reassessment.

Gideon is similarly confused:

> Ja. I know what you're saying. It burns you out hey? Kill somebody and sooner or later you end up like one of those landmine wrecks on the side of the road up there on the Border – burnt-out and bloody useless.
>
> [p 45]

The play provides no clear-cut solutions towards easing the angst of either man and it ends in mundane fashion as Gideon asks Martinus to help him start his car, but before that the night watchman perceptively offers some advice, much as Hester, at the end of *Hello and Goodbye,* told Johnny: 'Live happily. Try, Johnny, try to be happy.' As a result of Gideon's experience 'on the border' he has not been able to muster the will, or the energy, to re-establish the holding of pigeons he and his father once had and which gave them both such pleasure. In parody he repeats:

> 'You're alive Gid!'
> What a bloody joke. I'm as dead as the men I buried and I'm also spooking the place where I did it. [p 45]

During the dialogue of the night he has told Martinus about the pigeons and this forms the basis of the parting message:

> MARTINUS: I also want to see them. Those pigeon-
> birds. Flying round up there like you say. I also
> want to see that.
>
> GIDEON: What are you saying man?
>
> MARTINUS: I am saying to you that when Playland
> comes back here next time – Christmas and New
> Year – I want to do it like you said…look up in the
> sky, watch the pigeon-birds flying and drink my tea
> and laugh!
>
> GIDEON: Do you mean that?
>
> MARTINUS: I am saying it to you because I mean it.
> To hell with spooking! You are alive. So go home
> and do it. Get some planks, find some nails and
> a hammer and fix that hook. Start again with the
> pigeon-birds.
> (*Pause.*) Do you hear what I am saying Gideon
> le Roux?   [pp 46–47]

Gideon contributes to this with a final act of reciprocity: 'And you also hey. Get out of that little room man. Let old Andries spook there by himself tonight. Do you understand me Martinus Zoeloe?' [p 47] Martinus responds to say he does. We can believe that the next day Gideon will take the black man's advice and find a hammer and that such action, together with the joint effort involved in pushing the old jalopy, represents an early example of the reconciliation in the country about to come to pass.

Each has satisfied a need they both have. They have listened, not because apartheid rules have said they could – or should – but because of human nature. The Truth and Reconciliation Commission (TRC) was not set up until 1994, but Fugard in 1992 has already shown in the arena of a night watchman's camp one of the guiding precepts of that Commission: to provide an oppor-tunity for the silenced to speak out. In the South Africa of 1990, Gideon is still more privileged than Martinus, but until that eve of a new year he had also been silenced by a guilt that is not neces-sarily expunged as a result of talking to this black man – but it is eased. In most cases the TRC was unable to fully forgive or heal the wounds inflicted by apartheid, but for Martinus and Gideon, their own little truth commission enabled their true feelings to be shown – and Fugard saw his next play as a continuation of this.

A little truth commission

Between *Playland* and *Valley Song* was *My Life,* described as images and stories from the personal biographies of the lives of five young South Africans which was, according to Fugard, considered by some critics to be 'a little truth commission on its own'. The release of Nelson Mandela heralded an amazing change but at a minor level, observe the change that took place in the theatrical world between 1958 and *My Life.* Lewis Nkosi had to play Father Huddleston because it was not allowed to have black and white performers on the same stage; but for this piece in 1994 the audience sees a diversity of South Africans classified by the apartheid regime as: two blacks, one Coloured, one white and another of Indian extraction – which is precisely the point of the play. There are omissions of course – there are no men, no Moslems and no elderly – but that reflects Fugard's intent:

> ... I felt the one voice that was not being heard was that of young South Africans, and dammit all, they are the future. What we were doing was not for ourselves, my generation and beyond, because we were already too old to get the real benefit of it, we were doing it for those who were going to come after us. I had such a strong sense that nobody was really asking them to speak or listening to them when they did get a chance to speak. It's not all that easy you know to stand up and be heard.
>
> [Fugard 1996, p vii–viii]

The title of this book includes the words: 'Athol Fugard: His Plays...' which begs the question as to whether *My Life* is one of these. What eventuated was the result of Fugard choosing five young people, who all turned out to be female – but this was not deliberate – who were encouraged to keep a journal recording their everyday lives and to meet in a rehearsal room and tell their stories. Fugard took responsibility for the final choice of material that was taken to the stage, firstly at the Standard Bank National Festival of the Arts at Grahamstown in July 1994 and then to a National Schools Festival and finally to the Tesson Theatre in Johannesburg. A 'Schools Festival' was appropriate as the end result was more suited to such a venue than a conventional theatre. It is hardly a work of drama.

The text was published, together with *Valley Song*, in 1996, but unlike the work-shopped plays of the early 1970s, the words appear to be mostly those of the five girls. The earlier works had a text that was teased out by collaboration with relatively savvy 'men of the theatre' – or at least 'men of the world' – but the final text was essentially Fugardian. To repeat the view of Mark Gevisser in the South African *Mail and Guardian* on 26 May 1995: 'despite the many temptations, neither Kani nor Ntshona steals the show and both allow the lyricism of Fugard – unmistakeable even in his "workshopped" scripts – to shine through'. We cannot know, but there does not appear to be too much of Fugard in *My Life*; the words are essentially those of the five girls.

They talk about their dreams for the future and about the commonplace happenings in their lives. They comment on the subject of violence and how one of their number, the Indian, is a Tamil who is different from them because she believes in fate – destined to marry a Tamil boy and no one else. It is a brave experiment, but as in the case of *Orestes,* performance is more crucial than text and because of Fugard's apparently limited input to the words, this script does not have the resonance of his other dramatic output. However, what can be said for this minor aberration is that it must have assisted him in the important creation of Veronica in *Valley Song*.

The Playwright and the pumpkin seeds

Valley Song was the next Fugard play of the new South Africa – after *Playland* – where the strand of optimism the new political order brought in is, in most regards, on display. He wrote in September 1997:

> And then, finally, *Valley Song*. Possibly my most success-
> ful attempt at balancing the personal and the political in
> its examination of the inevitability of change, of loss and
> renewal. It is a play which ends...with a note of hope
> and affirmation.   **[Fugard 1998, p viii]**

This work returns to the oft-used family setting where we are given a nostalgic view of the past, eloquently rendered by the two characters, the first being Buks, a recognisable portrait of one of Fugard's 'good men', and the other, the playwright himself, referred to as the 'Author'. Both of these are written into the script with the instruction that they be presented on stage by the same actor.

In the performance at the Royal Court Theatre in January 1996, Fugard played both parts as he had done at the premiere in Johannesburg in August 1995, followed by Princeton and then New York. In the London showing he changed identities by a variation of diction, a more stooping posture and the alternating use of Buks' woollen hat. Fugard has suggested that the reason for the single actor was to underline how both the white and the Coloured in South Africa needed to be responsible for the success of the new politics in the country, although why this could not be projected using two actors is unclear. A more likely answer is that the author relished the theatrical challenge of presenting these two faces of his country in the one person. It does not create the sort of ambiguity he has looked for in the past but it does show that at the age of sixty-three his theatrical ingenuity was in good working order. Also, within the context of the story, the two men shown in the form of one actor stand, for a time at least, in oppo-sition to each other, but by the end of the play they are seen as brothers, in harmony in the campaign to retain the values of life in New Bethesda. As the Author says:

> Like your Oupa, I don't want to see you go. It means
> the Valley is changing and that selfish part of me doesn't
> want that to happen. It wants it to stay the unspoilt,
> innocent little world it was when I first discovered it.
>
> [P 53]

While in their possible confrontational role, Buks attempts to
appease the Author, whom he refers to only as 'Master' or the
'Whiteman', by presenting him with a wheelbarrow of vegetables.
Marius, in *The Road to Mecca*, did the same although in his case
this could have been a love offering or simply a kindly action or
even a sop to Helen to ease the prospect of her impending departure to the old people's home. In both cases these gifts are the
fruits of the New Bethesda soil, although in the earlier example
they can be considered, as root vegetables, as products of the
darker side of the South African landscape.

Buks is a man of the soil, a man of the Valley, and content with
his life while his alternative, styled as the Author, is dissatisfied
with his.

> ...sick and tired of the madness and desperate scramble
> of my life in the make-believe world of Theatre. I wanted
> to return to 'essentials', to the 'real' world and here was
> my chance to do it.
>
> I could see myself sitting on my stoep after a day of
> good writing – all prose now, no more nonsense from
> actors and producers and critics – sitting there on my
> stoep watching the sun set and admiring my land, finally
> at peace with myself.   [pp 30–31]

In comparison he tells the audience of the history of Buks'
existence:

> ...the young Buks stepped into his father's shoes and
> husbanded that land. And that's how it has been ever
> since. His life is rooted now as deeply in the soil as the
> old Walnut tree next to the windmill. When it's like that

between you and a piece of land, you end up being a
part of it.   [p 31]

Buks is a seventy-six year-old Coloured man who has lived in this
Karoo village all his life except for the years he spent in the army
during the Second World War. His daughter, Caroline, ran away
to Johannesburg where she dies in childbirth. Buks' wife, Betty,
goes to the city when a message is received that Caroline is ill and
returns with news of her death and their granddaughter, Veronica,
as a babe-in-arms. Buks, like his father, farms a few acres of land
not in his ownership that adjoins the Landman house, unoccupied and dilapidated, that Buks' father and Landman himself
built with their own hands. How deliberate was the choice of
name? Is he a 'man of the land' like Buks or a member of the
master race, the man who owns the land?

Veronica at sixteen has a talent for singing and dreams of a
professional career. Her desire to go to Johannesburg to pursue
this ambition pains Buks, who fears the same fate as befell his
daughter. He is also apprehensive at the prospect of a sale of the
Landman house and land which might bring to an end his life
as a farmer. The third character, the Author, does buy the property but, at the end of the play, reassures Buks on this point: his
concerns that he will be dispossessed are groundless. But not the
concerns about the ambitions of Veronica – Buks has to let her
go and be satisfied with the pumpkins he is going to continue to
grow. Echoing Isabel in *My Children! My Africa!*, the Author tells
Veronica that 'The future belongs to you now' [p 53].

Buks is no kin to any of the other Fugard people of mixed race
– the Coloureds – previously encountered. He could have been as
dispossessed as Morris, in so far as the land is concerned, if *Valley
Song* had been a bitter commentary on post-1990 South Africa
with Buks being evicted from his farmland because he has no title
– no piece of paper – but that is not to be. He is not forced out of
his home like Steve and the love shared with his wife, eloquently
revealed in the play, means that he is not going to follow along
the disastrous path taken by Errol Philander in *Statements....* But

then this play is unlike most of Fugard's earlier works that are so marked with pessimism. Buks, the fatalist, is a poor man and Veronica's ambition probably unachievable but the audience is sympathetic towards them. There is a well projected sense of hope and future contentment that we have not had so prominently from Fugard before. It is a pastoral poem, extolling the virtues of hard work and the need to allow talent to prosper – if possible. In this 'coming of age' story the recurrent confrontation between the young and the old is present, but in *Valley Song* it is a gentle skirmish with the Author acting as an umpire to ameliorate any wounds that are inflicted.

Fugard has said that *Valley Song* is all about dreaming and dreams. These are certainly present but they are generally of the affectionate and comfortable kind that do not need to be locked away in Styles' strong room. The Author says to Veronica:

> But what I do know is that dreams don't do well in this Valley. Pumpkins yes, but not dreams – and you've already seen enough of life to know that as well. Listen to me, Veronica – take your apple box and go home, and dream about something that has a chance of happening.   [PP 34–35]

Veronica does not heed his advice. The ambition of her friend Alfred is for an old second-hand bicycle and the Author recommends this, but not Veronica. She tells him that perhaps his life is over and he is ready to become a ghost – a ghost of the South African past that comes back, Scrooge-like, to haunt Buks when he believes he might be evicted from his akkers. Her response is the word 'Never' when the Author tries to picture her future:

> Okay, let's leave it at that. But for your sake I hope you don't remember tonight and what I've said to you in ten years time if like all the other women in the village you are walking barefoot into the veld every day with a baby on your back to collect firewood.   [P 55]

Buks is unlike Fugard's earlier portraits of Coloured men but Veronica is also very different from his other young people. At one end of the spectrum is Master Harold, privileged compared to Veronica, but unhappy, pessimistic, unsure of himself and possibly developing into the worst type of bigoted white racist. But that was the 1950s. Forty years later Veronica walks on stage.

Fugard may well have seen the 1986 play, *Have you seen Zandile*, based on the life of Gcina Mhlope. Zandile is a bright child and a possible precursor to Veronica. She dreams of being a teacher, but her life is one of hardship contrasting the urban environment of Durban and that of the Transkei, This play was a success at the Market Theatre and was also performed in Edinburgh where it won the Edinburgh Fringe First Award. However, what is more likely is that the creation of Fugard's post-apartheid heroine was crucially influenced by his involvement with *My Life*. Veronica has ambition, true love for her grandfather and a healthy realisation of the hurdles ahead if she is going to succeed as a singer but, importantly, in *Valley Song* she vividly represents the national hope for the future. Ten years later the wheel has turned again. In *Victory* we see the charming, but easily led Victoria, and the utter failure that is Freddie – and hopes are dashed.

Another difference with previous plays is music. Music has always been important in Fugard's life, as exampled by what he wrote in his *Notebooks* while working on *Playland*:

> Another one of those miraculous epiphanies that have blessed every play I have written. This time it happened while I was listening to Pergolesi's 'Stabat Mater' late last night – utterly ravishing, those two women's voices soaring in ecstasy and pain and love. I was thinking of the text – 'Stabat Mater dolorosa,' stood the mother full of sorrow – when suddenly I saw her in my mind's eye in a corner of the photograph: a black woman watching Gideon dump the bodies in the hole.
>
> [Barbera 1993, p 533]

However, music does not really feature on his stage until *Valley Song*. We are given an example of theatre in *The Island*, the dance floor in *'Master Harold'...and the boys* and poetry readings in *My Children! My Africa!*, but it is not until this upbeat post-apartheid play that he gives music a position centre-stage. It matches the mood of the work. Buks cannot read but he tries to recall some extracts from *Rigoletto* that he learned while guarding Italian prisoners of war:

> Lae donder mobili
> En soo moretsa
> Da da de da da da   [p 6]

But it is the singer Veronica who adds this new artistic dimension to a Fugard play.

She is like Fugard himself. He left home while still young, just as she wants to do. If Fugard had stayed in Port Elizabeth, would he have written the plays he did? He empathises with his young heroine; she may not have the inherent talent he had but she has to leave the Karoo and her grandfather to find out; and this raises a feature familiar to Fugard – romance. Sam instructs Willie on the subject, although away from the dance floor there is little to be romantic about in the 1950s; but in *Valley Song,* romance and love are as sturdy as Buks' pumpkins:

> And I love her? Oh, Betty...there is so much love for her inside me I don't know what to do with it. Could I have done more?   [p 47]

Buks' love for the Valley, and his granddaughter, shines through the play like a beacon, and even the disillusioned Author is drawn back to his roots, but for the girl, she has to leave. However, her attachment to the her home is lovingly rendered in her last song – however trite the words – which she prefaces with 'I love you, Oupa':

> You're breaking my heart
> Valley that I love.

You're breaking my heart
When I say goodbye.

You gave me a start
Valley that I love.
But now we must part
'Cause I'm on my way.

I'll sing all your songs
Valley that I love.
So that people will know
How beautiful you are.

The dream I've got
Is leading me away.
But Valley that I love
I'll come back one day.   **[p 50]**

I was twenty years old

An insight into the birth-pangs of the artistic imagination that
nurtures an act of writing is invariably of considerable interest in
understanding the work in question. These origins in the plays of
Athol Fugard have already been referred to: we can see his father
in *Hello and Goodbye*; he lived in the same Braamfontein as Milly;
and *A Lesson from Aloes* is based on people he knew. However, it
was not until *'Master Harold'...and the boys* that his own history
became the principal inspiration, and this is also the case with
The Captain's Tiger. This opened at the State Theatre in Pretoria
in August 1997, went to Princeton in 1998 and then transferred to
New York in January of the following year. It was later performed
at the Market Theatre, with Fugard himself playing the part of
the Author/Tiger. In the UK it was staged at the Orange Tree
in Richmond, although at this venue the Author and the Tiger
were played by different actors – a move that Fugard subsequently regretted. Nevertheless, the Orange Tree's 'theatre in the
round' was ideally suited for a play where the set is virtually a
blank space, totally different from the confined habitats of *Blood*

Knot, Hello and Goodbye and *The Road to Mecca*. The scene for *The Captain's Tiger*, as in *Valley Song*, is in dramatic contrast to these rooms – or an imagined prison cell or even a pig sty.

It has proved to be one of his least successful offerings – at least in the eyes of many critics – with such phrases being used as: 'Just an amiable exercise in nostalgia' to 'This tiger's got no bite.' A particularly damning comment was made by John Simon in the *New York Magazine* of 1 February 1999:

> ...the man is reduced to purveying ditchwater... And except for 100 minutes of trivial and pointless palaver, there is no play.   **[Wertheim 2000, pp 225–226]**

However, if the play is viewed from the vantage point of a knowledge of Fugard's past – and how this has been revealed in some of his more successful works – *The Captain's Tiger* is far from being a failure. It is an autobiographical picture of his time on board the *SS Graigaur*, the merchant ship he boarded in Port Said forty-five years ago. This picture is skilfully arranged for the theatre so as to reveal the pain involved in artistic creation – played out alongside the story of his mother's early life.

The adept staging does not hide an element of self-indulgence in the writing that renders it less successful than its brother, *Exits and Entrances,* where, more graphically, it is Fugard's theatre that is exposed rather than his own strengths, or frailties, as a writer. Perhaps because *The Captain's Tiger* is more pointedly autobiographical than any of the other plays, the writing does on occasions do less than justice to Fugard's genius with words. In particular, the description of him losing his virginity in Japan is not altogether convincing, particularly when using such phrases as: 'the bows lifting and falling in a rhythm as seductive as those hips that gave you such a good time in the last port.' **[p 6]** One can wonder if he used Eugene O'Neill as inspiration – O'Neill went to sea and had a problem with alcohol. Other seafaring writers are directly referred to, such as Melville, Conrad and Hemingway, but these references have no real pertinence to a story, the heart of which – to all intents and purposes – is set in the Eastern Cape.

The play is divided into sixteen scenes that all take place close to Number Four hatch aboard the merchantman and where the Author/Tiger sits at his writing table. In this character he is alternatively the sixty-five-year-old author and the Captain's servant, in his twenties. As the Tiger he strikes the ship's bell, eight times, and then sets the scene with a speech directed at the audience. This is followed by the text of the first ship-borne letter he writes to his mother. She is then imagined by him onto the stage as a young girl, Betty, as he begins a novel based on her life and titled *The Story of a South African Woman* – with homage to Olive Schreiner's famous book, *The Story of a South African Farm*. The third character in the play is a Swahili crew member known as the Donkeyman. He speaks little English and is illiterate but becomes fascinated by the Tiger's writing. He has a part to play within that section of the story that concerns the progress of the ship as it sails East, and as a near-silent foil to the young Tiger, but as an illiterate admirer of the writer at work, he is not altogether a convincing addition.

The ship visits a number of places on its journey from Port Said, including Ceylon, Japan and Fiji, but these are mainly irrelevant as the author's writing, and the appearance of his mother as the young Betty, result in a succession of imaginary scenes that are set in Middleburg and Port Elizabeth – and not other foreign parts. The transformation of a table – and a box to sit upon – next to Number Four hatch to an imagined South African landscape is adroitly achieved thanks to Fugard's descriptions. One scene in particular demonstrates this. The author decides that his heroine needs to go out into the veld to think things over but he dramatically converts this into his own scene:

> ...Gathering up her skirts and laughing aloud at herself, she skipped lightly over the last few yards of broken rock to the summit of the koppie. With her heart pounding from both her exertions and a sense of triumph at having made it to the top, she settled down on a warm rock to regain her breath.   **[p 22]**

Betty objects. She did not, or would not, make such a climb with thorny bushes tearing her stockings, but the author persists:

> I know it's a big...heroic image...but that's a deliberate choice. That is what I wanted, what the moment needs, what the story is all about – the Karoo woman as Hero, which is what my mother would have been if life had given her half a chance. You and Olive Schreiner. [p 32]

Betty's response is to tell him that what really happened was they were visited by an aunt from Port Elizabeth who wanted the young girl to return to that city with her. The author reluctantly accepts the truth even though he says 'there's no drama in it', because if he refuses, Betty threatens to leave him [p 33]. This is a nice touch. If the Fugard story is not truthfully and accurately told, the muse will depart.

At the end of the play the Tiger throws the manuscript overboard – as replicated in Fugard's past – because of the conflict between the reality of his mother's hard life and the romantic story he tries to tell. He eventually recognises the truth when, compared to the idealised picture of Betty that he has drawn up to now – based on the photograph in her bedroom of a pretty girl in a white dress – he paints a real picture of her and his father in later life:

> She's...sitting on the side of her bed...her tired old nightie clammy with sweat – the sweat of desperation... clutching her asthma spray with one hand, scratching her graying head with the other. She's trying to work out how she can make the few quid she's got in her bag, pay the café rent, and the boys' wages, and the baker, and the cooldrink man, and the Cadbury's man and all the other bloody parasites that feed off her life. She goes over that pathetic little bit of mental arithmetic again and again, but it never works out... She hasn't got enough... She'll never have enough. Her once beautiful, brown eyes are little pools of anxiety and fear. He is lying in his bed a

few feet away from her, reading old comic books with a
magnifying glass.

Those wonderful, blue eyes are still unclouded...
his fine aristocratic features and complexion smooth
and unlined... They have the repose of a death mask.
He stopped playing the piano a long time ago and she
doesn't dream any more.   [pp 57–58]

In telling the story of his mother, Elizabeth Magdalena Katerina
Potgieter, we see references to other plays. The Tiger tells Betty
that when he left home and hitch- hiked through Africa – it was
a compulsion:

Ever since I was small there's been this feeling inside
me, a sort of yearning for something.

The only thing I knew for sure was that I would never
find it at home. So you've got to leave. That's all there
is to it. You've got to go out there and try and find it
because all the time that feeling is there inside you, like
a bird in a cage wanting to be free.   [p 21]

This sentiment is echoed by Veronica in *Valley Song*. The scene
where Betty discovers that the object of her affections is a cripple
figures, naturally enough, in *'Master Harold'...and the boys*. Again,
when the author places Betty on the summit of the koppie and
gives this description – 'Spread out in front of her was a view
of the Karoo in all its glory – a landscape of muted purples and
browns, and dusty distance' **[p 22]** – we recall such a vision as was
shared by Mr M and Isabel at Wapadsburg Pass. Betty enjoys
the dance she attends but until she meets her husband-to-be she
says to herself, a little like Milly: 'But as the clock moved nearer
the witching hour when the dance would end and everyone go
home, a little voice inside Betty began to ask: Is this it? Is this
all?' **[p 52]**

The ship being in the doldrums symbolically coincides with a
time of writer's block but the real focus of the play is the magis-
terial way that Fugard uses the conjuring up of his mother as a

young girl to write on the rewards, failures and traumas of author-ship. The conversations they have with each other underlines that the writer has control, which the Tiger refers to as 'Creative Authority', but if that writing is not authentic, it will not do. In an interview with Dennis Walder in March 2002, Fugard, talking about *The Captain's Tiger*, commented on this:

> ...as time passes it will be appreciated for a lot of what it says about the craft of writing. How your page talks back to you. That is what I am dramatising there... An internal dialogue that goes on all the time in shaping the work of art. And in *The Captain's Tiger* I found the perfect way to dramatise that: by making my charac-ter come alive and take on a dialogue with the writer – happy with some of it, then very angry.

> **[Walder 2004, p 70]**

The picture of a supposedly fictional character threatening to depart the writer's imagination if angry with the words being written is a fascinating conceit, but is there another slant? Is this a reference to the need to find another subject now that the prin-cipal apartheid source is no longer available? Perhaps, but then in his next play, *Sorrows and Rejoicings*, he makes that source avail-able again – in a modern setting – with marked success.

The Homecoming

In the post-1990 period it is arguable that Fugard's finest work is *Sorrows and Rejoicings* – although not all critics held this view. However, when seen in London in 2002, the delicate relationship between the characters, affected as they had been in the past by the constraints of apartheid – particularly exile – married to the successful device of the man in the case appearing on stage at different moments in his life, provided a memorable night at the theatre.

While at university Allison, of English extraction, meets Afrikaner Dawid, who is a left-wing lecturer with ambitions to be a poet, and they marry. He takes his new wife to his family home in the Karoo where she meets the housekeeper, Marta, a Coloured woman who had been Dawid's mistress. They have a daughter, Rebecca. As a result of his political activities, Dawid elects to go into exile rather than be subject to a banning order. He believes that his poetic creativity will flourish away from apartheid South Africa but the opposite proves to be the case and as a result he begins to drink to excess. He eventually returns home where there is some form of reconciliation with his antagonistic daughter before he dies.

The plot requires the actor playing Dawid to appear as a broken man of fifty-one, then at the age of thirty-six 'full of energy and passionate conviction' [p 23], and later, when in exile, as a man under the influence of alcohol. We see him again in pyjamas and dressing gown just before he dies and finally at the end of the play when he is required to re-appear as the young Dawid on the night he first made love to Marta. This might seem an unwieldy device but on stage, as witnessed at the Tricycle Theatre with Marius Weyers in the role, it worked. And not just as a device – the appearance of Dawid in his different personas is integral, if not paramount, in the structure of the play. In an earlier draft there were no shifts in time; Dawid returns home at the beginning of the play and dies before the interval so that the second act is only concerned with the three women. We can only be pleased that this version was jettisoned.

The time is said to be the present but the introduction of Dawid at different stages in his life enables flashbacks to be created of cinematic quality. The stable time is just after Dawid's funeral when the three women in his life gather in the living room of his house in the Karoo. Marta is the most interesting of these. In the Fugard canon she is the true successor to Lena, with a similar singular spirit. She is sensitive to Dawid's aspirations as a poet but when he says, 'exile is going to give me back my voice, Marta' [p 24], she instinctively knows it is the wrong decision. She complains: 'it was all that politics that got him into trouble – he was meant to be a poet not a politician' [p 22], to which Allison, who realises the full tragedy of Dawid's life, replies: 'in this country you cannot separate the two' [p 22]. Fugard presaged this point of view in an address he made in 1990:

> The notion that there could be a South African story that doesn't have political resonance is laughable. When it comes down to it, any story, from any time in history, from any society, is political – if you take the word 'political' in its broadest and most meaningful sense. Every act of story-telling is in a sense a political action. Certainly this is so in South Africa, which is unbelievably politicized... Politics is there in everything we do in South Africa. So the notion of telling a story in South Africa and not being political is naïve. I know, particularly as I have an interest in the dispossessed of my country, with whom I identify very strongly, it is inevitable that there is going to be a political by-product to what I make.
> [Barbera 1993, p 385]

Dawid's tragedy appears to be mid-way between the case of Fugard himself, who refused the one-way exit permit and that of Breyten Breytenbach, who defied the system, returned from exile and was jailed for alleged terrorism: 'A traumatic event for the Afrikaner power base – their Shakespeare had gone as far as to try and launch a guerrilla army.' [Allister Sparks: Personal interview, October 2000.] As Fugard mentions in the 2002 interview with Dennis Walder referred to in the discussion on *The Captain's Tiger*, some of the greatest works in English have been produced by writers away from their home shores – Joseph Conrad being the prime example – but Dawid is no Conrad. The playwright could have avoided the loss of his passport if he had taken the exile option but he did not and while restricted to South Africa produced some of his finest work. Dawid does not have the strength to do this but his initial motives for leaving appear genuine enough:

> That is what I am going to try to do, Marta. That is why I am leaving the country. My writing is the only weapon I've got. Without it I'm useless. And that is

what that bloody banning order has made me... useless!
I can't read. I can't be published. I can't be quoted. You
know what comes next? 'So why bother to write, Dawid
Olivier?   [p 24]

However, he fails to understand how strong, and important, are
his roots – and his language. He recalls the guilt he felt when he
failed to return from London for his grandfather's funeral:

> ... I wanted to ask his forgiveness for not being there
> at the funeral... I wanted to make up for it by promis-
> ing him that when I died I would be buried with him
> and Ouma...but I couldn't remember any Afrikaans...
> I didn't want to speak to him in English, but I couldn't
> find the Afrikaans words I needed.
>
> Don't need Freud or Jung to work that one out, do
> we. Of all the fears I lived with over there, that was
> the worst. Dying in exile was one thing, but living in
> exile without your soul? Because that is what it would
> have been, not so? I mean, your soul speaks with your
> mother's tongue.   [pp 42–43]

So, not only does exile kill his inspiration, it destroyed his soul
– and his manhood. Another of Fugard's exiles was Steve in *A
Lesson from Aloes*, who is driven to leave, amongst other reasons,
because the security police 'laughed at his manhood'. Dawid
suffers similarly. He sees the banning order as being '...silenced
into impotence by the Government' and so conceives of a short
story about someone in his situation who cuts off his testicles and
sends them to the prime minister with a note: '"You took away my
manhood, so why not take these as well." That's when I knew I
had to leave' [p 25].

He inspires the love of two women, seen in the play as the
Chorus that defines him, but he is a flawed character, selfish and
weak, providing limited happiness for them. As Dawid's unsat-
isfactory life unfolds we see how much stronger was his love for
Marta than for his wife. He needed the Karoo to succour his

poetic muse, as well as the Afrikaner language which Marta, who was part of his world, could give him but which Allison could not. As Dawid says: 'your soul speaks with your mother's tongue' **[p 43]**. He tells Marta that he is not running away – 'I'm leaving because I want to fight' **[p 24]** – but when democracy comes, he opts out again and fails to vote in London, preferring to drown his sorrows in drink – an excuse which can hardly explain why in the Western Cape the Coloured population failed to vote in the ANC at the 1994 election.

The real 'Sorrows' in the play are not the fates of Marta and Rebecca but the failure of Dawid. He leaves Marta and their daughter Rebecca the stinkwood table but this only emphasises the differences in class and ethnic structure. Dawid waxes lyrical about the origins of the table, coming from a tree known as the King of the Knysna forest, and recalls how the family would sit at it to say grace and eat food. Marta, on the other hand, is only good enough to clean it, to shine it with her tears and take from it the 'scraps and leftovers' **[p 11]**, much as she has to accept in her relationship with Dawid. Rebecca hates the way her father has treated Marta and in anger calls her mother 'An Old Stinkwood Servant'.

However, she is rather more than that. To continue the comparison with Lena, she owns only what she can carry but Marta finishes up as the proprietor, in trust for her daughter, of the Karoo property – and the important prop in the play, the stinkwood table. However, as suggested in an article by Marianne McDonald, is this table and the property a metaphor for the new South Africa that has been handed over to the likes of Marta. Will she and her fellow citizens keep well their country – and the table – or sell it, or burn it? **[Theatre Forum, 2002 p 11]**.

In the context of 'burn it' there are a number of references to fire in the play. When it is revealed that Rebecca has burnt all of the poems left behind by her father, this prompts Allison to recall that in London he tried to write a piece entitled, *The Fires of South Africa*. She remembers some lines:

Fires of sorrow

Fires of hate
Incendiary tears
Ignite our fate   **[p 50]**

Boesman and Lena's fate is to be treated as white man's rubbish.
When the white man set fire to their Korston *pondok*, Boesman
says they were not just burning down their dwelling: 'There was
something else in that fire, something rotten. Us! Our sad stories,
our smells, our world.' **[p 229]** However, the strongest fire of all
was the love Dawid engendered in Marta:

> There was a fire inside him and little Marta Barends
> warmed her life by sitting as close to it as she could. I
> suppose some people would say she got too close and
> got burnt.   **[p 38]**

In contrast, Lena asks Boesman why he hits her: 'To keep your
life warm? Learn to dance, Boesman. Leave your bruises on the
earth.' **[p 237]**

Marta's first words in the play are: 'That's right nothing has
changed' **[p 6]**. This refers to the Karoo house but it might
also be true for herself and her people in the new South Africa
– 'nothing has changed'. Allison tries to justify Dawid's life by
saying: 'Without people like him, Marta, you would still be living
in the old South Africa' **[p 22]**, to which Marta replies: 'I still am'.
However, as in so much of Fugard's work, there is hope. During
Dawid's last flashback appearance he quotes Eugène Marais from
his *Song of South Africa*: 'South Africa gives nothing but demands
everything' **[p 53]**. Marta understands this. She has been the giver
but the reconciliation with her daughter at the end of the play is
her final reward; Rebecca is the property bequeathed by Dawid
she cherishes the most, the 'Rejoicings' that counter Dawid's
'Sorrows'. Not so for Lena. She has no living children.

There was an interval of over thirty years between the first
performance of *Boesman and Lena* and *Sorrows and Rejoicings,* but
there are some striking similarities in the two plays, not least
in the weakness of the two male characters and the strength of

the females. Here Marta represents a continuation of Fugard's portraits of strong and ultimately rebellious women. Both Lena and Marta are based on people from his own life: the origins of Lena have already been described while Marta is partially based on servants Fugard knew in the Karoo. The play is dedicated to Mary Benson, who was the model for Allison, and to Katrina and Dudu, two Karoo housekeeper friends of his.

Marta is not however featured in the play as a housekeeper, but as an object of love. It might just be possible to discern love as one element in the reason why Lena stays with Boesman, but in *Sorrows and Rejoicings,* love is a primary theme. Milly, Hester and Lena are sad spirits, albeit resilient ones, but Marta is more phlegmatic and at ease with herself than Fugard's other Amazons. It therefore seems reasonable to suggest that, although ironically *Sorrows and Rejoicings* was the first of his plays to be entirely written outside South Africa, Fugard has followed Albie Sachs' advice and written about love.

In 1989 Sachs – a white South African Jewish lawyer and a leading member of the ANC, later a Justice of the Constitutional Court of South Africa – propounded that using culture as a weapon in the freedom struggle should be banned. This controversial statement, that first appeared in the *Weekly Mail* in February 1990, was made in a paper, *Preparing ourselves for Power,* that was composed for an ANC in-house seminar on culture. From this paper:

> In the first place, it results in an impoverishment of our art. Instead of getting real criticism we get solidarity criticism. Our artists are not pushed to improve the quality of their work, it is enough that it be politically correct. The more fists and spears and guns, the better. The range of themes is narrowed down so much that all that is funny, or curious or genuinely tragic in the world is extruded.
>
> ... Instead, whether in poetry or painting or on the stage, we line up our good people on the one side and the bad ones on the other...you can tell who the good

ones are, because in addition to being handsome of appearance, they can all recite sections of the Freedom Charter or passages of Strategy and Tactics at the drop of a beret.

... And what about love? We have published so many anthologies and journals and occasional poems and stories, and the number that deal with love do not make the fingers of a hand. Can it be that once we join the ANC we do not make love any more, that when the comrades go to bed they discuss the role of the white working class?   [de Kok and Press 1990, pp 20 & 21]

Fugard's portrait of Marta is, in basic terms, an example of post-apartheid writing in so far as 'time and place' are concerned but is it in fact, 'the same old story'. Perhaps so; but there is also a strong sense of reconciliation in the latest play that reflects the new mood in the country. Allison returns to London, where she is happiest, while Marta is left with her memories – but above all the play celebrates the reconciliation of mother and daughter in the new South Africa. Rebecca spends nearly all of the play standing in the doorway to the living-room where the action takes place – even if converted at one point to a space in London occupied by a drunken Dawid. Fugard's experience with the girls in *My Life* – and continuing from the creation of Veronica – would have helped him in constructing Rebecca and Victoria in *Victory* – because we can see in Marta's daughter an example of the new liberated South African who has to decide whether to come into this new world – or remain on the threshold. However, at the end of the play, the text has them leaving the room together and evidently when the play was performed in New York, Marta has her arm around Rebecca. Reconciliation in word and deed.

Fan the flame of your purpose. Make it burn as big and bright as you can

The purpose referred to is Fugard's passion for the stage that he, at last in his career, demonstrates not in the quality of his plays, but in a drama that makes a direct reference to it. This is *Exits and Entrances*. It would fit comfortably in Chapter Eight of this book, 'Art and Rebellion', as it is passionately concerned with the art of theatre represented from a position centre-stage by the actor, 'André' and from the wings by 'The Playwright'. Some of Fugard's familiar themes are present: human relationships, disillusionment, Christian faith – or the absence of it – and some references to the presence of politics and race outside the theatre; but nevertheless this play, unlike his other works, has the world of dramatic art as the over-arching subject.

The two characters in the play are André Huguenet, often referred to as the Afrikaner Laurence Olivier, and 'The Playwright' – Fugard as a young man. The play is neatly staged. Fugard's characteristically simple and unchanging set is used to represent the room of a Port Elizabeth apartment where the writer works in 1961 and as dressing rooms at the Labia Theatre in Cape Town in 1956 and the Opera House in Port Elizabeth in 1961. The first performance was at the Fountain Theatre in Los Angeles on 13 May 2004 and it was then seen at the Edinburgh Festival in 2007 – with the original cast – where *The Times* theatre critic, Benedict Nightingale, called it 'an intelligent and touching play'.

Reference is made in his review to Ronald Harwood's *The Dresser* but this is not altogether pertinent. Harwood's play concerns a long-term relationship between a grand old man of the theatre, based on Donald Wolfit – Harwood, who was born in South Africa, worked with Wolfit's touring Shakespeare company – and his faithful dresser. In the original production these parts were played by Albert Finney and Tom Courtenay, but in the Fugard piece the intercourse between the two men on stage is there to flesh out the career of each, rather than to show what they do, or have done, together. Comparison can also be made to David Mamet's play *Life in the Theatre*, which concerns two people in somewhat similar circumstances to those in *Exits and Entrances* – but in the American play we have an 'All about Eve' situation, where in time the junior actor eclipses the senior one. In the Fugard play the decline of André is charted but the main thrust shows the younger man, influenced by the older, progressing as a writer rather than a performer.

True to Fugard, there is again an offstage character in this play who has some relevance to the professions of both writer and actor, but this time he is a presence of some eminence, namely Eugène Marais, whose own life is featured in the film Fugard made with Ross Devenish, *The Guest*. André meets him when filling in time between acting roles and employed as a reporter on a Pretoria newspaper, where Marais also worked. André and The Playwright have been discussing what is home for them. The former explains that for him it is the stage while The Playwright prosaically says: '...the Sea Point flat where I live with my wife' [p 19]. In later life he might well have agreed with the vision of home as presented by Marais:

> ... I asked him where his 'home' was. He smiled and then held up the sheet of blank paper that was on his desk in front of him.
>
> ... Afterwards I thought a lot about that moment and I did finally get his meaning. He was a writer. A great writer. Words on paper is what his life had been all about. That blank sheet of paper was his real home.
>
> [p 20]

On another occasion André tells Marais of his dreams for a significant Afrikaner theatre. Marais gives these aspirations his blessing with the words: 'Fan the flame of your purpose. Make it burn as big and bright as you can.' André then passes these words, and the blessing, onto The Playwright.

Fugard demonstrates the triumphs of André while contrasting acting and writing. The rise and fall of the actor's career is documented on stage as he moves from a majestic Oedipus to play the Cardinal in *The Prisoner* by Bridget Boland. In the earlier role, The Playwright recalls:

> ...the most awful cry that any member of that audience had ever heard. It sounded as if he had somehow

> reached down into himself and was dragging his geni-
> tals up through his body and throat... And that was not
> just one memorable performance! Oh no. André knew
> it was the moment of the play, so he hit that mark with
> uncanny accuracy virtually every night.   [p 8]

This example of grand theatre is then contrasted with the Cardinal
who is being humiliated and made to scrub floors by a totalitarian
government in a mid-European country. André explains that his
apprenticeship for this more humble role was served when he was
reduced to working as the manager of a Pretoria cinema when a
stage role could not be found:

> The lobby of the Pigalle turned out to be a blessing in
> disguise, because as things worked out, it was actually a
> rehearsal room for the performance you saw tonight.
> ...terrified that one of my admirers from the past would
> come in and see where the great André Huguenet had
> ended up, dying every day of humiliation and shame, I
> was in fact preparing for my farewell performance.
>   [p 29]

In contrast to André's big dramatic picture, with its ups and
downs, the progress of the writer's career is shown in more modest
tones.

The Playwright tells André, in somewhat brutal terms, that his
crippled father is about to die. When asked what is wrong with
him, the son says: 'Nobody needs him any more. None of us have
any space for him in our lives', and as a consequence 'he is dying
of unimportance' [p 25]. They then move on to discuss writing
and the Playwright talks of a play about two brothers that has
just been finished. This provokes a dialogue that highlights the
difference between the full-blooded Afrikaner and Fugard, only
half Afrikaner:

PLAYWRIGHT: One is light skinned, one dark...

ANDRÉ: And both of them no doubt nose-pickers who speak the English language badly [...]

PLAYWRIGHT: They live in a *pondok* in one of the local slums... [...]

ANDRÉ: I give up! You're not taking me seriously. Is it perversity that makes you devote the glorious energy of your young life, of whatever talent you've got, to crawling into stinking *pondoks*? Why? Explain to me.

PLAYWRIGHT: It's a world of untold stories. For any writer that's a gift from the gods

ANDRÉ: Gift from the gods? What you've described to me is a nightmare. [...] But just remember you're a white man and try telling stories about your own people.

PLAYWRIGHT: If I find a good one I will.

ANDRÉ: What do you mean? You've already got it. It's staring you in the face [...] Your father, for heaven's sake [...] There'd be a good role for me in that one! And what's more you've already got your title: *A Man of No Importance*.

PLAYWRIGHT: [...] You know André, that phrase you used... 'our people'. If you don't mind me saying so, that is exactly what is wrong with our theatre – with this whole damned country for that matter. Because as far as I'm concerned the people of the slums are also 'my people'. I can't pretend they don't exist. [...]

ANDRÉ: And do you think your plays, or anybody elses for that matter, are going to make a difference?

PLAYWRIGHT: I don't know. But wasn't that the hope you had for your theatre...once upon a time? Wasn't it going to 'wake up the Afrikaner and make him think'? Your words! [...]

ANDRÉ: [...] Wake up the Afrikaner and make him think? Did I really say that? What a fool! Look at

them. It's worse now than when I started out thirty-
five years ago. The guardians of the *volk* have locked
up this country and thrown away the key. If you
think they are going to allow any changes, you've
got another guess coming.

PLAYWRIGHT: If that was true, if I really believed
there was nothing we could do to change it... I don't
know...maybe it would be time then for a suicide
pact between us.   [pp 26–28]

On stage are two artistic white men. There is a relationship
between them – not familial as in so many Fugard examples –
but of mentor and pupil/admirer, more akin to Helen and Elsa.
Within the play they are not seen to be affected by the apartheid
policies of the 1950s and 1960s – although The Playwright returns
from London because of Sharpeville and they do have different
attitudes towards the dispossessed – but what they do represent is
the other apartheid within the white community. This has already
been explored in comparing Piet and Gladys, but in this play the
two opposites are intellectuals. Fugard as The Playwright may not
be a true representative of the English-speaking stock – he is half
Afrikaner anyway – but he writes in English and from the English-
liberal viewpoint. André on the other hand, with Eugène Marias
as shadow, is Afrikaner to the core. It is he who dreams of using
the theatre to: '...break the shackles that the *vervloekte* dominees
and politicians were forging around our minds and souls', but he
is only concerned with the minds and souls of the Afrikaner.

This mantle was then assumed by Fugard who, rather more
successfully, used his theatre to try and break the bonds that
bound up the mass of the South African dispossessed. In an interview published on the web by 'Tonight' (Western Cape) on 25
May 2004, Fugard said: 'Looking back, I realise that André's
vision of theatre was ultimately too limited. It did not encompass
all South Africans. The only way forward, then as now, is by inclu-
sion; by having a vision that truly embraces our multicultural

identity. A theatre for the Afrikaner was really not enough. It was not what South Africa needed then and not what it needs now.'

However, the play shows the affection they have for each other so there is another example of reconciliation on view. Less difficult to achieve perhaps than between Gideon and Martinus but there had been, and to an extent there still is, a wedge between these two white communities that *Exits and Entrances* shows can be bridged.

Richard Hornby sees another aspect of this divide. In an article in the *Hudson Review* of 2005 he considers that André represents the aesthete in dramatic art that 'elevates and ennobles' contrasting with that of Fugard, 'realistic and moral, teaching audiences about social problems'. He accepts that these are not always in opposition to each other but the South African situation renders these two definitions much more complex. Hornby goes on to say that in *Exits and Entrances* Fugard has straddled both but in the local context, it seems more relevant to consult Ian Steadman's view discussed in Chapter Nine and consider the continuum in Fugard's work from *My Children! My Africa!* – that Steadman saw as the first play of the plays to be both liberal and liberating – to his post-apartheid work. Although *Exits and Entrances* shows once again that Fugard is not principally a political writer: we only need to wait for the next one, *Victory*, to return to that grazing ground.

A Hollow victory

While *Exits and Entrances* was on stage at the 2007 Edinburgh Festival, Fugard's latest play, *Victory*, was being performed during the Peter Hall season at the Theatre Royal, Bath. The audience for this new play could have complained that they were getting little value for the price of the ticket as the action on stage was all over in less than one hour – with no interval – but it is a powerful work that puts Fugard back into his best scenario: the after-effects of politics and their impact on human relationships. Unusually for him the set is in no way minimalist. The scene is an overcrowded, somewhat shabby, sitting room in what would appear to be a house of some substance. The property is that of Lionel Benson, a retired teacher who is clearly a book-lover. The set is dominated, left and right, by bookshelves that tower over the stage; the designer has clearly decided that they are to be both practical and symbolic as the top shelves are out of reach of even the most gargantuan set of a library steps.

The books themselves represent the possessions of the privileged white man and they are used to demonstrate this when, at the start of the play, the two intruders onto this scene drags piles of them from the lower shelves to be scattered around the floor and used as a target for urine. These two are both Coloured, Victoria (Vicky), whose mother, now deceased, was Lionel's cleaner – and friend – for many years, and the young girl's disreputable boyfriend, Freddie Blom. This unhappy youth, hyped up with dagga, has broken into the house firstly to vent his resentment on the fact that in the new democratic South Africa the white man still enjoys all the privileges while he has nothing, and also to steal money to enable him to leave the Karoo to join a Cape Town gang. Vicky is a reluctant housebreaker but she is so besotted with Freddie she joins the enterprise to discover the money she believes the house contains.

Lionel returns unexpectedly and the two intruders tie him to a chair while they continue to act out their pointless search. Lionel is not concerned for his possessions – or his personal safety. What devastates him is that the daughter of his friend should have betrayed him – leading to him expressing his despair, as Fugard is doing, that the 'Rainbow' nation has failed to deliver on its promises. The play ends in a melodramatic fashion – unlike anything Fugard has written before – with Lionel being shot by accident, Freddie fleeing the disaster leaving Vicky on her knees facing the audience and singing quietly and forlornly as the curtain falls.

In the programme produced for the presentation at Bath, Fugard introduces the play using a short article entitled 'Writing Victory'. In this he properly compares his new creation, Victoria, with Veronica in *Valley Song* – he could also have referred to Rebecca in *Sorrows and Rejoicings* – and goes on to raise the question as to what the latest play says about the state of South Africa today:

> I won't pre-empt your response to this play by trying to give you an answer to that question. Even a superficial acquaintance with the news coming out of South Africa must however make you realise that your answer will depend on whether you are an embattled white living in a maximum security enclave in one of our cities, or a destitute black trying to survive the squalor of one of our many slums...our euphemistically called 'informal settlements'.

The play, in microcosm, is about the contrast between these two environments. He ends his piece:

> My subject has always been the desperate individual, and, tragically, there are more than enough of them in the new South Africa.

Despite this, we leave the theatre with the final picture of Vicky expressing some sense of hope and wondering if her creator's somewhat jaundiced view is a product of the fact that he now spends most of his time in California. The gap between the 'haves' and the 'have nots' in South Africa is still unacceptably wide but Vicky is not going to become a Lena and if Freddie is indicted for burglary, he will get a fair trial and will not be digging holes in the beaches of Robben Island. Whatever, outside of the main theme of the drama we are left regretting that the play's brevity means that the early years of Lionel are not fleshed out, nor his relationship with Vicky's mother. Were they just good friends – faithful servant and benevolent employer – or was there a closer attachment? Or, in the context of the play's principal message of betrayal and the frustration of the under-privileged young, does the history of Vicky's mother really matter? The final chapter of this book tries to answer that question.

ELEVEN

What's changed?

Hands burn
for a stone, a bomb,
to shiver down the glass.
Nothing's changed.

Tatamkhula Afrika

I t is nearly six years since I sat in a studio theatre in Dublin and listened to Athol Fugard and now I find myself in another intimate theatrical space in London watching a revival of *Hello and Goodbye*. This venue is the Trafalgar Studios 2, part of the former Whitehall Theatre, famous in the past for Brian Rix and what became known as the 'Whitehall Farces'.

From the analysis in Chapter Four it is clear that *Hello and Goodbye* is not a farce. It is one of Fugard's minimalist but powerful domestic dramas that deals with a dysfunctional South African family. In this particular production one of the causes of this dysfunction has been more emphasised than in earlier stagings, namely the strict Calvinist religion that so powerfully controlled the lives of the members of this family; but this emphasis does not distort the impact the play has today, any more than it would have in the 1960s. At the Trafalgar Studios 2 the British actors provide the dialogue in South African accents but no one can escape the fact that forty years after the play was written, Johnnie and Hester are to be found today perhaps amongst the 'trailer trash' of the USA, in the affluent suburbs of cities in Austria – or anywhere. Families still fall apart, all over the world, and at any time. *Hello and Goodbye* refers to specifics within the South African political and social landscape, but the outcome of similar family breakdowns do not require these; the shortcomings in the characters of this brother and sister – and particularly in their parents – are formed by universal human frailties. Apartheid cannot be blamed, and is hardly even alluded to in the play, and I conjecture that as we have seen, for instance, *The Merchant of Venice* located in the dealing room of a twenty-first century city bank and a *Romeo and Juliet* replete with motor cycles, will the next revival of *Hello and Goodbye* be given in a Northern accent (shades of David Storey), or in the drawl of the Southern USA (courtesy of a Tennessee Williams)?

But back to London of 2008. This was a production of which Fugard would have been proud, even though his script has a 'Johnnie' and not a 'Johnny', as shown in the latest programme. The intimacy provided by the small acting area of this studio theatre lends itself to a set design that gives a striking representation of the tawdry lounge-cum-kitchen or kitchen-cum-bedroom at 57A Valley Road. This intimacy also adds strength to the acting of Rafe Spall and Saskia Reeves who well understand the characters the playwright has created and presents them to us with bravura performances.

Some current critics felt that Hester's acceptance of her brother's falsehood about the father was a flaw in the work, but an opposite viewpoint carries some weight. When she does enter the bedroom and discover the truth, this moment provides a denouement that, however expected, moves in two directions: firstly as an oblique anti-climax when she realises her journey to say 'Hello' to Johnnie and collect her share of the compensation has been wasted; but it then also provides the 'Goodbye' with that elusive Fugardian glimpse of hope as she wishes her brother well, and he closes the play with the word 'Resurrection'. However, this mildly upbeat ending raises the question, as it has always done, as to whether their sorry lives are likely to be resurrected in a better form in the future? This then naturally echoes the larger one for South Africa in the twenty-first century: has the world Fugard has given us changed and if so, is it for the better – or is the society still creating Lenas and Hesters?

Is this query capable of answer? As I am enjoying seeing a Fugard play on stage again, in the English studies being taught to my fourteen-year-old grandson he is, and so am I, being introduced to the poetry of Tatamkhula Afrika, who provides the heading for this concluding chapter. It comes from a poem entitled *Nothing's Changed* that records the poet's feelings on returning to the wasteland that was once District Six in Cape Town, where he used to live. It is a bitter piece contrasting a 'whites-only' eating establishment with a working man's café, but the title refers to his view, post-apartheid, that democracy has brought little change to the underprivileged in South Africa. It would appear this poet's history and background places him in a sound position to judge. He had a long life – born in 1920, died in 2002 – and served in the Second World War. Although he would be classified as Coloured, after the war he was accepted as a son by a conservative Afrikaner family and in this guise he was known as Jozua Francois Joubert. After working in South-West Africa he came to Cape Town, joined the ANC and became a Muslim. He was imprisoned, more than once, for his political activities and within the ANC given the name, Tatamkhula Afrika, which translates as grandfather – or great father – of Africa. The poem, *Nothing's Changed,* was written just after the fall of apartheid.

Marta, in *Sorrows and Rejoicings,* repeats this. When she tells Allison she is still living in the old South Africa, she invites her rival to: '...walk around the village tomorrow and see how much of the "new South Africa" you can find.' Allison contemplates re-visiting the village school, whereupon Marta says: 'Same old building. Government keeps promising us money to do it up, but I'll believe it when I see it.' This would seem to indicate that Tatamkhula Afrika's pessimism is shared by Fugard, and his latest play, *Victory*, does little to change that view. On the other hand the overall mood of his post-1990 writings is less bleak than some of his earlier plays. *My Life* projects a positive impression and we can believe that the young Veronica and the young Rebecca will not finish up like so many of their predecessors: '...walking barefoot in the veld every day with a baby on your back to collect firewood.' Furthermore, these expressions of pessimism ignore the mammoth task involved in effecting real change and discounts what has actually been achieved in South Africa since 1990. The gap between the rich and the poor is still very evident, but there are now more black South Africans amongst the former – thanks, to some extent, to the policies of Black Empowerment. As an example, even within Anglo-American, the conglomerate that in the past has epitomised white capitalism in the country, it has recently been announced that part ownership in this undertaking will be passed into the hands of black companies. This can be seen as a major breakthrough, even if this dilution is in fact a trade-off for the renewal by the government of some mining licences.

However, this book is not a discourse on South African politics and capitalism, pre- and post-apartheid. What is more relevant is to consider what changes have taken place on the Fugard stage since Mannie Manim opened the curtain to reveal *No-Good Friday* on 30 August 1958, until the audience settled into their seats, nearly fifty years later, at the Theatre Royal in Bath. In that half a century Fugard has provided a new major work for the theatre at intervals of around one every two years, and he shows no signs of stopping. In the *Telegraph Revue* of 4 August 2007 he writes about his work at the time that *Victory* was about to open in Bath:

> Writing went well today. I smelt the end of one of the plays. I realise that I wanted to end it with an image of a rainbow. I work every day though I still feel insecure about what I've written and sometimes wonder whether I haven't conned everybody.

I began this book expressing some admiration for Athol Fugard – I am far from being conned – and intend to sing the same song whilst engaged in this final analysis, where I choose to concentrate on the cast of the plays, rather than the works themselves. This book, perhaps inevitably, has developed to be more a treatise on his people than anything else, and I contend that this is a pleasing outcome. At one level it could be said that almost all literature is only concerned with humankind and certainly Fugard's humankind is of infinite interest. They are mostly what can be described as 'small people' but in Fugard's hands many of them have become unforgettable, if not giants of the stage.

Have these changed over time? Fugard's career has not shown a steady development throughout his life. Like all artists there are peaks and troughs – what he refers to as 'aberrations' – but if it is clear that some of his plays are more valuable than others, there is a consistency about the quality and authenticity of his characterisations that is very precious. As I have already argued in the case of Hester and Johnnie, that authenticity does not depend on a South African context; Lena is another Mother Courage and Sam would have found favour in the eyes of Tolstoy. It is a galaxy of vibrant people; no one in this playwright's lexicon is bland.

Many of them share very similar traits. Look at defiance and courage. In his plays it is defiance against formidable opponents, even if in many cases these are so often unseen. We do not have on stage the bulldozer that demolishes Boesman and Lena's last habitat, but we are made painfully aware of the many destructions in the past. We can imagine Helen's neighbours and the warders who control the lives of John and Winston just as vividly as the specific threat, standing in the wings, posed by Ethel, and her brother. Queeny sees her chance of real happiness walk out of her shebeen because, like a number of Fugard's masculine creations, Johnny does not have the same supply of courage that she has. Both Lena and Hester's futures are grim, to say the least, but the itinerant rescues her relationship with her companion and the frustrated prostitute still has room to sympathise with her unhappy brother.

We may find it difficult to believe that the two murderers have found any satisfactory measure of forgiveness on that New Year's Eve in 1989, or that Marta can still love the man who has treated her so ill, but never mind incredulity, we care. That is what Fugard has achieved throughout his career; he has compelled the viewing public to be concerned about his people. We tolerate, or overlook, the flaws in Mr M, because he is an unforgettable character. When the candles are lit we see the same radiance in Miss Helen as do Elsa and Marius. She is not a stereotyped heroine; she is a wizened old lady, but in Fugard's hands she becomes, to forgive the hyperbole, a mixture of Cleopatra and Joan of Arc. And then there is love. As he said at our meeting in November 2002: 'I always write about love.' How true. His love stories are never conventional. Mr M dies because of an unarticulated love for Thami; and who but Fugard would have set his most poignant story of romance in the mud alongside the Swartkops River? So often the lovers are incongruous in their contrast to each other. Frieda and Errol are obvious examples, but Helen and Elsa, although both women, are extreme opposites in so far as age and political viewpoints are concerned. The affection between a middle-aged black man and a white boy in South Africa is doomed to failure, but perhaps the ultimate tragedy is that of Sophia. Has any writer better made clear the difference between being the loved and being the lover? Sophia is the lover, but it brings little joy when this passion is not reciprocated.

It could be said that although his characters continue in brilliance, the stories become smaller and shorter. His latest plays are more miniatures, more personal, than the great political masterpieces of *Boesman and Lena* and *My Children! My Africa!* This is no doubt a reflection of advancing years, but there has been no diminution in quality. What is seen is that as the words get fewer, the people get younger – and that shall be the epitaph to this book.

Except for Master Harold and the schoolchildren in *My Children! My Africa!*, all of his earlier creations are well out of puberty, but in the new South Africa the picture changes. Not, however, completely. In the UK production of *Victory*, Lionel was played by Richard Johnson – a veteran of the stage and a founder member of the Royal Shakespeare Company – and André Huguenet is hardly a stripling. There is still plenty of variety but things have changed. The baton of 'courageous pessimism' that Fugard has carried for so long has now been handed over to the courage and hopefulness of the young. As I conclude the writing of this book we do not know whether the next President of the USA might be a black man – or a woman – so in South Africa, is it possible to see in the future a Rebecca as that country's next leader? Fugard would applaud such a happening; final recognition for one of his 'strong women'.

Glossary

Abakwetha	Recently circumcised Xhosa initiates to manhood
Aina	An exclamation of pain
Beneukt	Unreasonable, contrary
Boetie	Brother
Donner	'bastard'
Hodoshe	'carrion fly' – nickname of Chief Warder at Robben Island
Hotnot(s)	An offensive mode of address to a Coloured person
Kaal	Naked
Maak sy bek oop	'open its mouth'
Meid	A non-white girl. Servant
Moeg	Tired. Weary
Moer	Obscene exclamation – womb
Ou boeta	Address to older brother
Ouma	Grandmother
Pondck	Shack
Sies	Exclamation of disgust
Sies wêreld	Exclamation of disgust towards the world
Swartgat	Abusive name for black man – black arse
Vat jou goed en trek	'take your things and go'
Verkrampte	Ultra-conservative
Vlenterbroek	Torn trousers
Voetsek	A rough command to be off
Voortrekker	Boer pioneer – member of the Great Trek
Weg werald kom brandewyn	'go away world, come brandy'

Bibliography and References

Works by Athol Fugard referred to in the text

BLOOD KNOT: *Port Elizabeth Plays* (Oxford, Oxford University Press, 2000), 51–123

BOESMAN AND LENA: *Port Elizabeth Plays* (Oxford, Oxford University Press, 2000), 191–247

THE CAPTAIN'S TIGER: *The Captain's Tiger: A Memoir for the Stage* (New York, Theatre Communications Group, 1999)

THE COAT: *Township Plays* (Oxford, Oxford University Press, 2000), 121–145

DIMETOS: *Interior Plays* (Oxford, Oxford University Press, 2000), 107–164

EXITS AND ENTRANCES: *Exits and Entrances* (New York, Dramatists Play Service, 2005)

THE GUEST (with Ross Devenish): *Interior Plays* (Oxford, Oxford University Press, 2000), 165–215

HELLO AND GOODBYE: *Port Elizabeth Plays* (Oxford, Oxford University Press, 2000), 125–189

THE ISLAND: *Township Plays* (Oxford, Oxford University Press, 2000), 193–227

A LESSON FROM ALOES: *Interior Plays* (Oxford, Oxford University Press, 2000), 217–270

MARIGOLDS IN AUGUST (with Ross Devenish): *Marigolds in August and The Guest* (New York, Theatre Communications Group, 1992)

'MASTER HAROLD'...AND THE BOYS: *Port Elizabeth Plays* (Oxford, Oxford University Press, 2000), 1–49

MY CHILDREN! MY AFRICA!: *Plays One* (London, Faber and Faber, 1998), 149–247

MY LIFE: *My Life and Valley Song* (Johannesburg, Witwatersrand University Press, 1996)

NO-GOOD FRIDAY: *Township Plays* (Oxford, Oxford University Press, 2000), 1–54

NONGOGO: *Township Plays* (Oxford, Oxford University Press, 2000), 55–120

ORESTES: *Theatre One*, Stephen Gray (ed) (Johannesburg, Ad Donker, 1978), 81–93

PEOPLE ARE LIVING THERE: *Interior Plays* (Oxford, Oxford University Press, 2000), 1–74

A PLACE WITH THE PIGS: *Playland and A Place with the Pigs* (New York, Theatre Communications Group, 1993)

PLAYLAND: *Playland and A Place with the Pigs* (New York, Theatre Communications Group, 1993)

THE ROAD TO MECCA: *The Road to Mecca* (London, Faber and Faber, 1985)

SIZWE BANSI IS DEAD: *Township Plays* (Oxford, Oxford University Press, 2000), 147–192

SORROWS AND REJOICINGS: *Sorrows and Rejoicings* (New York, Theatre Communications Group, 2002)

STATEMENTS AFTER AN ARREST UNDER THE IMMORALITY ACT: *Interior Plays* (Oxford, Oxford University Press, 2000), 75–106

VALLEY SONG: *Valley Song* (London, Faber and Faber, 1996)

Achiron, Marilyn (1986), 'Athol Fugard' in The *Cosmopolitan* (New York,)

Ait-Hamou, Louisa (1990), *The Divided Self and Separate Audiences* (York, PhD thesis. University of York)

Alden, Chris (1998), *Apartheid's Last Stand* (London, Macmillan)

Amato, Rob (1984), 'Fugard's Confessional Analysis: *"MASTER HAROLD"...and the boys'* in *Momentum: On Recent South African Writing* Daymond, M J; Jacobs, J U & Lenta, Margaret (eds) (Pietermaritzburg, University of Natal Press)

Ashcroft, Bill; Griffiths, Gareth & Tiffin, Helen (eds) (1997), *The Post-Colonial Studies Reader* (London, Routledge)

Attridge, Derek & Jolly, Rosemary. (eds) (1998), *Writing South Africa Literature, apartheid and democracy, 1970-1995* (Cambridge, Cambridge University Press)

Banham, Martin (Ed) (1995), *The Cambridge Guide to Theatre* (Cambridge, Cambridge University Press)

Barber, James (1999), *South Africa in the Twentieth Century: A Political History – In Search of a Nation State* (Oxford, Blackwell Publishers)

Barbera, Jack (ed) (1993), *Twentieth Century Literature Athol Fugard Issue* (New York, Hofstra University)

Barnes, Clive (1974), Sizwe Banzi 'Is a Message From Africa' in *The New York Times* 14 November (New York, The New York Times)

Barnett, Ursula (1983), *A Vision of Order: A Study of Black South African Literature in English (1914–1980)* (London, Sinclair Browne)

Beckett, Samuel (1979), *Waiting for Godot* (London, Faber & Faber)

Beinart, William (2001), *Twentieth Century South Africa* (Oxford, Oxford University Press)

Beinart, William & Dubow, Saul (1995), *Segregation and Apartheid in Twentieth Century South Africa* (London, Routledge)

Benjamin, Walter (1988), *Understanding Brecht* (London, Verso)

Benson, Mary (1961), 'South African's Play about Things as They Are' in *The Times* 12 December (London, The Times)

Benson, Mary (1977), 'Keeping an Appointment with the Future' in *Theatre Quarterly 7.28* (Oxford,)

Benson, Mary (1997), *Athol Fugard and Barney Simon: Bare stage, a few props, great theatre* (Randburg, Ravan Press)

Benson, Mary (1990), *A Far Cry: The Making of a South African* (Harmondsworth, Penguin Books)

Benson, Mary (ed) (1987), *Athol Fugard's Notebooks: 1960–1977* (London, Faber & Faber)

Bentley, Kin (1990), 'Lisa makes London debut in dad's play' in *The Eastern Province Herald* 4 September (Port Elizabeth, The Eastern Province Herald)

Biko, Steve (1988), *I Write What I Like* (Harmondsworth, Penguin Books)

Billington, Michael (1971), '*Boesman and Lena*' in *Plays and Players* 18.49 (London, MultiMedia Publishing)

Billington, Michael (1974), '*Sizwe Bansi*' in *The Guardian* 9 January (London, The Guardian)

Bloom, Harry (1961), *King Kong – An African Jazz Opera* (London, Collins)

Blumberg, Marcia (1991), 'Languages of Violence: Fugard's *Boesman and Lena*' in *Themes in Drama – 13: Violence:* Redmond, James (ed) (Cambridge, Cambridge University Press)

Blumberg, Marcia (1998), 'Re-Staging Resistance, Re-Viewing Women: 1990s Productions of Fugard's *Hello and Goodbye* and *Boesman and Lena*' in *Staging Resistance* by Colleran, Jeanne & Spencer, Jenny (eds) (Ann Arbor, University of Michigan Press)

Blumberg, Marcia (1993), 'Fragmentation and psychosis' in *Themes in Drama: 15: Madness,* Redmond, James (ed) (Cambridge, Cambridge University Press)

Blumberg, Marcia & Walder, Dennis (eds) (1999), *South African Theatre As/And Intervention* (Amsterdam-Atlanta, Rodopi)

Boal, Augusto (1985), *Theatre of the Oppressed* translated by Charles A and Maria-Odilia Leal McBride (New York, Theater Communications Group)

Boraine, Alex (2000), *A Country Unmasked: Inside South Africa's Truth and Reconciliation Commission* (Oxford, Oxford University Press)

Branford, Jean (1980), *A Dictionary of South African English* (Cape Town, Oxford University Press)

Brecht, Bertolt (1991), 'Questions from a worker who reads' in *The Poetry Anthology* (Milton Keynes, The Open University)

Brecht, Bertolt (1998), *Collected Plays: One* (London, Methuen)

Brecht, Bertolt (2001), *The Measures Taken and Other Lehrstücke* edited by John Willett and Ralph Manheim (New York, Arcade Publishing)

Breytenbach, Breyten (1984), *The True Confessions of an Albino Terrorist* (London, Faber & Faber)

Breytenbach, Breyten (1986), *End Papers* (London, Faber & Faber)

Breytenbach, Breyten (1999), *Dog Heart: A memoir* (London, Faber & Faber)

Brink, André (1983), *Mapmakers* (London, Faber & Faber)

Brink, André (1990), 'All of Me' in *Leadership* (9.3)

Brink, André (1993), *Looking on Darkness* (London, Random House)

Brink, André (1996), *Re-inventing a Continent* (London, Secker & Warburg)

Brink, André & Coetzee, J M (1987), *A Land Apart* (Harmondsworth, Penguin Books)

Brook, Peter (2000), 'Listening to the silence' in *ZA at Play* (*Mail & Guardian* On-line: 11 February)

Brustein, Robert (1991), *The Theatre of Revolt: Studies in modern drama from Ibsen to Genet* (Chicago, Ivan R. Dee)

Bunting, Brian (1969), *The Rise of the South African Reich* (Harmondsworth, Penguin Books)

Campschreur, Willem & Divendal, Joost (1989), *Culture in Another South Africa* (London, Zed Books)

Camus, Albert (1971), *The Rebel* translated by Anthony Bower (Harmondsworth, Penguin Books)

Camus, Albert (1975), *The Myth of Sisyphus* translated by Justin O'Brien (Harmondsworth, Penguin Books)

Camus, Albert (1983), *The Outsider* translated by Joseph Laredo (Harmondsworth, Penguin Books)

Cary, Joyce (1976), *Mister Johnson* (Harmondsworth, Penguin Books)

Childs, Peter & Williams, Patrick (1997), *An Introduction to Post-Colonial Theory* (Hemel Hempstead, Prentice Hall)

Christopher A J (1994), *The Atlas of Apartheid* (London, Routledge)

Clingman, Stephen (1990), 'Revolution and Reality' in *Rendering Things Visible,* Trump, Martin (ed) (Athens (USA), Ohio University Press)

Clingman, Stephen (1993), *The Novels of Nadine Gordimer* (London, Bloomsbury)

Coetzee, Ampie (1990), 'Literature and Crisis' in *Rendering Things Visible,* Trump, Martin (ed) (Athens (USA), Ohio University Press)

Coetzee, J M (1996), *Giving Offense* (Chicago, University of Chicago Press)

Cohen, Derek (1978), 'Athol Fugard's *Boesman and Lena'* in *Journal of Commonwealth Literature* 12.3 (London, Sage Publications)

Cohen, Derek (1991), 'Athol Fugard and the Liberal Dilemma' in *Brick* 40 (Toronto, Michael Redhill)

Coleridge, Samuel Taylor (1952), *Kubla Khan:* in *The London Book of English Verse,* Read, Herbert and Dobree,Bonamy (eds) (London, Eyre & Spottiswoode)

Colleran, Jeanne (1988), *The Dissenting Writer in South Africa: A Rhetorical Analysis of the Drama of Athol Fugard and the short fiction of Nadine Gordimer* (Ohio, PhD thesis. Ohio State University)

Colleran, Jeanne (1995), 'Athol Fugard and the problematics of the Liberal Critique' in *Modern Drama* 38.3 (Toronto, University of Toronto Press)

Colleran, Jeanne (1995), 'Resituating Fugard: Re-think-
ing Revolutionary Theatre' in *South African Theatre Journal 9.2*
(Stellenbosch, South African Theatre Journal)

Colleran. Jeanne & Spencer, Jenny (eds) (1998), *Staging Resistance:
Essays on Political Theater* (Ann Arbor, University of Michigan Press)

Coplan, David (1985), *In Township Tonight: South Africa's Black City
Music and Theatre* (Harlow, Longman)

Couzens, Tim (1985), *The New African: A Study of the Life and Work of
H I E Dhlomo* (Johannesburg, Ravan)

Coveney, Michael (1973), 'Challenging the Silence' in *Plays and
Players* 21.2 (London, MultiMedia Publishing)

Crow, Brian with Banfield, Chris (1996), 'Athol Fugard and the
South Africa " workshop' play"' in *An introduction to post-colonial
theatre,* Crow, Brian (ed) (Cambridge, Cambridge University Press)

Crowder, Michael (1987), 'Whose Dream Was It Anyway? Twenty-
Five Years of African Independence' in *African Affairs* 86.342
(Oxford, Oxford University Press)

Davenport. T R H (1989), *South Africa A Modern History* (Bergvlei,
Southern Book Publishers)

Davis, Geoffrey & Fuchs, Anne (eds) (1996), *Theatre and Change in
South Africa* (Amsterdam, Harwood Academic Publishers)

Davis, Geoffrey V (1999), 'Of 'Undesirability' The Control of
Theatre in South Africa during the Age of Apartheid' in *New Theatre
in Francophone: and Anglophone Africa* Fuchs, Anne (ed) (Amsterdam
– Atlanta, Rodopi)

Davis, Geoffrey V (ed) (1997), *Beyond the Echoes of Soweto: Five plays
by Matsemela Manaka* (Amsterdam, Harwood Academic Publishers)

Daymond, M J, Jacobs, J U & Lenta, Margaret (eds) (1984),
Momentum: On Recent South African Writing (Pietermaritzburg,
University of Natal Press)

De Klerk, W A (1975), *The Puritans in Africa* (London, Rev. Collings)

De Kok, Ingrid & Press, Karen (eds) (1990), *Spring is Rebellious*
(Cape Town, Buchu Books)

Deacon, Harriet (ed) (1996), *The Island: A History of Robben Island
1488–1990* (Claremont, David Philip)

Denniston, Robin (2000), *Trevor Huddleston: A Life* (London, Pan
Books)

Derrida, Jacques & Tlili, Mustapha (eds) (1987), *For Nelson Mandela*
(New York, Seaver Books)

Dhlomo, Herbert (1985), *H I E Dhlomo Collected Works* (Johannesburg, Ravan Press)

Dubow, Saul (1990), 'Race, civilisation and culture: the elaboration of segregationist discourse in the inter-war years' in *The Politics of Race, Class and Nationalism in Twentieth Century South Africa* Marks, Shula & Trapido, Stanley (eds) (Harlow, Longman)

Dubow, Saul (1995), *Scientific racism in modern South Africa* (Cambridge, Cambridge University Press)

Durbach, Errol (1984), 'Sophocles in South Africa' in *Comparative Drama* 18.3 (Kalamazoo, West Michigan University)

Durbach, Errol (1987), '"*Master Harold...and the boys*": Athol Fugard and the Psychopathology of Apartheid' in *Modern Drama* 30.4 (Toronto, University of Toronto Press)

Durbach, Errol (1989), 'Surviving in Xanadu: Fugard's *A Lesson from Aloes*' in *Ariel* 20.1 (Calgary, University of Calgary)

Edgar, David (1997), *Plays:1* (London, Methuen)

Ellison, Ralph (1965), *The Invisible Man* (Harmondsworth, Penguin Books)

Eyre, Richard & Wright, Nicholas (2000), *Changing Stages: A View of British Theatre in the Twentieth Century* (London, Bloomsbury)

Fanon, Frantz (1986), *Black Skin, White Masks* translated by Charles Lam Markmann (London, Pluto Press)

Fanon, Frantz (1970), *Toward the African Revolution* translated by Haakon Chevalier (Harmondsworth, Pelican Books)

Fanon, Frantz (1990), *The Wretched of the Earth* translated by Constance Farrington (Harmondsworth, Penguin Books)

February, Vernon (1991), *Mind Your Colour* (London, Kegan Paul)

Fenton, James (1980), 'A protest before our very eyes' in *The Sunday Times* 13 July (London, The Sunday Times)

Fletcher, Jill (1994), *The Story of South African Theatre 1780–1930* (Cape Town, Vlaeberg)

Fletcher, John & Spurling, John (1978), *Beckett: A study of his plays* (London, Eyre Methuen)

Foley, Andrew (1994), 'Courageous Pessimist' in *New Contrast* 22.4 (Cape Town, South African Literary Journal)

Foley, Andrew (1996), *Liberalism in South African English Literature 1948–1990: A reassessment of the work of Alan Paton and Athol Fugard* (Durban, PhD thesis. University of Natal)

Forster, E M (1972), *Two Cheers for Democracy* (Harmondsworth, Penguin Books)

Foucault, Michel (1991), *Discipline and Punish* translated by Alan Sheridan (Harmondsworth, Penguin Books)

Freire, Paulo (1996), *Pedagogy of the Oppressed* translated by Myra Bergman Ramos (Harmondsworth, Penguin Books)

Fuchs, Anne (1990), *Playing the Market: The Market Theatre Johannesburg 1976–1986* (Chur, Harwood Academic)

Fugard, Athol (1978), *Orestes* in *Theatre One* Stephen Gray (ed) (Johannesburg, Ad Donker)

Fugard, Athol (1985), *The Road to Mecca* (London, Faber and Faber)

Fugard, Athol (1983), *Tsotsi* (Harmondsworth, Penguin Books)

Fugard, Athol (1984), '*Sizwe Banzi is Dead*' in *A Night at the Theatre* Harwood, Ronald (ed) (London, Methuen)

Fugard, Athol (1987), *Selected Plays* (Oxford, Oxford University Press)

Fugard, Athol (1993), *Playland and A Place with the Pigs* (New York, Theatre Communications Group)

Fugard, Athol (1993), 'Some Problems of a Playwright from South Africa' and 'Recent Notebook Entries' in *Twentieth Century Literature Athol Fugard Issue* (New York, Hofstra University)

Fugard, Athol (1994), *Cousins A Memoir* (Johannesburg, Witwatersrand University Press)

Fugard, Athol (1996), *My Life and Valley Song* (Johannesburg, Witwatersrand University Press)

Fugard, Athol (1996), *Valley Song* (London, Faber and Faber)

Fugard, Athol (1998), *Athol Fugard: Plays One* (London, Faber and Faber)

Fugard, Athol (1999), *The Captain's Tiger: A Memoir for the Stage* (New York, Theatre Communications Group)

Fugard, Athol (2000), *Interior Plays* (Oxford, Oxford University Press)

Fugard, Athol (2000), *Port Elizabeth Plays* (Oxford, Oxford University Press)

Fugard, Athol (2000), *Township Plays* (Oxford, Oxford University Press)

Fugard, Athol (2002), *Sorrows and Rejoicings* (New York, Theatre Communications Group)

Fugard, Athol (2005), *Exits and Entrances* (New York, Dramatists Play Service)

Fugard, Athol & Devenish, Ross (1992), *Marigolds in August and The Guest* (New York, Theatre Communications Group)

Gainor, J Ellen (ed) (1995), *Imperialism and Theatre* (London, Routledge)

Gilbert, Helen & Tompkins, Joanne (1996), *Post-Colonial Drama* (London, Routledge)

Goddard, Kevin (ed) (1992), *Athol Fugard: A Resource Guide, English Olympiad* (Grahamstown, National English Literary Museum)

Golding, William (1979), *Darkness Visible* (London, Faber & Faber)

Gordimer, Nadine (1978), *The Conservationist* (Harmondsworth, Penguin Books)

Gordimer, Nadine (1994), *Something Out There* (London, Bloomsbury Publishing)

Graver, David (1999), *Drama For A New South Africa* (Bloomington, Indiana University Press)

Gray, Stephen (ed) (1978), *Theatre One* (Johannesburg, Ad Donker)

Gray, Stephen (1990), '"Between Me and My Country": Fugard's *My Children! My Africa!* at the Market Theatre, Johannesburg' in *New Theatre Quarterly* 6.21 (Cambridge, Cambridge University Press)

Gray, Stephen (ed) (1982), *Athol Fugard* (Johannesburg, McGraw Hill)

Gray, Stephen (ed) (1993), *South African Plays* (London, Nick Hern Books)

Green, Michael (1984), '"The Politics of Loving": Fugard and the Metropolis' in *English Academy Review* 2 (Johannesburg, The English Academy of South Africa)

Green, R J (1969), 'South Africa's Plague: One View of *The Blood Knot*' in *Modern Drama* 12.4 (Toronto, University of Toronto Press)

Green, Robert J (1968), 'Athol Fugard: Dramatist of Loneliness and Isolation' In *Teater S.A.* Vol No. 2 (Cape Town,)

Green, Robert J (1976), 'Politics and Literature in Africa: The Drama of Athol Fugard' in *Aspects of South African Literature,* Heywood, Christopher (ed) (London, Heinemann)

Grotowski, Jerzy (1991), *Towards A Poor Theatre* edited by Eugenio Barba (London, Methuen – Drama)

Gunner, Liz (ed) (1991), *Politics and Performance Theatre, Poetry and Song in Southern Africa* (Johannesburg, Witswatersrand University Press)

Gussow, Mel (1982), 'Witness' In *New Yorker* (New York, New Yorker)

Harwood, Ronald (1984), *A Night at the Theatre* (London, Methuen)

Hornby, Richard (2005), 'Impresario' in *The Hudson Review* 58.2 (New York, The Hudson Review)

Hauptfleisch, Temple (1997), *Theatre and Society in South* Africa (Pretoria, J L van Schaik)

Hauptfleisch, Temple & Steadman, Ian (1991), *South African Theatre: Four plays and an introduction* (Pretoria, Kagiso Tertiary)

Hauptfleisch, Temple, Viljoen, Wilma & Greunen, Céleste Van (1982), *Athol Fugard: A Source Guide* (Johannesburg, Ad Donker)

Head, Bessie (1993), *The Cardinals* (Oxford, Heinemann)

Henry, William A III (1989), 'On the Front Line of Anger' in *Time* (Time Inc.)

Hobson, Harold (1963), '(Knock)ings at the Door: Anti-Apartheid at the Arts' In *Sunday Times* 24 February (London, Sunday Times)

Hofmeyr, Isabel (1990), 'Building a nation from words' in *The Politics of Race, Class and Nationalism in Twentieth Century South Africa* Marks, Shula & Trapido, Stanley (eds) (Harlow, Longman)

Horn, Andrew (1997), 'South African Theatre Ideology and Rebellion' in *Readings in Popular African Culture* Barber, Karin (ed) (Oxford, James Currey)

Hornby, Richard (1990), 'Political Drama' in *The Hudson Review* 43.1 (New York, The Hudson Review)

Jameson, Fredric (1996), *The Political Unconscious* (London, Routledge)

Jameson, Fredric (2000), *Brecht and Method* (London, Verso)

Jeyifo, Biodun (ed) (2002), *Modern African Drama* (New York, Norton)

Johnson, R W (2004), *South Africa: The First Man, The Last Nation* (London, Weidenfield & Nicolson)

Jones, Laura (1994), *Nothing Except Ourselves: The Harsh Times and Bold Theater of South Africa's Mbongeni Ngema* (New York, Viking)

Jordon, John O (1993), 'Life in the Theatre: Autobiography, Politics, and Romance in *'Master Harold'...and the boys'* in *Twentieth Century Literature: Athol Fugard Issue* (New York, Hofstra University)

Joubert, Elsa (1987), *Poppie Nongena* (New York, First Owl Book)

Kani, John (ed) (1994), *More Market Plays* (Johannesburg, Ad Donker)

Kannemeyer, J C (1993), *A History of Afrikaans Literature* (Pietermaritzburg, Shuter & Shooter)

Kauffmann, Stanley (1974), *'Sizwe Banzi Is Dead, The Island'* in *The New Republic* 21 December (New York, The New Republic)

Kavanagh, Robert (1985), *Theatre and Cultural Struggle in South Africa* (London, Zed Books)

Kavanagh, Robert (ed) (1981), *South African People's Plays* (London, Heinemann)

Kerr, David (1995), *African Popular Theatre* (London, James Currey)

Kerr, Walter (1980), 'A History Lesson From Miller, A Social Lesson From Fugard' In *The New York Times* 30 November (New York, The New York Times)

Khan, Naseem (1971), 'Athol Fugard: (I'm more interested in talking about rubbish than politics)' in *Time Out* 23–29 July (London)

Kiewiet, C W De (1975), *A History of South Africa* (London, Oxford University Press)

King, Robert (1993), 'The Rhetoric of Dramatic Technique in *Blood Knot*' in *South African Theatre Journal* 7.1 (Stellenbosch, The University of Stellenbosch)

Kirby, Robert (1982), *It's a Boy* (Sandton, Triad Publishers)

Krog, Antjie (1999), *Country of My Skull* (London, Vintage)

Kruger, Loren (1999), *The Drama of South Africa* (London, Routledge)

Lange, Margreet de (1997), *The Muzzled Muse: Literature and Censorship in South Africa* (Amsterdam-Philadelphia, John Benjamins)

Larlham, Peter (1991), *Black Theatre, Dance and Ritual in South Africa* (Ann Arbor, UMI Research Press)

Leigh Hunt, James Henry (2004), 'Abou Ben Adhem' in *The Times Book of English Verse* (Glasgow, HarperCollins)

Lelyveld, Joseph (1985), *Move Your Shadow* (New York, Times Books)

Lelyveld, Joseph (1983), *'Master Harold* Stuns Johannesburg Audience' in *The New York Times* (New York, The New York Times)

Lessing, Doris (1994), *The Grass is Singing* (London, Flamingo)

Levy, Frank (1973), 'Fugard's Boesman and Lena Physical and Metaphysical Exhaustion' in *Yale/Theatre* 4.1 (New Haven, Yale University)

Lodge Tom (1983), *Black Politics in South Africa* (London, Longman)

Loomba, Ania & Orkin, Martin (1998), *Post-Colonial Shakespeares* (London, Routledge)

Maake, Nhlanhla (1992), 'Multi-cultural relations in a post-apartheid South Africa' in *African Affairs* 91.365 (Oxford, Oxford University Press)

Mackay, E Anne (1989), 'Fugard's *The Island* and Sophocles *Antigone* Within the Parameters of South African Protest Literature' in *Literature and Revolution* Bevan, David (ed) (Amsterdam-Atlanta, Rodopi)

Mandela, Nelson (1999), *Long Walk to Freedom* (London, Abacus)

Maponya, Maishe (1995), *Doing Plays For A Change* (Johannesburg, Witwatersrand University Press)

Matshikiza, Todd (1982), *Chocolates for my Wife* (Cape Town, David Philip)

Matshoba, Mtutuzeli (1971), *Call Me Not a Man* (Johannesburg, Ravan Press)

Maylam, Paul (1990), 'The Rise and Decline of Urban Apartheid in South Africa' in *African Affairs* 89.354 (Oxford, Oxford University Press)

McClintock, Anne (1995), *Imperial Leather* (New York, Routledge)

Mda, Zakes (1990), *The Plays of Zakes Mda* (Johannesburg, Ravan Press)

Mda, Zakes (1993), *And the Girls in their Sunday Dresses* (Johannesburg, Witwatersrand University Press)

Mda, Zakes (1993), *When People Play People: Development Communication Through Theatre* (Johannesburg, Witwatersrand University Press)

Mda, Zakes (ed) (1996), *Four Plays* (Florida Hills, Vivlia Publishers)

Memmi, Albert (1990), *The Colonizer and the Colonized* translated by Howard Greenfield (London, Earthscan Publications)

Merrett, Christopher (1994), *A Culture of Censorship: Secrecy and Intellectual Repression in South Africa* (Cape Town, David Philip)

Mhlope, Gcina, Vanrenen, Maralin & Mtshali, Thembi (1988), *Have You Seen Zandile* (London, Methuen)

Millin, Sarah Gertrude (1986), *God's Stepchildren* (Craighall, Ad Donker)

Modisane, Bloke (1965), *Blame Me on History* (London, Panther Books)

Mphahlele, Ezekiel (1959), *Down Second Avenue* (London, Faber and Faber)

Mtwa, Percy; Ngema, Mbongeni & Simon, Barney (1983), *Woza Albert* (London, Methuen)

Munro, Margaret (1981), 'The Fertility of Despair: Fugard's Bitter Aloes' in *Meanjin* 40.4 (Melbourne, Melbourne University Press)

Ndebele, Njabulo (1991), *Rediscovery of the Ordinary* (Johannesburg, COSAW)

Ngcobo, Lauretta (1999), *And They Didn't Die* (New York, The Feminist Press at the City University of New York)

Nicol, Mike (1991), *A Good-Looking Corpse* (London, Secker & Warburg)

Nightingale, Benedict (1973), 'Sparks of Life' in *The New Statesman* 28 September (London, The New Statesman)

Nightingale, Benedict (1999), 'White out of black' in *The Times* 12 April (London, The Times)

Nixon, Rob (1994), *Homelands, Harlem and Hollywood: South African Culture and the World Beyond* (New York, Routledge)

Nkosi, Lewis (1973), 'The Rhythm of Violence' in *Themes of Drama An Anthology* George E Wellwarth (New York, Thomas Y Crowell Company)

Nkosi, Lewis (1983), *Home and Exile* (Harlow, Longman)

Nkosi, Lewis (1987), *Mating Birds* (New York, Harper & Row)

Nuttall, Sarah & Coetzee, Carli (eds) (1998), *Negotiating the past: The Making of Memory in South Africa* (Oxford, Oxford University Press)

O'Brien, Anthony (2001), *Against Normalization: Writing Radical Democracy in South Africa* (Durham, Duke University Press)

Omond, Roger (1985), *The Apartheid Handbook* (Harmondsworth, Penguin Books)

Orkin, Martin (1991), *Drama and the South African State* (Manchester, Manchester University Press)

Orkin, Martin (1988), 'Body and State in *Blood knot/The Blood Knot*' in *South African Theatre Journal* 2.1 (Johannesburg, South African Theatre Journal)

Orkin, Martin (ed) (2001), *At the Junction: Four plays by the Junction Avenue Theatre Company* (Johannesburg, Witwatersrand University Press)

Orwell, George (1955), *Nineteen Eighty-Four* (Harmondsworth, Penguin Books)

O'Sheel, Patrick (1978), 'Athol Fugard's "Poor Theatre"' in *Journal of Commonwealth Literature* 12.3 (London, Sage Publications)

Pacheco, Patrick (1982), 'Fugard's Rites of Passage and Plays of Pain' in *The Wall Street Journal* (New York, The Wall Street Journal)

Peck, Richard (1992), 'Condemned to Choose, But What? Existentialism in Selected Works by Fugard, Brink, and Gordimer' in *Research in African Literatures* 23.3 (Austin, University of Texas)

Perkins, Kathy (ed) (1998), *Black South African Women: an anthology of plays* (London, Routledge)

Plaatje, Solomon (1987), *Native Life in South Africa* (Harlow, Longman)

Platzky, Laurine & Walker, Cherryl (eds) (1985), *The Surplus People* (Braamfontein, Ravan Press)

Reid, John (1991), *Athol Fugard: A Bibliography* (Grahamstown, NELM)

Rich, Frank (1980), 'The Stage: *Aloes*, Fugard on Apartheid' in *The New York Times* 18 November (New York, The New York Times)

Rich, Frank (1989), 'Generation Gap in Fugard's *My Children!*' in *The New York Times* 19 December (New York, The New York Times)

Rive, Richard (1986), *'Buckingham Palace' District Six* (Cape Town, David Philip)

Roberts, Sheila (1982), ''No Lessons Learnt': Reading the Texts of Fugard's *A Lesson from Aloes* and *'Master Harold'...and the boys*' in *English in Africa* 9.2 (Grahamstown, Rhodes University)

Roux, Edward (1964), *Time Longer Than Rope: A History of the Black Man's Struggle for Freedom in South Africa* (Madison, The University of Wisconsin Press)

Sampson, Anthony (1999), *Mandela* (London, Harper Collins)

Sanders, Mark (2002), *Complicities: the intellectual and apartheid* (Durham, Duke University Press)

Sarinjeive, Devi (1987), *Fugard's Situations: An existentialist study of selected plays by Athol Fugard 1958–1972* (New York, PhD thesis. University of Columbia)

Saunders, Christopher (ed) (1988), *Readers Digest Illustrated History of South Africa: The Real Story* (Cape Town, The Readers Digest Association of South Africa)

Savage, Michael (1986), 'The imposition of Pass Laws on the African population in South Africa 1916–1984' in *African Affairs* 85.339 (Oxford, Oxford University Press)

Schuster, Lynda (2004), *A Burning Hunger: One Family's Struggle Against Apartheid* (London, Jonathan Cape)

Schwartz, Pat (1988), *The Best of Company* (Craighall, Ad Donker)

Seidenspinner, Margarete (1986), *Exploring the Labyrinth* (Essen, Verlag Die Blaue Eule)

Seymour, Hilary (1980), '*Sizwe Bansi is Dead*: a study of artistic ambivalence' in *Race and Class* XXI.3 (London, Sage Publications)

Shava, Piniel Viriri (1989), *A People's Voice: Black South African Writing in the Twentieth Century* (London, Zed Books)

Sheckels, Theodore F Jr (1996), *The Lion on the Freeway: A Thematic Introduction to Contemporary South African Literature in English* (New York, Peter Lang)

Sher, Anthony & Doran, Greg (1997), *Woza Shakespeare* (London, Methuen)

Simon, Barney (ed) (1997), *Born In The RSA: Four Workshopped Plays* (Johannesburg, Witwatersrand University Press)

Slabolepszy, Paul (1985), *Saturday Night at the Palace* (Johannesburg, Ad Donker)

Slabolepszy, Paul (1994), *Mooi Street and other moves* (Johannesburg, Witwatersrand University Press)

Solberg, Rolf (1990), *Alternative Theatre in South Africa: Talks with Prime Movers since the 1970s* (Pietermaritzburg, Hadeda Books)

Sophocles (1998), *Antigone, Oedipus the King* and *Electra:* Hall, Edith (Ed) (Oxford, Oxford University Press)

Sparks, Allister (1991), *The Mind of South Africa* (London, Mandarin)

Sparks, Allister (2003), *Beyond the Miracle: Inside the New South Africa* (Johannesburg, Jonathan Ball Publishers)

Steadman, Ian (1984), 'Alternative Politics, Alternative Performance: 1976 and Black South African Theatre' in *Momentum: On Recent South African Writing:* Daymond, M J; Jacobs, J U & Lenta, Margaret (eds) (Pietermaritzburg, University of Natal Press)

Steadman, Ian (1989), 'Fugard's new play – reality's the antagonist' in *Weekly Mail and Guardian* 30 June – 6 July (Johannesburg, Weekly Mail and Guardian)

Steadman, Ian (1991), 'Theater Beyond Apartheid' in *Research in African Literatures 22.3* (Austin, University of Texas)

Steiner, George (1984), *Antigones* (Oxford, Clarendon Press)

Stone, Brian & Scorer, Pat (1977), *Sophocles to Fugard* (London, British Broadcasting Corporation)

Swan, Christopher (1982), 'Dramatist Athol Fugard: struggle – and hope – in a grim context' in *The Christian Science Monitor* 13 April (Boston, The Christian Science Monitor)

Tennyson, Alfred Lord (1952), *In Memoriam* in *The London Book of English Verse:* Read, Herbert and Dobrée, Bonamy (eds) (London, Eyre & Spottiswoode)

Themba, Can (1999), *The Suit* (Johannesburg, ViVa Books)

Thompson, Leonard (1985), *The Political Mythology Of Apartheid* (New Haven, Yale University)

Thompson, Leonard (1990), *A History of South Africa* (New Haven, Yale University Press)

Trump, Martin (ed) (1990), *Rendering Things Visible: Essays on South African Literary Culture* (Athens (USA), Ohio University Press)

Tucker, Percy (1997), *Just The Ticket* (Jeppestown, Jonathan Ball Publishers)

Tynan, Kenneth (1963), 'Under the Influence' in *The Observer Weekend Review* 24 February (London, The Observer)

Vandenbroucke, Russell (1986), *Truths the Hand can Touch: The Theatre of Athol Fugard* (Craighall, Ad Donker)

Vandenbroucke, Russell (1992), 'Fugard and the Politics of Human Dignity: A Note on *Boesman and Lena* and *The Island*' in *Perspectives on South African English Literature* Chapman, Michael; Gardiner, Colin & Mphahlele, Es'kia (eds) (Johannesburg, Ad Donker)

Villiers, Marq de (1990), *White Tribe Dreaming* (Harmondsworth, Penguin Books)

Visser, Nicholas (1993), 'Drama and Politics in a State of Emergency: *My Children! My Africa!*' in *Twentieth Century Literature: Athol Fugard Issue* (New York, Hofstra University)

Visser, Nicholas & Couzens, Tim (1985), *Introduction to H I E Dhlomo: Collected Works* (Johannesburg, Ravan Press)

Walder, Dennis (1984), *Athol Fugard* (London, Macmillan)

Walder, Dennis (1992), 'Resituating Fugard: South African Drama as Witness' In *New Theatre Quarterly* 32 (Cambridge, Cambridge University Press)

Walder, Dennis (1994), 'South African Drama and Ideology: The Case of Athol Fugard' in *Altered State? Writing and South Africa* Boehmer, Elleke, Chrisman, Laura and Parker, Kenneth (eds) (Sydney, Dangeroo Press)

Walder, Dennis (1997), 'Questions from a White Man Who Listens' in *South African Literary History: Totality and/or Fragment* Reckwitz, Erhard; Reitner, Karin & Vennarini, Lucia (eds) (Essen, Verlag Die Blaue Eule)

Walder, Dennis (1998), *Post-colonial Literatures in English History, Language, Theory* (Oxford, Blackwell Publishers)

Walder, Dennis (2000), 'Suffering Visions and Present Bearings: Fugard's Theatre of the Interior' in *History and Theatre in Africa:* Hutchinson, Yvette and Breitinger, Eckhard (eds) (Bayreuth, Bayreuth African Studies)

Walder, Dennis (2001), *Mandela's Books and the Strong-Room of Dreams: Reflecting on the Value of Literature*, Inaugural Lecture (Milton Keynes, Open University)

Walder, Dennis (2003), *Athol Fugard* (Tavistock, Northcote House)

Walder, Dennis (2004), 'On the Threshold of the Future' in *African Theatre: Southern Africa* Martin Banham *et al* (eds) (Oxford, James Currey)

Watson, Graham (1970), *Passing for White* (London, Tavistock Publications)

Weales, Gerald (1978), 'The Embodied Images of Athol Fugard' in *The Hollins Critic*, XV.1 (Roanoke, Hollins University)

Weales, Gerald (1993), 'Fugard Masters the Code' in *Twentieth Century Literature: Athol Fugard Issue* (New York, Hofstra University)

Wertheim, Albert (1987), 'The prison as theatre and the theatre as prison: Athol Fugard's *The Island*' in *The Theatrical Space: Themes in Drama* 9 Redmond, James (ed) (Cambridge, Cambridge University Press)

Wertheim, Albert (1988), 'The Lacerations of Apartheid: *A Lesson from Aloes*' in *Text and Presentation*, Hartigan, Karelisa (ed) (London, University Press of America)

Wertheim, Albert (1995), 'Witnessing Destruction and Survival in South Africa: Athol Fugard's *A Lesson from Aloes*' in *The Writer as Historical Witness*, Thumboo, Edwin & Kandiah, Thiru (eds) (Singapore, UniPress)

Wertheim, Albert (2000), *The Dramatic Art of Athol Fugard* (Bloomington, Indiana University Press)

West, Rebecca (1949), *The Meaning of Treason* (London, Macmillan)

Wolpe, Harold (1989), *Race, Class and the Apartheid State* (London, James Currey)

Wood, James (2004), 'Damned if you do' in *The Times Literary Supplement* 3 September (London, The Times Literary Supplement)

Woods, Donald (1979), *Biko* (Harmondsworth, Penguin Books)

Wortham, Christopher (1983), 'A Sense of Place' in *Olive Schreiner and After* Van Wyk Smith, Malvern and Maclennan, Don (eds) (Cape Town, David Philip)

Yeats, W B (1982), 'He wishes for the Cloths of Heaven' in *The Collected Poems of W B Yeats* (London, Macmillan)

Young. Robert J C (1996), *Colonial Desire: Hybridity in Theory, Culture and Race* (London, Routledge)

Zunes, Stephen (1999), 'The role of non-violent action in the downfall of Apartheid' in *The Journal of Modern Africa Studies*, 37.1 (Cambridge, Cambridge University Press)

Index